HOW TO LEARN FROM PROJECT DISASTERS

To

our silent partners

Sudershan and Dorothy

How to Learn from Project Disasters

rue-life stories with a oral for management

O.P. Kharbanda

E.A. Stallworthy

G

Gower

The Sydney Opera House

The theme of this book is epitomised by our frontispiece, a photograph of the Sydney Opera House, showing its sailing roofs. All the criticism is levelled at its cost and the time that it took, as compared with the original estimates. No one seems to criticise those original estimates, or those who made them, accepting that the actual time and cost were perhaps the real cost, and the time that it should have taken, to build such a marvellous *development project* – for that is what it most certainly was. Originally estimated in 1967 to cost $A 6 million, it was completed in 1973 for $A 100 million. But of course the scope of the final figure was utterly different from that of those first estimates, and escalation had also taken its toll.

The original concept was by Utzon, an architect from Denmark, chosen in open competition from some 200 entries from more than 30 countries. Whether his dream ever became reality remains an open question. Nevertheless, one writer has called this building 'the other Taj Mahal' and despite all the criticism it is today in full use. The building that graces Bennelong Point on the shores of Sydney Harbour is so much more than an opera house. The complex has four performing halls, together with an Exhibition Hall, a Reception Hall, five rehearsal studios, two restaurants, six theatre bars, lounge areas, a library, a green room for the artistes, various administrative offices and 60 dressing rooms – in all, nearly one thousand rooms of various shapes and sizes.

Engineers will be interested to know that the total electrical demand is some nine megawatts, the major load being the air conditioning, rated at some 550 tonnes. Electrical engineers would appreciate that the next most important load is the complex lighting installation. Mechanical engineers will be fascinated by the winches that raise and lower the scenery and lighting. There are more than one hundred, together with revolving platforms and lifts for scene changes. Even the acoustics engineer can meet something novel: there are halo-like devices suspended over the stage in the Concert Hall that can be raised and lowered – by more winches – to improve the acoustics. They are called 'acoustic clouds' and help the musicians to hear their own music before the echoes reach them from the distant walls.

What can be concluded from all this? The project cost is some sixteen times more than originally was thought, but is most certainly a *development project*, although never described as such; and we all know what development projects cost, particularly when compared with the very first estimates. We cite some interesting examples in this book. The record shows that 'cost' was one of the criteria in the selection of the design. The chairman of the assessors is on record as saying: 'the winning scheme is by far the cheapest to build'. He could still be right, and he most certainly can never be proved wrong, for they only ever built the one! That in itself is a little lesson that can always be borne in mind when you are making cost comparisons.

As we go through our case studies, we highlight the importance of 'human relations' and learn that the cost implications of not allowing project managers to 'manage' can be considerable. Many of the problems here were created by the 'committees' who sought to govern. Committee followed committee, administrative bureaucracy grew ever stronger, till Utzon, whose creation this was, finally left Australia in disgust. Peter Hall, the architect who took over from him, described Utzon as the only architect 'technically and ethically able to complete the Opera House as it should be completed'.

We have highlighted in this brief history some of the many, many problems that lead to project cost and time overrun, that lead to disaster. These are the problems which we deal with in detail as we review the various case histories we have gathered together here in this book from around the world. Despite everything, they finished with a building of great grace and beauty, the Sydney Opera House.

— ☐ — ☐ — ☐ — ☐ — ☐ — ☐ —

Frontispiece photograph reproduced by kind permission of Ove Arup Partners, London, who were closely identified with the design and construction of the Sydney Opera House.

Published by Gower Publishing Company Limited,
Aldershot, Hants, England

Reprinted 1984

British Library Cataloguing in Publication Data

Kharbanda, O.P.
  How to learn from project disasters.
  1. Industrial project management – Case studies
  I. Title   II. Stallworthy, E.A.
  658.4'04   HD69.P75

  ISBN 0-566-02340-7

Printed and bound in Great Birtain by
Biddles Ltd, Guildford and King's Lynn

Contents

Preface

Overruns in time and cost are customarily seen as a failure in project management and when extreme can well be a 'disaster'. Such overruns, unfortunately, are the norm rather than the exceptions that they ought to be. There are other factors, such as politics, changing technology and the economic climate, largely outside the control of the project team, which can also play a significant role, but project management remains their responsibility.

A substantial cost overrun can well prove disastrous not only to the project but also to the contractor involved. As we demonstrate in this book, a cost overrun threatened the survival of a major British contractor (Chapter 6) and another practically 'wiped out' one of the largest American contractors (Chapter 7). The crash of giants such as Lockheed and Rolls Royce in 1971 resulted from a cost overrun on a *single* project. A more than ten-fold overrun must be a disaster – yet such cases continue to reach the headlines. For instance, there is the Vienna General Hospital, with the contract awarded in 1960, for completion in 1968 at a cost of some $317 million. Now it may be completed by 1986, and carries a price tag of nearly $4 billion. The Sydney Opera House, which serves as our frontispiece, is another well-known and widely publicised example. Estimated to cost $A6 million in 1967, it was finally completed in 1973 for a total cost of some $A100 million. Some of the multi-billion synthetic oil projects now on the drawing board could, unless we listen *now*, meet the same fate.

Man is so obsessed with his need for success that project disasters are usually just filed away. The management literature is replete with success stories, but hardly any attention is paid to failures, let alone to the lessons they could teach us. It is true that 'failed', 'bankrupt' and 'bust' are not pleasant words, but they nevertheless are a reality in the corporate world. The number of such disasters has been on the increase, yet this vital aspect has been largely neglected until recently.

A serious study of corporation failure and collapse only began in the seventies. Now the subject is no longer taboo but is publicly debated from time to time and interest is bound to gather momentum in the eighties. The study and analysis of some typical projects that have overrun in cost and time, as presented here, should lead to the better management of future projects. Lessons can and should be learned from one project to another, from one organisation to another.

Man learns by experience, and one can learn most from one's mistakes. And he is a wise man indeed who can learn not only from his own mistakes but from those of others. This is what we have set out to do. We have sought out projects of varying complexity, size and location, if only to demonstrate that no one is immune. The choice of projects is inevitably somewhat arbitrary, but our combined spheres of work, in various fields and several continents, have helped us to present and analyse a fairly wide spectrum of diverse projects.

This book adds, we think, a new dimension to the literature on project management. If earlier we, among others, have been telling you 'How to do it', now the emphasis is on 'How not to do it!' We normally hear how things ought to be done, very seldom how they ought not to be done. But learning from past failures can be far more effective than any amount of preaching.

If we are to learn from the past, we must listen. That is why our closing chapter carries the plea: 'Let's listen now – or we shall never learn'. It is most difficult to get people to listen, let alone learn. It is our sincere hope that the present work will help in this direction.

O.P. Kharbanda
E.A. Stallworthy

Acknowledgements

While writing this book we found a certain measure of support, but also a degree of reluctance in providing clarification or information on the projects we wished to review. Examples of the response we received are quoted in the text. One reluctant correspondent said:

> I also think we shall be wanting to analyse the lessons to be learned within our own management structure *before unfolding* to a wider audience.

Another insisted that the project must not be identified. We thought that the lessons it held were so valuable that we brought it to you just the same, omitting the name of the plant and other identifying data.

Much of the data for our case studies has been culled from information widely scattered in the technical press and sometimes, even, in the popular press. Precise acknowledgement of our sources has sometimes been impossible, although we have done what we could, where we could. This you will find in the 'References' section at the end of each chapter. In addition, we have received specific information and data from individuals and organisations, duly acknowledged, if we were permitted to do so, at the appropriate place in the text. Not all this information was offered to us without hesitation. For instance, to quote once again:

> Naturally, we are most anxious that the project is handled with care. From the tone of your letter, and knowing your reputation, we are confident that you will present the undertaking in a fair light.

Let us be fair. Some of our correspondents were so anxious to help that they telephoned us from places as far away from us as North America and South Africa to furnish clarification on specific points or to give additional information sought by us. We owe them special thanks.

The bibliography at the end of the book is offered both as a source of reference and also as part of our acknowledgement. It will, we hope, serve as a source of reference to those of our readers who may wish to follow up certain aspects of this vital subject. The notes in the bibliography are intended to convey the 'flavour' of each reference, so far as that is possible in a few words.

OPK
EAS

Illustrations

PART ONE

SETTING THE SCENE

1 Project cost control

A great many books have been written about cost control and thousands of papers on various aspects of this subject have been published, but little has been said about the context in which all this occurs. There is a great gulf between theory and practice. We are going to look in some detail at the context in which, and for which, all this writing has been done. Let us see what it means to the practice and philosophy of project cost control and so learn from the practice to put the theory in its proper place. The contrast, one might almost call it conflict, between theory and practice is as old as time. It is possible to go back nearly two thousand years and find an example that is as 'up-to-date as today', and similar examples could surely be drawn from the engineering works of the early Egyptians, the Babylonians and the Chinese, thousands of years before that, had we the data.

Our example is a noted engineering work called Hadrian's Wall. This wall is well known to those living in the United Kingdom, but to those who live elsewhere it should be explained that it was built by the Romans nearly two thousand years ago, right across the north of England, from coast to coast, on the instructions of Emperor Hadrian, to keep out the barbarians from the north – the Scots! It was not a defensive wall, like the wall around a castle, because the Romans fought their battles on open ground. Rather, it was an administrative boundary, to control movement between the two countries. There are some people, even now, on both sides of the border, who wish it had not fallen into disuse.

Hadrian's Wall

Along Hadrian's Wall there are what are called 'mile castles', with

3

gateways. These gateways were built at regular intervals of a mile, even when there was a near-precipitous drop outside the gate, making that particular gate useless. Presumably the 'design criteria' for the wall were written in Rome by someone who did not foresee the possibility that the wall would be built across mountainous country, and stated that a gateway had to be constructed every mile. Then, just as is found today with the construction of a process plant, the design criteria had to be followed rigidly. The men on the job went on and built a gate every mile, whether that gate was going to be of any use, or not (Ref. 1). See the photograph taken from the air, Figure 1.1.

It may be seen as just noted, that the reader is given the

Figure 1.1 Hadrian's Wall, a view from the air
This aerial photograph of Milecastle 39, taken from Professor D.G.B. Jones' booklet 'Hadrian's Wall from the Air', allows one to see clearly the way the ground falls away outside the gate to the north (top), with no possibility of a road or path to the gate. The track shown veers away to the left. (Photograph reproduced by permission of the Department of Archaeology, University of Manchester.)

reference, the authority for this 'case history' from the engineering works of the Romans. These references may be found at the end of each chapter, in addition to the bibliography at the end of the book, which gives the more general background reading on the subject. All case histories throughout this book are from real life. Those to be discussed have been drawn from the process design and engineering developments of the past ten years or so, rather than the past ten thousand, but we can already learn from our first case study, Hadrian's Wall. We can ask ourselves, for instance, in relation to the plant, or the factory, the production unit with which we are presently involved – either running it, or building it, or designing it:

Have we unnecessary equipment?
Have we unnecessary procedures?
Have we unnecessary design rules?

Have we? Or have you never asked yourself that particular question? If it has never occurred to you to ask it, then start asking it now. You might save quite a lot of money.

The world is our oyster

Although we are writing about cost control in relation to the construction of new manufacturing facilities, our examples will spread rather wider than that because of the lessons to be learnt. In every manufacturing facility today, whether we are talking about chemicals, pharmaceuticals, food, metals, or factories for mass-produced items such as cars, refrigerators or toys, we come up against process plants at some stage. We are involved, therefore, in the sequential steps of process development, process design, detailed design and engineering, procurement, construction and commissioning. This is all familiar ground to the cost engineer, and is the field in which he should exercise his arts from the very start to the bitter end. Figure 1.2 illustrates what might be called the 'thought processes' associated with this progress of events, and the role of cost control in the accumulation of data and the interpretation of data is demonstrated. As already stated, this activity – project cost control – is carried out in the real world. When that world is looked at, it can be divided into under-developed countries (if that term may be employed), developing and developed countries. This is well-known terminology, but we are going to go one step further, and discuss an 'over-developed'

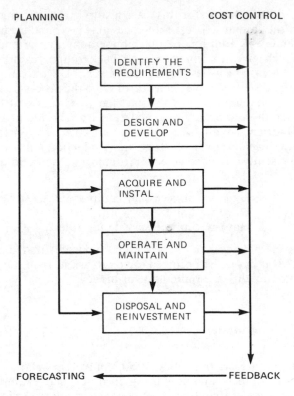

PLANNING   COST CONTROL

IDENTIFY THE REQUIREMENTS

DESIGN AND DEVELOP

ACQUIRE AND INSTAL

OPERATE AND MAINTAIN

DISPOSAL AND REINVESTMENT

FORECASTING   FEEDBACK

Figure 1.2 The work cycle
A diagrammatic representation of the work flow through the life of a project. The control of cost and time is seen as a continuing function throughout.

country. Surely you do not need to be told which one that is. All these countries or areas of the world are very different, and the design and construction of a process plant ought to be considered, and related to, the particular country in which it is going to be built. We are not talking of the estimating aspect, or the profitability aspect, although those are significant factors. As will be seen, the matter is far more complex than that.

What we shall do is to look at the implications of designing and building in these various areas, and the way in which they affect the work of the cost control engineer in particular. Since our primary concern is project cost control, let us look first of all at those who can, and should, control cost. Then, after that, we will take a look at the world in which they work.

What *is* cost engineering?

Traditionally, the most significant skills in the various stages of development leading to the building of a new process plant have been those of the design engineer. However, various developments and changes have been taking place in recent years which, while not detracting from the necessity of mastering the increasing complexity of the design and engineering aspects of a project, have led to a better understanding of the need for a corresponding high level of skill, training, experience and know-how in project management, if a project is to be brought to a successful conclusion. Cost engineering is a vital part of project management.

Cost engineering, whether it be applied within the chemical process industry or any other industry, unfortunately varies widely in its application at the present time. The levels of the people providing cost engineering input can vary from purely clerical operations to the total financial management of a project. One of the prime factors that determines the degree of influence which the cost engineer can have is the effectiveness of his input in relation to the successful financial management of a project. Those then who are the directive force in the cost engineering department have to ensure that their service and that of their staff is both effective and beneficial. Too often, while paying lip service to cost *control*, what is actually being offered is a cost *monitoring* service. It is the difference between a dynamic forward-looking approach and a passive assessment of past history.

To assist those engaged in cost engineering there is now available a rapidly growing literature on the subject, with a great many very sophisticated techniques, employing computer programs. There can be a great gulf between the theory so presented and successful practice. This gulf *can* be bridged – by experience, if not by our own experience, then by the experiences of others. This is the purpose of our series of case studies. This is the way the cost engineer can learn, and the only way he will learn. Wherever we looked, in every one of our case studies, cost control was supposed to be the 'name of the game'. Financial accountability was supposed to reign supreme, but the projects were *not* built within the budget, nor within the time target first promised. Why not?

Cost control is everybody's business

Who controls cost? Those who incur those costs. This includes everyone connected with the project, whether at site or at head office, together with all the suppliers and subcontractors. Cost control is in effect the prevention of waste and since waste is caused by people, it can only be controlled by people. Most of the waste is potential to begin with: a design that has not been optimised. That is where cost control must start: in the design office. Leaving it till construction starts is far too late.

Each member of a project team is in a position to affect, and thus control, cost. But he cannot act in isolation, because then there would be 'too many cooks' and everyone knows what that leads to. So a Project Manager is appointed, and his function can be likened to that of the conductor of an orchestra. The best result is achieved when all involved in the project are working in harmony, following the lead (baton) of the Project Manager. Each individual has his own, and valuable, part to play; if any one were missing there would be something lacking. But they must play in unison. The conductor succeeds because he has direct and instant communication with every member of his orchestra. The Project Manager needs that too: both with his 'orchestra', all who are working on the project, and with the 'music' they are making – the results of their work. That is why it is so important for the results of their work, in terms of cost control reports, to come immediately after the event. 'Echoes' spoil the music! But is the project team and all who work on the project with them, master of the situation? They are still like that orchestra; put them in a hall with poor acoustics, and then see what happens. Let us think a little further about this matter of 'control'.

The real constraints

Our basic concern at the moment is to try and bring home the all-pervading importance of cost control, but it is very easy indeed to be unable to see the wood for the trees. This is always a potentially dangerous situation and can be of major significance with multi-project developments – and we get more and more of them these days. The bigger the investment, the more sophisticated the systems that are employed. Hereby a delusion develops. The flow of data can create the illusion that events are 'under control'. In fact, they have their own momentum. The real trick in effective project *management* – rather than *control* – is to find out where that momentum is taking one.

Any company proceeding to implement a series of capital projects operates under two basic groups of constraints: one internal, the other external. The internal constraints are largely the result of company policy (or lack of policy). The external constraints motivate some of the internal constraints and also constrain the contractors, subcontractors, manufacturers, suppliers and others who contribute either directly or indirectly to the progress of the project.

While a project is under study and during the early stages of design and order placement, the internal constraints are all-important to the progress of the project. Once, however, the project is largely committed, the external constraints assume a dominating role. What are these external constraints? They have been summarised (Ref. 2) as follows:

Social
Inflationary
Geographical
Political

The relative impact and importance of these several factors will vary from country to country. Typical social constraints are the availibity of natural resources, the availability of labour, the quality of labour, the population trend and the quality of life in the country concerned. These factors influence the frequency of strikes; the availability of transport to the site; the need to build toilets, canteens, or even housing, on the site; the ability to ship products from the site. All these determine the decision to build and the speed with which the project is brought to completion.

Despite easy communications and many other similarities, there is still a great difference between building a process facility in the United Kingdom and elsewhere in Western Europe. Why? The fundamental reason is geographical: the water that separates and still insulates the islands of Great Britain, even though in one place it is only 20 miles (30 kilometres) wide. This was and still is a critical constraint.

All the efforts to overcome these constraints, or work within them, are ultimately reflected in what is accomplished, what is built. Plotted over time, this always takes the form of an S-curve, and the end result of the constraints leads inevitably to the 'law of the S-curve', which will be looked at shortly. A law! If there is a law, who controls costs? We shall be a long way along the right path if we can but recognise our limitations, and work within them. It has never helped to attempt the impossible.

The role of the S-curve

When we start to design and build something of any size or

complexity we find that the several processes, or stages, that bring us, finally, to the completed installation, do not proceed by 'leaps and bounds'. As a result we have that classic cost control tool, the S-curve and especially the S-curve for value of work done. So true, so constant, so universal is this type of progress, in form and shape, that we are able to talk about 'the law of the S-curve' (Ref. 3). This is an empirical fact and finds its fullest expression in the growth of the value of work done on the project. Figure 1.3 illustrates typical curves of this type. All are part of 'value of work done' except the curve marked 'committed'. The sum of the three separate areas of effort (design, delivery of materials and construction) gives the S-curve for value of work done for the project as a whole, and it is that curve that follows the law most closely.

For all investments in new manufacturing facilities, the efforts involved in process and detailed design and engineering, procurement, expediting, and the supervision of construction in the field find their ultimate reflection in a mounting complexity of worked materials on the site. It is the end result of all this, as it grows, when measured in monetary terms, that produces the S-curve for the value of work done. For any area of capital investment, and for a particular project development and management approach, the S-curve is essentially always the same and it is this fact – an empirical fact – that enables a sound forecast to be made of the progress of the work over time. The significance of this statement will be more fully appreciated if our earlier remarks on the real constraints are borne in mind. For the law to be seen in action, value of work done must be clearly and consistently defined, and recorded as defined. The techniques to achieve this constitute the basic work of the cost control engineer and are the subject of the host of books and papers on cost engineering to which we have already referred.

When expressed in percentage terms, the S-curve for 'value of work done' *always* follows the same path. This is an empirical statement, based on the analysis of a substantial number of completed installations over the years. With a different organisation, and a different type of plant, the S-curve will be somewhat different also, but each time that particular organisation deals with a project, the S-curve will follow substantially the same path. History repeats itself; thus we talk of a 'law'.

With so much in a sense already controlled through circumstance and technique of approach, and so not in the hands of project management, one could almost dare ask the question: What is left for the cost control engineer, or even the project manager to do? Certainly, they have a real and important role to play because the

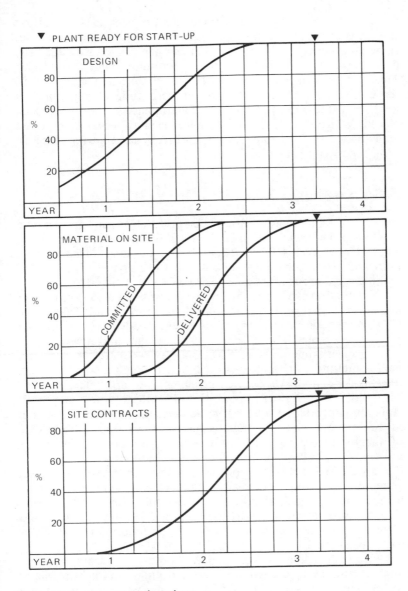

Figure 1.3 Progress per project phase
Typical progress in terms of value of work done for the three phases into which every project can and should be subdivided.

S-curve has been developed in the context of their exercising their functions in a proper manner. Were they to abandon their role, something entirely different would happen. After this analysis, perhaps they will see that their role is not quite what they thought. This is a fundamental issue to be raised time and again as we scrutinise and reflect upon the various case studies. If we can only learn from these examples where the emphasis *should* have been placed, where the effort *should* have been applied, then we are really on the road to managing our project and achieving effective project cost control.

Simple is beautiful

There is a contemporary ethos 'that technology can do virtually anything'. The result of this thinking is that when technology encounters problems, or creates problems, the solution is sought in more and better technology. This is rather like saying: 'The cure for bad management is more management.'

This situation can be seen at the present time in the field of project management and project cost control. A symposium is held in the USA. Hundreds of cost engineers attend, and nearly a hundred papers are presented. The year is 1974. We are told how to inter-relate project estimates and CPM schedules; we are told that we can have computerised two-dimensional progress reports – once a week if we like! Yet at the very same time one of the papers dares to have as its title: 'Can we really control multi-million dollar projects?' Another paper tells us that 'the advancement in technology, in scientific management ... has reached a peak in the entire history of mankind. We have had a glorious past and a glamorous present.' Yet, only six months later a brochure arrives from one of the specialised software companies offering these wonderful systems, comparing them with what is happening at present: 'shoddy project planning, slipped schedules, overrun budgets, sloppy coordination, seat-of-the-pants management ...' It would seem that, in their opinion at least, the situation is grim indeed, with vast scope for improvement.

They are not alone in that opinion. Another six months pass by, another summer is reached, and another symposium is held. Many of the same faces are seen, and there is another set of 50 or more papers. What are they saying this year? Just listen, and learn:

> The project network method is the most powerful technique yet developed for *planning* and *scheduling* a project. But ... it has not proved as useful for *monitoring* and *controlling* a project.

And again:

> Whilst remarkable advancement has been achieved in the area of net-
> working techniques and sophisticated reporting, the rate of *successful
> utilisation* of such systems has not attained a comparable growth.

The emphasis is, of course, ours.

There is no doubt at all that the need for effective project cost
control, in its turn the primary result of good project management,
grows by the year. The plants that are being built get bigger – much
will be said about that in Chapter 15 – and they are also becoming
ever more sophisticated and complex. Over the past ten years, costs
have practically trebled, and the size of plant built in the process
industries has also trebled in many cases. This leads to a
proliferation of joint ventures, sometimes across national
boundaries. Then particularly in the developing countries, the
government also takes a hand, and the position gets even more
complex. There are more parties to be consulted, more design
constraints to remember, more cost items to control. The end result
is, to use a well-known proverb, that one 'cannot see the wood for
the trees'. What then is to be done?

This section is headed with the words 'simple is beautiful', and
this is what must be recognised and then applied. We must ensure
that cost control techniques are serving a purpose, and are not
merely ornaments, like some of those 'mile castles' in Hadrian's
Wall. To help us in this, we can eventually come to the conclusion,
as we demonstrate in Chapter 15, that *'small* is beautiful' as well.
Then, if we build small, and mistakes are made – and they will be –
at least, they will only be little ones! Before relating the case histories, a look should be taken at the world about us. Networking
techniques and computerised reports, are a symptom, rather than a
result. They are symptomatic of what happens in the course of
development and the best way to see the result is to look at those
countries that have gone furthest along this road, the nations of
Western Europe and the USA. Where has it taken them?

Where are they going?

In the United States of America

In the USA the art and science of the cost control of projects are
well understood, have been the subject of detailed, widespread and
comprehensive development over a great many years. Do their
projects, then, stay within budget? It seems not. They still have

their problems, as the quotations from their literature on the subject clearly demonstrate. Why?

One fundamental reason is summed up by the following comment, taken from a talk on attitudes to industry in the United Kingdom and the United States (Ref. 4):

> What are we doing in the UK and the United States to free enterprise capitalism? I suggest in the UK we are trying to tax it to death and in the US you are trying to regulate it to death.

The annual meeting of the American Association for the Advancement of Science held in San Francisco late in 1979 was pervaded by pessimism and gloom. The consensus of opinion then was that the United States was going backwards, not forwards. A report on the various symposia that were held (Ref. 5) concluded that the USA was rapidly becoming a technologically second-class country, was on the brink of nuclear war and had little chance of meeting its future energy needs unless some drastic action was taken very soon.

These sentiments came not from just one speaker but from a wide spread of the influential people gathered there, leading figures in the American science establishment. In fact, the tone was set by what is called the 'keynote address': the paper that begins the meeting. The speaker told his audience that in the USA 'innovative and entrepreneurial spark is dying as in area after area our lead is closed by other nations'. He found this especially worrying because the US economy and social structure were as he said, 'rooted in the generous availability of the fruits of technology'. One of the main themes was energy: energy resources and the cost of energy. Another speaker, discussing the oil crisis, viewed the decade then beginning with 'almost unmitigated gloom'. That was oil; the 'International Monetary System' was also under pressure. Energy was taking, in the USA, and indeed worldwide, an ever larger share of the gross national product, draining ever more from the economy it was supposed to support.

These are all factors which affect the design and construction of process plants and their subsequent profitable operation. They are thus matters of immediate concern to the cost engineer. What are the lessons for him? It may be hoped that a few lessons can be learned from this 'over-developed' country in the next chapter.

On the other side of the Atlantic

In the United Kingdom major investment has taken place in the last ten years or so in what are called 'North Sea Projects'. These are the oil platforms in the North Sea, with the associated pipelines and plants designed to collect and process the gas and petroleum that has been found there in such abundance. These projects enter a field of high technology and have had very special environmental hazards to overcome. But does that justify the situation disclosed in relation to project cost control? We think not. One writer (Ref. 6) calls what has been going on 'a Wagnerian financial opera'. He says:

> It is a recognised problem of operators that accurately forecasting the final cost of a project is very difficult and creates a problem of investment analysis and in deciding the correct economic indicators. It is also a well-known fact that many of the North Sea Fields which have been developed were *grossly* underestimated.

The facts are:

20% of North Sea fields were up to 200% overrun.
30% of North Sea fields were up to 100% overrun.
50% of North Sea fields were up to 50% overrun.

The key ingredients that cause it all are:

1 Optimistic budgets based on limited technical definition;
2 Excessive construction/approval delays;
3 Unscheduled hazards/scope changes/claims;
4 General mishandling of the project;
5 Spiralling inflation;
6 Unstable currency exchange disparities.

Not much there about environmental hazards, is there? We do not propose to enter into the 'whys and wherefores' of all this at the moment. They will come in detail when the case studies are examined. For the moment, it is enough to realise that a problem exists: a problem by no means confined to North Sea projects or to the UK. The problems are worldwide. We shall meet the same elements as those cited above time and again, in different contexts, and perhaps with different emphasis as we move on from case study to case study.

References

1   Breeze, D.J. and Dobson, B., *Hadrian's Wall,* Penguin Books, 1978, p. 38.
2   Guthrie, K.M., *Managing Capital Expenditure for Construction Projects*, Craftsman Book Co. USA 1977.

3   Kharbanda, O.P., Stallworthy, E.A. and Williams, L.F., *Project Cost Control in Action,* Gower, Aldershot, Hampshire, 1980.

4   Hodgson, M., 'Attitudes to industry in the United Kingdom and the United States'. A talk by the Chairman of ICI given to the American Chamber of Commerce in London on 14 November 1978. (Available on request from ICI Ltd.)

5   *New Scientist* editorial titled 'Science in San Francisco', in the 17 January 1980 issue.

6   Sinclair, M., 'The Economic Problems of North Sea Projects – a Wagnerian Financial Opera', *The Cost Engineer* (UK) 19(1) 1980, p. 22.

2 Killed by kindness

Before we come down to cases we want to get a 'feel' for the conditions in which the cost control function has to work. As has been seen already, the 'climate' in which a process plant, or any other type of manufacturing installation, is built has significance both in terms of cost and the ability to control that cost. These days we talk freely about 'developing' and 'developed' countries. We think we can also see one step further: we think we can also see what might be called an 'over-developed' country. That country is, we believe, the United States of America.

In the USA the art and science of the cost control of projects are well developed and well understood. It has been learnt the hard way, by experience over several decades. There are networks, such as CPM, PERT, PRECEDENCE and a host of others. These techniques have been developed in great detail and are widely used. Each company and contractor has his own favourite network or networks and each has developed a set of techniques and procedures to suit his own particular requirements. The owner tends to use one type of approach, the contractor another, but the basic principles are the same. Even the good old barchart remains in fashion for it is still the simplest and a very effective method of presenting the overall picture in an easily understood format. Every contractor, even the smallest, has a distinct planning and scheduling section in his organisation, with a cost control activity. Some have developed very sophisticated techniques, using a computer, visual display units (VDUs) and the like scattered through their offices and even on the construction sites. The VDU now appears on the site along with the teleprinter.

All these procedures have been described at length in numerous books and papers, to which we ourselves have contributed. Our

17

own contribution has been to advocate simplicity. We have advocated manual techniques, and have exhorted our readers to 'KISS' their efforts – Keep It Simple, Stupid. There is another version, 'keep it stupid, simple', but we wonder whether that applies any more. Most contractors are in fact well aware that simple techniques, introduced early, are far more effective than complex techniques introduced late. The more complex methods may well eventually provide more accurate information, but it then comes too late to influence the situation. If we may liken our project to a patient, he may by then already be dead and beyond revival. No amount of artificial respiration, with or without oxygen, will then help.

In the USA at least the techniques of project cost control have been learnt, and are being applied. But this does not seem to mean that there are no delays or cost overruns on projects where these techniques are being utilised, and by those who know how to use them. One has only to scan the financial and technical press to see that this is most certainly *not* the case. What has gone wrong? The techniques of project cost control are well known and rigorously applied, yet projects still get into financial difficulties and cannot be completed on time.

We have already spoken of the constraints which apply, and in fact govern the situation with which the cost engineer is confronted. To set the scene, let us begin by quoting a past President of the United States, Thomas Jefferson. As long ago as 1816 he said:

> I place economy amongst the first and most important virtues. A public debt is the greatest danger to be faced. If we can prevent government from wasting the labour of the people under the pretence of caring for them, they will be happy.

What has actually happened since then? Some 150 years later the Congressional Directory tells us that the USA has 40 major regulatory bodies, all busy 'caring for the people'. How has this come about?

Enter Ralph Nader

Ralph Nader, a lawyer, seems to have made a career of fighting for causes which he believes to be just, on behalf of the community, in its capacity as consumers and citizens. The centre he first set up has now grown enormously, employing technical staff in all categories. This enables the centre to study thoroughly all aspects of any problem, analyse each one in great detail, and so build up a strong, sound case on the behalf of the citizens. There seems to be no dearth of funds for the taking up of seemingly good causes and they have had a great measure of success. The organisation commands great respect in government, industrial, civic and other circles. Ralph Nader is acknowledged, even by his bitterest opponents, to have 'influenced more people than anybody else' in this area of public relations. He has also been descirbed as a 'force, wherever he chooses to be a force'.

Ralph Nader first shot into public life in 1965, through the medium of his best-seller, a book with the title: *Unsafe at Any Speed: the Designed-in Dangers of the American Automobile*. The main theme of this book was the Chevrolet Corvair, decried as 'one of the nastiest handling cars ever built'. That sentence spelt the death knell of the Corvair. On this background he is a man feared by industry, small or large, and especially the major enterprises. General Motors, one of the biggest companies in the world, had him investigated by private detectives and he took them to court on the issue. The verdict went in Nader's favour, the GM president publicly apologised and Nader netted $270 000 as damages, to recompense him for the 'invasion of his privacy'. From then on there was no going back for Nader and his policies.

To continue with the Nader saga; he founded, in 1968, the Center for the Study of Responsive Law (consumer). The purpose of this centre was to generate public and official discussion of some of the central issues of the times. These issues included: air and water pollution; food and pesticide regulations; and anti-trust regulations. The present projects of the centre include a major conference on nuclear power and a project on critical mass energy while among groups organised within the centre are the Centre for Concerned Engineering and the Health Research Group.

The centre has served as an information resource, supplying data and help to the press, government officials and concerned individuals and groups throughout the United States, and even around the world. A Public Interest Research Group was founded in 1970, bringing together professionals drawn from a wide variety of disciplines to examine and report on technical issues such as automotive safety, emission control, environmental protection and clean water.

It can be seen from this that the net is cast very wide indeed. Some of the issues taken up and the battles fought and won are included in the next section. Although the Nader Group was not directly involved in all of them, they have played a major role in the entire movement. The Group operates entirely from funds provided by donations and the payments for Nader's public appearances. The Group has established itself in colleges and universities, while a number of young people (called Nader's Raiders) have taken up voluntary work for the centre. Its efforts are now being directed at grass roots level all over the country, instead of concentrating on Washington. The generic issue, the environment, is being translated into concepts that the common man can understand. It is now a very effective voice for a wide range of consumer causes. We have seen the cause; let us now study the effects.

Is any chemical safe?

The public attitude has been changing drastically, moulded by the media. If we were to judge only the news items, no chemical, and no factory producing chemicals, is safe. We set out below a short list of 'culprits', arranged in alphabetical order for convenience, and to demonstrate our own neutrality. The list is a random selection from news items in the technical press:

Acrylonitrile:
   Causes a drop in productivity. A 90% reduction in the exposure level has been ordered on an 'emergency temporary' basis.
American Cyanamid:
   A safety plan covering women at its lead-pigment-using facilities has been found to be faulty.
Armco and Republic Steel:
   The companies will have to spend $370 million for pollution control at the jointly owned Reserve Mining Co.
Cancer:
   Some organic chemicals present in much of Britain's drinking water are said to cause cancer. Fly ash may be a possible cause of cancer in men.
Car manufacturers:
   Ford Motor have been asked to recall 64 000 vehicles to rectify a defect in the emission-control system. Crysler Corporation had to fix pollution-control equipment on some of their 1978 cars by 29 April 1980 or stop selling them. General Motors agreed to pay £170 000 for improper assembly of pollution control equipment.
Damages and fines:
   Civil fines up to $5 million for firms spilling hazardous chemicals. There is a $40 billion damages' law suit, led by a veteran of

the Vietnam War against five US companies, on account of cancer claimed to be caused by a defoliant known as Agent Orange, used by the USA in Vietnam between 1962 and 1971.

Ethylene oxide:
This is used to kill germs on medical instruments and bandages, but may itself be a danger to human health.

Hair dyes:
Many of the permanent hair dyes now have to carry a warning to the effect that they contain a chemical which causes cancer in test animals.

Hexachlorophene:
This chemical could cause birth defects. Pregnant women are warned to avoid soaps containing this disinfectant.

Infertility:
The pesticide DBCP is cited as a possible cause.

Nitrites:
A total ban on nitrites in food is proposed.

Ozone:
New environmental problems are anticipated owing to the growing use of methylchloroform, and its assumed effect on the earth's ozone layer. This follows earlier restrictions on the use of trichlorethylene.

Phthalate ester plasticiser:
Identified as an environmental contaminant as widespread as the now notorious DDT and PCB.

Pentachlorophenol:
Monsanto are to close their plant in Wales on the orders of the British government.

Polyvinyl chloride:
Air Products to close their Calvert City plant.

Sulphur dioxide:
The Supreme Court refuses to hear a challenge to the SO_2 emission limits set for industry in rural areas.

Why dwell at such length on these seemingly disconnected items of news? What have they to do with project cost overruns, and the failure of projects? Simply because they are *not* unconnected. The fear, whether it be real or imaginary, of the adverse effects of chemicals such as those in the above sample list, is countered by regulations that are mandatory for the process industries. Not only does the US government spend vast sums of money on environmental control activities, nearly $10 *billion** as long ago as

* 1 billion = 1,000 million

1976, but those on the other side have to spend even greater sums. Public and private spending to meet Federal air pollution standards was estimated to be in excess of $13 billion in 1977. This was divided between the provision of new pollution control equipment and the cost of operating that equipment. To take specific cases, Ohio Edison had to spend $450 million for pollution control at their W.H. Sanis power plant, US Steel had to spend $25 million to reduce air pollution at their Fairfield, Alabama plant, and Monsanto say they will have to spend $2.4 million on a new information system merely to keep 'tabs' on the health of its 50 000 employees, spread over some 200 plant installations.

As we see from all this, the cost burden is there and the money has to be found. Plants take anything from two to five years to build and they have to meet the regulations current at the *end* of that period, not those at the beginning. To meet these requirements, costs can and do escalate substantially as a plant is being built, so rapid is the change. This is illustrated by Figure 2.1, which is an expansion of the diagram given in the previous chapter (Figure 1.1). You can see that we now have what we like to call a 'lump of lead' in the middle of the sequence of events, described as scope changes, leading to extra work and claims. If only the changes could be made before the detailed design and construction starts, they would cost far less. But changes made as the work progresses escalate out of all proportion, as is illustrated in Figure 2.2. The later the change, the more expensive it becomes.

But even the intrinsic cost of the measures that have to be taken is growing. A few years ago the specific cost of safety and preventive measures to protect the *environment* only (not the workers in the plant) might have been some 5% of the capital investment. Today it is climbing towards 20% of the investment. Thus an ever-growing proportion of total investment is required to meet the various regulations that have been imposed, and are still being imposed. This investment brings no return in terms of reducing product cost, it just adds to it. For the cost engineer it has become an 'unknown'; no wonder his budget estimate is overrun. No wonder, particularly with plants of but marginal profitability, that they finish up making a loss. Until environmentalists and governmental bodies start to take a more pragmatic view of the situation, new investment will become progessively less attractive, until it becomes completely unprofitable. If you think that we are exaggerating, or overstating the case, just look at what has already happened in the nuclear industry.

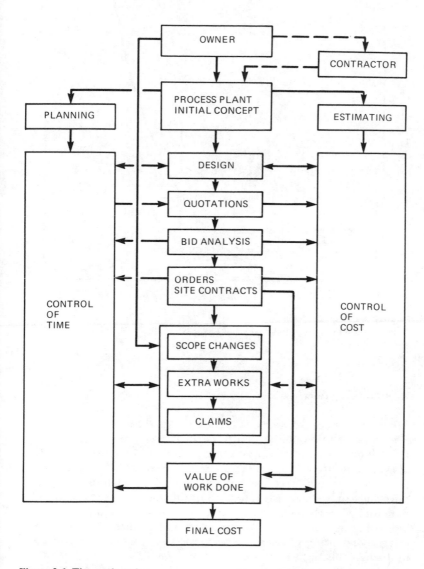

Figure 2.1 The work cycle
A more detailed diagram than that presented in Figure 1.1. The complicating effect
of scope changes on the work flow through the life of the project can be clearly seen.

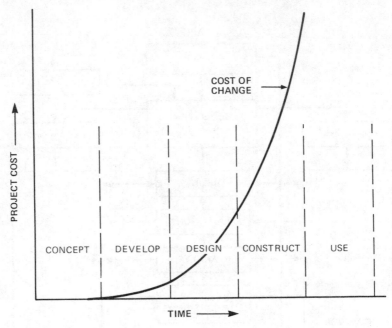

Figure 2.2 The cost of change
The cost of change rises dramatically, the later such changes are made during the life
of the project.

Regulations galore!

There are, of course, facts; there are things that can be measured.
For instance, air quality continues to deteriorate in Washington,
DC. Some eight million out of the nine million residents of the state
of Michigan are carrying the same toxic chemicals in their bodies
that have caused liver cancer in cattle. But what are the implications of such facts? Interest groups may well exaggerate the
potential of such facts to the point of outrage, aided by an ever-
increasing bureaucracy in Washington and a variety of interested
parties who bring pressure to bear upon government by constant
lobbying. This has led to over-reaction, resulting in an exponential
increase in the number of regulations. The regulatory process has
indeed been likened to an octopus, its long arms strangling growth
and destroying the innovative process for which the chemical
industry has for so long been noted. The main reason for the
present situation is a complete *distrust* of the industry, allowing the

flames of public misconception to be continuously fanned. Opinions both inside, and more particularly, outside the Government tend to become polarised, extremes develop and sound decisions are thereby inhibited.

If we look at the matter in what might be called 'physical' measurable terms, in Washington EPA employees have risen from some 8 000 in 1971 to more than 12 000 today. Administrative costs have risen six-fold over the same period, being now of the order of $5 billion. On the other hand the US chemical industry has already spent some $7 billion on pollution control facilities and is expected to spend another $6 billion during the first five years of this decade, to meet *existing* rules. The proposed new rules could escalate this cost to some $11 billion. Indeed, an independent estimate by the Council of Enviromental Quality indicates that the total cost to both government and industry of meeting the regulations during the next ten years will be some $360 billion. These figures are not consistent, but they are the figures that have been published. At least something of the order of magnitude of cost involved is seen, not one cent of which will be *productive*, merely *protective*. What is the inevitable end result of this developing situation? The cost engineer says:

No profits – No growth – No progress

What can be done? Very little. The chemical industry can try to take its case to the public, participate in the development of legislation, seek to ensure that it is realistic, and legislators must listen. When we turn to the nuclear power industry, we find the same picture, but taken to an extreme.

Nuclear regulations beat them all!

There is no doubt at all that the nuclear power plant sector of industry suffers from over-regulation, over-exposure and over-reaction, and will continue to do so. The Department of Energy and the Nuclear Regulatory Commission (formerly the Atomic Energy Commission) are charged with the safety of nuclear power plant installations. Initially and inevitably the codes and standards of the industry were those of the chemical industry, coupled with some vague guidelines regulating the construction of nuclear power plants. Later, the high risk associated with this particular type of installation was more fully appreciated, and more definitive guidelines were laid down. This led to an exponential growth in the number of regulations, as illustrated in Figure 2.3. This growth

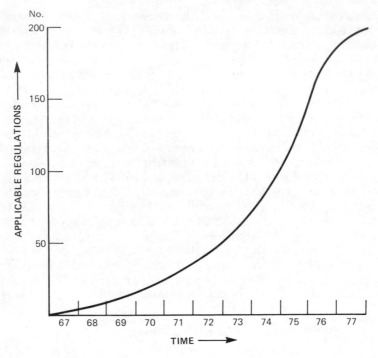

Figure 2.3 Regulations
This graph illustrates the growth in the cumulative total of regulations in relation to nuclear power plants since the late sixties. (With acknowledgements to the Tennessee Valley Authority – Ref. 1.)

occurred while plants were under construction, and so led to disruption and a lot of 'heart searching' in relation to the plants being planned. The end result was enormous cost and time overruns on the projects in hand, and the postponement or cancellation of projects in prospect. The background and the results of all this have been well documented (Refs. 1 and 2). The problem of cost was further accentuated by the unprecedented (for the USA) inflation over the years 1973–75, coupled with the increased governmental and public concern highlighted earlier.

As a consequence of all this, the cost and planning engineers were groping in the dark. Nuclear facilities had to be considered as a genre on their own, and no parallel could now be drawn with the conventional power stations, or even with the earlier nuclear power stations. To aid poignancy to the problem, this alarming growth in new codes, regulations and guidelines occurred during a period of unprecedented escalation in the cost of equipment, materials and wages. The main contractors in the nuclear power plant field suffered heavily, since their quotations were based on their earlier experience. They found out that the fine print of the regulations was going to be rigidly enforced and the extent of their error is illustrated in Figure 2.4. As a result of the technical elaboration required to comply with the regulations, materials were delayed, and actual costs exceeded first estimates by a factor of three or more, as illustrated in Figure 2.5.

Then came the widely publicised accident in 1979 at Three Mile Island. Despite the apparent over-regulation and apparent over-cautious approach an accident could still happen, and this was a great setback for the industry. It could have been far more serious than it was, apparently, and knowledgeable circles asserted that a major catastrophe was averted by sheer good luck, *not* by design. The verdict of the enquiry made the following points, among others:

> The operating utility did not have sufficient knowledge and expertise, or personnel, to operate the plant and maintain it adequately;

BROWNS FERRY UNITS 1–3 ESTIMATE COMPARISONS

Basic quantities	Initial estimate	Actual
Concrete	270 000 cubic yards	470 000
Excavation	850 000 cubic yards	5 000 000
Electric cable	6 000 000 lin. feet	22 200 000
Conduit	900 000 lin. feet	1 700 000
Craft manhours		
Total	12 000 000	36 300 000
Per gross kw	3.5	10.5
Schedule		
Award NSSS	June 1966	June 1966
Start construction	September 1966	September 1966
Fuel load first unit	July 1970	June 1973
Construction time	46 months	81 months

Figure 2.4 Estimate comparisons
This table shows the basic 'volumes' for the Browns Ferry Nuclear Power Station. It reflects the discrepancies caused by the estimator being unaware of the volume of future changes in scope. (With acknowledgements to the Tennessee Valley Authority – Ref. 1.)

THE MOVEMENT IN THE CAPITAL COST ESTIMATE OF THE
TENNESSEE VALLEY AUTHORITY NUCLEAR PLANTS
FOR THE PRODUCTION OF ELECTRICITY

Nuclear power station	Original estimate	Latest cost
Browns Ferry	100	233
Séquoyah	100	433
Watts Bar	100	*291
Bellefonte	100	284
Hartsville	100	*411
Phipps Bend	100	*186
AVERAGE	About ...	300

*Note: This is an estimate, assuming the construction programme
to be completed by 1986, but completion of these three
plants has now been deferred.

Figure 2.5 The movement in the capital cost estimate
The reason for the increase in the capital estimate varies, but the difference between
the first estimates and the final cost is divided between scope changes, schedule
delays and inflation. (With thanks for permission to publish from the Tennessee
Valley Authority.)

> The Nuclear Regulatory Commission was so preoccupied with
> licensing that it had not monitored the safety aspects properly;
> Fundamental changes are required in organisation, procedures and
> practices at nuclear power stations.

The accident was ascribed to design flaws, coupled with human
error. Had the regulations been strictly enforced, then the accident
could have been avoided. It was likened to what is called a 'near
miss' with commercial airliners. We get scared, but we do not quit
flying. Rather, we analyse the experience, seeking to ensure that it
will not happen again. So the incident was bound to lead to some
changes in design and operational procedures, and also the mode of
regulation adopted by the Nuclear Regulatory Commission, and
these *will* have a cost impact.

The initial public reaction was an over-reaction, and there was a
great strengthening of the hands of the 'No Nukes' (no nuclear
power stations) movement, spurred on by the Nader Group. There
was a sudden shadow over nuclear power worldwide, and particularly in Japan, Germany and France. Retrospectively, we see that
this has been only a short term reaction. There is no doubt that
nuclear power is here to stay, both in the USA and elsewhere, but

the safeguards, and hence the cost, are going to go up. We shall continue to see cost and time overruns, for we are sure that the cost engineer, despite all his efforts, will fail to keep pace with actuality. Or more properly, perhaps, his pessimistic view will be rejected by management. Once again, no one will believe him till it is too late.

Where do they go from here?

Fundamentally we can only hope that the nuclear regulations, old and new, will be applied with logic and commonsense, rather than blind rigidity as in a story that appeared in the *Washington Post* in March 1980. The paper reported the case of a small contractor who had fallen foul of the American Department of Labour because 5 per cent of the four labourers working for him 'were not women'. As a result he had been ordered by the Department to maintain a written Equal Opportunity Employment policy, to appoint an EEO officer with a written job description, to keep records of his encouragements to minority female employees to seek promotion and, all in all, to comply with the 43 different rules laid down by the faraway bureaucrats. A further note: it has been calculated that the costs of complying with such Utopian fantasies, which involve more clerks, more records and more reports, were of the order of more than $100 billion as long ago as 1977. They are most certainly far higher today.

Returning to the theme of nuclear power, the current dependence of the USA is of the order of 15%, ranging from a high of about 25% in the Northeast to a low of about 5% in the Far West. With the dwindling resources of oil there is no doubt that commercial development of nuclear power will continue. This means that to counteract the sweeping proposals of the regulatory bodies, industry will gear itself up for a counter-offensive. This will inevitably lead to a number of court battles, minor and major, with the two sides failing to listen to one another, emotions running high. What is the answer? There is only one answer, although we doubt whether it will be sought – *moderation*. The opposing groups take extreme positions and there is no one, it seems, to intervene and moderate the arguments. The fears are real enough. A case highlighted internationally illustrates what can happen. It was called the 'love canal case'. A community living near the Niagara Falls, the honeymooners' paradise, was found to be invaded by chemicals from a waste dump long buried and forgotten. The family life of the community was thereby threatened. This was a fact, and industry cannot ignore its responsibilities in this field. But there was over-reaction. *All* such dumps must be cleaned up, they said. Effluents must be *completely* free from toxic chemicals, but such measures are not practically possible and can result in unnecessary and prohibitive costs.

Hence our plea for moderation. Unfortunately, the 'man in the street' has no conception at all of the way in which the fruits of the chemical industry have been woven into his daily life, especially in the USA. The industry contributes very substantially to his daily well-being, but the media only highlight the bad news. You will remember the proverb, 'Bad news travels fast'. Chemical producers should not have to apologise for, and excuse, what they do. True, they work to make a profit, but most managements have a highly developed sense of public responsibility and do what they can, within the constraints in which they have to work. So we urge that the chief executive officers of chemical companies create an on-going dialogue, where the good as well as the bad is brought to light. Both sides must be heard, not just the vociferous one.

The economy has to slow down

We can see that over-development, such as seems to have occurred in the United States, can bring in its wake many peculiar problems, some of which we have discussed here in a little detail. A law operates, as always, whereby as one group of problems is solved, another set is created. The chief problems that now have to be faced, with all their consequences, are those created by very rapid growth and over-affluence. To see what has happened over the past ten years or so, study Figure 2.6. Here fuel prices and interest rates in the USA are compared with the cost of construction works. We can see that while the cost of construction has doubled, both fuel costs and interest rates have trebled. These factors are worldwide and not limited to the USA and they have a powerful effect on the economy. Further, what we might call the 'imbalance' is most difficult for the cost engineer. He is happiest when all his curves run parallel. Then he *really* knows where he is.

Leading economists the world over seem to be convinced that the standard of living of the average American *must* decline, if inflation is to be controlled. The economy demands still faster formation of capital assets to satisfy demand, a process which diverts funds from the consumer, the social services and the improvement of the environment. The end result: a reduced standard of life. There is no longer money for everything.

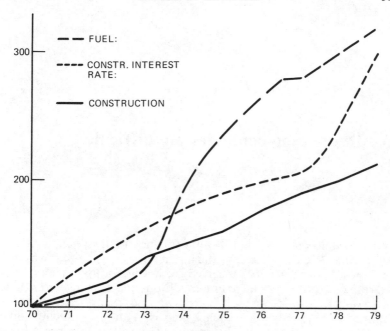

Figure 2.6 Cost escalation over time
Here we compare the ways in which fuel costs and construction costs have varied; at the same time interest rates have also shown a steady climb.

References

1   Willis, W.F., 'TVA's First 10 Years of Nuclear Plant Design and Construction Experience', *Cost Engineering* (USA), Vol. 21, 1, January/February, 1979.
2   Liddle, C.J., 'Estimation or Procrastination?' *Engineering and Process Economics*, Elsevier Publishing, Amsterdam, 3, 1979, pp. 165–173.

3 Developing countries are difficult

When people visit a foreign country for the first time such a visit is often described as 'a leap into the unknown'. That, indeed, was the title of a booklet we once received from a motoring organisation, warning us of the very different conditions and circumstances that we would meet once we took our car abroad. And a '*leap* into the unknown' is exactly what such a step is. You are suddenly confronted with a completely different world. In that confrontation, you realise that *you* have to conform, to do otherwise would be fatal.

In the industrial sphere the same thing has been happening, only it is the technology of the Western nations that 'suddenly' appeared in what are called the 'developing nations'. But there was no attempt at all to conform to local conditions; it was assumed that Western technology could be applied 'lock, stock and barrel' within these countries, as the saying goes. But it could not. Outlooks were different, the *needs* were very different. What went wrong? This is written for the edification, in particular, of project managers and cost engineers. Was it the fault of the cost engineers? Or was it perhaps poor project management? Something certainly has gone wrong, for so many of the projects have cost far more, and taken far longer, than anyone ever expected. Let us see what really happened.

Financial management

We can quote from a typical paper presented at a meeting of the Association of Cost Engineers. The paper carriers the title 'Effective Cost Engineering of Chemical Plants' (Ref. 1). The question was posed: 'What is good financial management, or effective cost engineering?' We were told the answer. There were said to be four critical elements in a good project, without which a project would not be effectively managed. These are:

1   to build the *right* projects;
2   – at the *right* time
3   – at the *right* place
4   – at the *right* price

If any one of these four elements is missing, then we are in deep trouble. When we turn to the developing countries, it would seem that most of the time not one, but all four of these elements were missing (Ref. 2). This sad result stems from the sort of thinking propounded by the leading financiers – and it is they, after all, who control the funds that allow plants to be built. Dr. Kaldor, for instance, argues thus:

> If we can only employ a limited number of people in wage labour, then let us employ them in the most productive way, so that they make the biggest possible contribution to the national output, because that will also give the quickest rate of economic growth. You should not go deliberately out of your way to reduce productivity in order to reduce the amount of capital per worker. This seems to me nonsense because you may find that by increasing capital per worker tenfold you increase the output per worker twentyfold. There is no question from every point of view of the superiority of the latest and more capitalistic technologies.

But, as Dr. Schumacher, having quoted Dr. Kaldor, goes on to demonstrate, in developing countries this apparently logical approach is a great mistake (Ref. 3). It is probably also a mistake for developed countries, but that would take time to demonstrate. We cannot enter into Dr. Schumacher's arguments now, but we shall touch on some of the points he makes later, in Chapter 15, Small *is* beautiful. For the moment, let us at least recognise that to build plants incorporating the latest in technology in developing countries is almost invariably a wrong choice of project, time and place. That is why the fourth element, cost, which is the direct responsibility of the cost engineer, also goes wrong. And there is just nothing, then, that he can do about it, as shall be seen. The first three elements are pre-requisite to the fourth.

Developing countries

In order to see something of the scope and scale of our subject, we

thought that we would compare the developed and the developing
countries in terms of energy use, and this is done in Figure 3:1. This
data was abstracted from a paper on the social and political aspects
of energy (Ref. 4). The immediate inference to be drawn from the
data is that the developing countries cannot achieve the standard of
living currently enjoyed in the developed countries, basing their
approach to their development on the oil and gas technology that is
the foundation of the prosperity of the developed countries. This
echoes what we have said already: any such attempt is doomed
before it starts. Yet that is the approach we see at the present time,
almost everywhere.

	Population 1975 millions	Increase % per year	Potential population year 2000 millions	Energy usage ratio
DEVELOPED NATIONS				
U.S.A.	210	0.6	250	50
Western Europe	472	0.5	550	30
DEVELOPING NATIONS				
Asia	2200	2.4	4200	15
Africa	375	2.6	800	5

Figure 3.1 The scale of the problem
The implication of the above table is that the developing nations cannot match the
developed nations while trying to base their industry on current oil and gas
technology. (Developed from data given by F.S. Patton – Ref. 4.)

It would however appear that this brutal fact of life is slowly –
but so very slowly – being recognised. Another paper (Ref. 5)
reminds us that the back yards of communities all over the Third
World are littered with the rusted remains of what development
experts considered best for the people there. We already have some
spectacular failures in relation to attempts to persuade a rural
people to adopt a foreign technology, even when it has been provided free of charge. Another aspect is taken up in a paper about
ethanol, or ethyl alcohol: just alcohol, to the uninitiated (Ref. 6).
As petroleum prices increase some countries may find that the production of ethylene from an agriculturally based feedstock, and
one of the basic chemical 'building blocks' in this modern world,
could well be a viable alternative. This theme is taken up in a little
more detail in Chapter 15, since it is part of our exhortation to keep

things simple, but for the moment let us but note that before 1945 a significant proportion of the world's ethylene production was in fact derived from ethanol. The process was then long established, and it was only the fact that cheap petroleum-derived hydrocarbons made the process uncompetitive that caused that particular route to disappear almost overnight.

There is more than the technology to get right. The price has to be right as well. Here we can quote a moral tale (Ref. 7). The scene is the Works Minister's office in a west African capital and tenders are being opened for a sewage treatment plant. The lowest of six tenders is found to be some 30% higher than the consultant's estimate. He has to explain within 24 hours, in relation to a feasibility study he completed two years earlier and has long forgotten in detail. What is the true answer? His contingencies were cancelled, and he was optimistic. Escalation has also taken its toll. On the other hand, the contractors are justifiably pessimistic. The owner, who can never be blamed, also added a multitude of 'frills and gingerbread'. But the consultant has to contrive an answer that protects him while not condemning the owner. This is what is going on all the time. The project cost has already overrun the estimate on which the action decision was based, and the work has not even started. It will overrun that first estimate still more before it is finished. In all probability it will finally cost twice that first estimate. This situation is rather like that presented in those novels that are written so that we can see the same events through the eyes of a number of different characters. Each of the four parties usually involved – the owner, the international bank lending the money, the consulting engineer and the engineering contractor – has his own view of what is going on. Almost invariably, the situation is made far worse by a complete inability to see, listen to or act upon the other parties' point of view.

With this background in mind, let us see what actually happens. A few examples have been chosen, rather at random, from various developing countries. Saudi Arabia, India and Korea have been selected. There is no wish to criticise any country or its policies, nor the projects and contractors we highlight. It is not even claimed that our examples are representative; they are only illustrative. While the three countries just mentioned are all termed 'developing countries', each differs significantly. Our particular interest is project cost control, and this is the angle from which we are going to look at the examples chosen. In that context, Saudi Arabia has never heard of it, India is conscious of it but has to learn how, while Korea has indeed learnt how to control costs. Korea like everyone who ever learnt a lesson, learnt it the 'hard way', but that is the best way – probably the only way. We are trying to make that learning process easier, by getting our readers to learn from the experience of others rather than their own, but that will only happen if you *really listen*!

The King Feisal Specialist Hospital, Riyadh

This hospital is a wonderful example of all that is the latest in technology, but what did it cost and what is its use? The hospital is claimed to be the world's most advanced and it has certainly been a showpiece for visitors to Saudi Arabia. It was intended to translate into practice a 'dream' of King Feisal. He wished to provide the latest that medicine, engineering and modern technology could provide for the health care of the people in his country. Unfortunately, the King did not live to see his dream fulfilled. Indeed, although the hospital is now completed and in 'operation', his dream is still not fulfilled. He died a few weeks before the hospital was finally opened, in 1975.

Perhaps that was just as well, since the hospital is now described as a 'white elephant', a classic example of 'everything that has gone wrong with modern technology'. These are the words of Dr Kenneth Williams, the British physician who planned the hospital and helped to create it. He now laments: 'It was a fascinating case study in the uncontrolled use of money'. First estimated to cost some $10 million, the final price tag is believed to be $250 million and one can but wonder, in retrospect, whether these figures could ever relate to the same project (Ref. 8). It may be thought of as a showpiece, but what does it actually show? It shows the way in which the latest technology, together with greed on the part of contractors and medical hardware suppliers from the various countries involved, can escalate health care cost to dazzling heights, unless there are sound, proper, strict cost control systems at all levels.

This 250-bed hospital is the very first in the developing countries with an integrated, computerised technological system. There are 18 computers, and the system processes all sorts of data, from a patient's case history to planning the menus, and finally printing the bill. Cardiac patients are each 'hooked' into their own individual computer terminal, thus registering the vital data, such as body temperature, blood pressure and pulse rate. Intensive care patients are televised on a 'closed circuit' system so that doctors and other personnel can maintain a close watch while sitting in their offices. Operations are filmed and recorded on video tape in full colour. With such comprehensive automation one would surmise that far fewer staff would be required as compared with the average hospital, and that the doctors would have 'all the time in the world' to devote to their patients. Far from it! The total staff numbers some 1200 and is still increasing. The patients have become mere numbers, lost in the complexity of the machine. The personal touch, so essential for confidence in the staff, and cure, is completely missing.

Although this hospital was originally a British concept, it was actually built by a Lebanese contractor, using technology and hardware from America, Britain, Europe and Japan. It is now managed by the Hospital Corporation of America. This health care project became a political football, the hospital a stadium and the patients merely spectators! For the person who first planned the project, Dr Williams, the dream now only exemplifies an escalation in health care costs that brings no reward, the transformation of a noble cause into greed and corruption, while at the same time the patient, for whom it was all being done, has been dehumanised.

What is the moral? It is surely this, that it is completely out of place to transplant modern technology into a developing country. Without cost control, all involved had a 'field day'. Everybody is happy except the patients themselves, for whom the hospital was actually built. Because it is so out of place, the hospital remains completely vulnerable. One fuse blown, one spare part missing, and a technician has to be flown across the world to make an on the spot investigation. Meanwhile, the patient goes home, or goes . . . ?

India – overruns the rule, not the exception

It is unfortunately true – will we never stop saying it? – that most projects overrun on both time and cost. Pick up any newspaper, any day, and you are likely to find at least one project in the news for this reason. Here is a typical extract. It relates to a hydroelectric power plant project. We highlight a few of the points made in the article (Ref. 9):

> *Kalinadi Project Delay doubles cost*
> The giant Kalinadi project on which Karnataka has set its hopes of meeting the State's endemic power shortage has yet to take off. It is almost a decade since work on this project began and it should have been completed long ago. After eight years, having been bogged down by frustrating delays, man-made and natural, the first 135 MW unit, one of the six planned in the first stage, is expected to . . .
> The delay has severely hampered the growth of industry in the area. The cost has escalated staggeringly, from Rs. 1260 million to Rs. 2760

million, despite the best efforts and the latest techniques, like PERT
and CPM. The contractors lacked tunnel-laying experience, there was
silting and heavy rainfall.

BHEL (Bharat Heavy Electricals Ltd.) have not kept up the
delivery schedule and there is a severe 'mismatching' of equipment.
Generators are not working properly. This is an amazing and
challenging undertaking from the point of view of engineering and
technology.

Such drastic delay in a basic industry such as power generation,
has a snowballing effect. The consuming industries, with plants
ready and waiting, cannot commission them. And this is not the
end of the road. There is the cost of the power itself. The energy
cost was estimated in the project report at Rs. 0.05 per unit. This is
now going to be higher by some three to four times, quite apart
from escalation. How viable will those user plants now be, with
profits based on the fantastically low figure of Rs. 0.05 per unit
(£1 = Rs. 18)?

This story is typical. A complete catalogue of such projects could
fill a book, but we would not wish to weary you. To let you see that
in India it really is true that overruns are the rule, a selection of projects from only one industry is presented in Figures 3.2 and 3.3.
Figure 3.2 relates to the series of fertiliser projects of the erstwhile
Fertiliser Corporation of India, now split up into five different
companies based on the geography of India and the function of
the plants. Figure 3.3 spells out the history of one particular project, Korba, where the delays and changes in policy have made this
project a 'non-starter', even though Rs. 300 million have now
been spent. No great effort was needed to compile Figure 3.2; our
problem was to limit the list to manageable proportions. The main
causes for the delays detailed are set out in Figure 3.4. These are all
causes which will be very familiar to our readers, which could have
been avoided or minimised with planning, control and experience.

Does departmental execution save money?

How does the Western world manage its affairs when it comes to
building process plants? There is no doubt that the 'managing contractor' concept has demonstrated its sucess time and again,
whether or not we have a 'turn-key' contract. The fundamental
approach is to place *all* the work in one hand. This requires confidence and trust because whatever the outcome the owner will
always suffer far more than the contractor. Formal contracts do
not help. While detailed contracts are drawn up, they are seldom

INDIAN FERTILISER PROJECTS

Location	Approval Date	Approval Budget Rs.m.	Completion Sched.	Completion Actual	Completion Cost Rs.m.	Overrun Time	Overrun Cost
Barauni	12–67	351	11–71	1977	923	2.45	2.55
Bhatinda	8–74	1384	1–78	1979	2405	1.36	1.75
Durgapur	2–66	381	12–69	1977	1022	3.00	2.65
Gorakpur	6–72	118	4–75	1976	184	1.30	1.56
Haldia (1)	11–71	880	10–75	1982	2997	2.25	2.77
Namrup (E)	12–67	295	1–71	1976	749	2.30	2.53
Nangal II	10–72	756	3–76	1978	1339	1.66	1.77
Panipat	2–75	1397	5–78	1979	2213	1.38	1.60
Ramagundam (2)	10–69	712	7–75	1980	2329	2.00	3.35
Sindri (M) (3)	1–73	889	2–78	1979	1832	1.50	2.06
Sindri (R) (4)	12–67	230	10–71	1981	597	3.30	2.65
Talcher (2)	10–69	705	7–75	1979	2320	2.00	3.35
Trombay IV (4, 5)	9–74	440	4–77	1979	763	1.77	1.74
Trombay V	10–75	1114	4–78	1981	1798	2.20	1.61

Rs.m. = Million rupees.   Type of development:
Where indicated   (M) = Modernisation
(R) = Rehabilitation
(E) = Expansion
otherwise, new installations.

Notes: (1) Plant mechanically complete. Not commissioned due to lack of adequate power. A captive power plant since installed. Breakdown of compressors brings further delay.
(2) Projects physically completed, but operating problems continue, leading to low capacity utilisation. Each plant requires an additional boiler & gasifier, total extra cost Rs. 1000 million, but this is the price of new technology.
(3) Completed, but shut down due to chemical snags.
(4) Completed, but design and equipment deficiencies remain. Modifications are in hand.
(5) Commissioned, but basic design deficiencies are reported.

Figure 3.2 Indian fertiliser plants
This table sets out the 'overrun' in both cost and time for a series of fertiliser plants, showing that this is a continuing factor over the years.

THE KORBA FERTILISER PLANT, INDIA

1968	Feasibility Report
1969 Oct.	Project 'approved'.
1972 Jan.	'Go-ahead' given by the Government. Estimate Rs. 721 million, including Rs. 202 million in foreign exchange. Target completion date: June 1974.
1973 Apr.	Foundation stone laid by the Prime Minister of India.
1973 Sept.	Agreement made with Techno Export for the Air Separation Plant.
1974 Jan.	Proposals cleared by the Project Investment Board.
1974 June	Project cleared by Central Cabinet.
1974 Nov.	Action on project slowed down. Revised cost estimate Rs. 1183 million, with a completion date of December 1978.
1975 Mar.	Allocation of funds for 1975 reduced to minimum required to meet earlier commitments. No fresh orders to be placed for equipment.
1975 Sept.	First major Indian delivery made – of electric motors.
1975 Dec.	First shipment of air separation plant received.
1976	Efforts made to cancel orders already placed. Project to be 'kept in suspense' until after successful commissioning of Talcher & Ramag and coal-based plants (1979/1980)
1979	Total expenditure Rs. 221 million.
1982 Apr.	Project abandoned. Total cost = Rs. 300 million.

Figure 3.3 The Korba Fertiliser Plant (India)

referred to, except perhaps as a contract is closed out, to settle claims and variations. In fact, the best executed projects are those without an elaborate contract document. The owner/contractor relationship often develops to such an extent that work is started well before the contract is signed, and it is the spirit, rather than the letter, that prevails.

It is still true in the Western world that quite often 'a handshake is the equivalent of a legal contract' and as such is more binding than any written document. To quote one small example (from *Fortune,* March 1978): 'Nearly half of the hamburger patties, which sell by the billions, come from a company nobody ever heard of. The company has been built quite literally on a handshake ... it never had a contract'.

INDIAN FERTILISER PROJECTS

TECHNICAL DETAILS

Location	Tons/day Ammonia	Urea	Feedstock	Main problems in execution
Baranni	600	900	Naphtha	Equipment failures
Bhatinda	900	1500	Fuel oil	Low estimate, scope changes
Durgapur	600	900	Naphtha	Equipment failures
Gorakphur	200	300	Naphtha	Equipment deliveries, labour problems
Haldia	600	500	Fuel oil	Piling, floods, equipment deliveries
Korba	900	1500	Coal	See Fig. 3.3
Namrup (E)	600	1000	Gas	Equipment failures
Nangal II	900	1000	Fuel oil	Revisions, equipment failures, heavy rains
Panipat	900	1500	Fuel oil	Low bearing capacity of soil, equipment deliveries
Ramagundam	900	1500	Coal	Approvals, equipment deliveries
Sindri (M)	900	900 (+AS)	Fuel oil	Equipment deliveries
Sindri (R)	–	1130*	–	Equipment failures, inferior pyrites
Talcher	900	1500	Coal	Power shortage
Trombay IV	–	1100 **	Gas	Revisions to the specifications
Trombay V	1250	820	Gas	Engineering, Bombay Port congestion

Notes: E = Expansion   M = Modernisation   R = Rationalisation
(+AS) = plus ammonium phosphate   * = triple phosphate
** = nitro-phosphate
Both inflation and escalation are common factors to the overruns on all the plants.

Figure 3.4 The problems highlighted
Here we survey the same plants as were listed in Figure 3.2, detailing the main problems encountered during execution that caused delay.

As yet India has failed to learn from these experiences, costing her much time and money. Much of the delay, and hence cost, in the cases set out in Figures 3.2 and 3.4 can be attributed, either directly or indirectly, to what we shall call 'departmental execution'. This means that the project is not given out in its entirety. Certain elements of work are retained and handled by a government department – quite often, a number of different government departments. This arrangement has the inherent disadvantage that it lends itself beautifully to 'passing the buck' to one or more of the numerous subcontractors also involved, or the other way round. For instance, the original unit at Trombay was let almost completely on a 'turn-key' basis, but certain activities, including the provision of foundations, remained the responsibility of the owners. Later, the compressor foundations were found defective, in that they were not properly designed to cope with the vibration. The contractor then used this fact as a shelter for the substantial delay which would have occurred in any case. This incident led to prolonged argument and even international litigation. Meanwhile, the cost burden on the project was such that its very viability was in question. Delay in project completion hurts all the parties involved, but the owner suffers most – chiefly in terms of loss of interest and loss of production. The contractor suffers largely from a loss of reputation. To show how important this aspect is to the contractor, we can quote a West German process plant contractor who claims, in a recent advertisement, that some 60% of his current work is repeat business from satisfied owners!

It must not be forgotten that engineering contractors acquire their expertise in project execution over a period of years. This is the know-how by which they make a living. The owner, on the other hand, has very different functions and strengths. His competency lies in the efficient operation of the plant and the selling of its products. How foolish, then, to take over some of the functions that are properly those of the contractor. There is a better course, a viable middle course, which in India seems very slow in coming. This is the development of experienced Indian main contractors, stepping into the shoes of the contractors from abroad who have dominated the Indian scene for so long. There are Indian contractors who have demonstrated their competence outside India, and they should be encouraged at home.

In this respect it would indeed be well if India could take a lesson from Korea where construction services have been exported on a very substantial scale – some $10 billion of orders booked in 1978 – and this has helped develop their engineering and construction skills at home. The first major petrochemical complex in Korea had

Toyo Engineering of Japan as prime contractors, but the latest petrochemical complex is to have Korea Engineering as prime contractors. So they move on. But not India. What is the problem?

In India individuals excel

An oriental, but not Indian management expert is on record as saying:

$$1 \text{ Indian} = 2 \text{ Japanese}$$
$$2 \text{ Indians} = 1 \text{ Japanese}$$
$$3 \text{ Indians} = confusion$$

We think that there is an element of truth in this, and that it pinpoints the problem. To the extent that it is true, it becomes a constraint that cost engineers and management have to reckon with and overcome. This is not the place, nor are we competent to analyse its significance in depth, but our own personal experience, particularly outside India, is that given opportunity individual Indians can and have excelled in their respective fields. Yet, in terms of team work and team effort, there is much left to be desired.

It is undoubtedly true that project execution and project cost control depend for their successful execution entirely on the combined efforts of the entire project team. There has to be an integrated whole, including not only the construction team on site, but also the home office staff concerned with design, engineering, procurement, expediting and the financing of the project. The members of this team belong to a wide range of disciplines and have very diverse functions. With their different backgrounds – engineering, buying, accounting – all radically different in concept, effective communication is a *must* for proper project control, and this is never easy. In India it seems, and perhaps for the reason we have indicated, not to be seriously attempted. We see the other extreme more often than not – departmental execution, a project handled in bits and pieces. The outcome is seen in the projects we have highlighted. When their history is studied – and we take two cases in some detail, first in Chapter 8 and then later in Chapter 13 – we see the same things time and again: lack of decision, changes in decisions, delays in delivery. The common factor behind these failings is undoubtedly a lack of proper team effort.

Why do we emphasise this? To learn from our failures in order to turn past failure into future success. Now we see as key factors in success: team work, forceful project management. We are by no means the first to say this. A recent text on management published by the American Management Association had the strange title: 'Huddling – the Informal Way to Management Success'. According to the author, results are not produced by organisations but by *people*. What sort of people? A very special kind of people, people who are 'huddlers', capable of working together informally in small groups resulting in intimate, work-oriented encounters between a few people at a time, who draw together and confer in order to get things done. 'Huddling' is in effect a synonym for 'team effort'. Perhaps more of us, especially in India, need to learn the art of huddling. Perhaps your last project failed because there was not enought huddling. Think about it, watch the project you are now busy with and ask yourself: Do we huddle? If not, perhaps you are on the way to another overrun!

Time is money

Another fundamental in project cost control is that 'time is money'. When you take time, you are spending money, and project prolongation is a major factor in most project cost overruns, particularly in India. The problem with time, however, is that you cannot help spending it, although it is a precious resource. Moreover, once spent, it is irrecoverable. It may be trite, but it is true; the clock can never be put back. This is the very first lesson for the cost engineer, but one yet to be learnt seriously in India. In the words of Omar Khayyam:

> The Moving Finger writes; and, having writ,
> Moves on; nor all your Piety nor Wit
> Shall lure it back to cancel half a Line

Let us translate time into money, to see what it can mean. With a project costing Rs. 100 million, one month's delay will incur a *direct* loss, due to extra interest, of Rs. 1.25 million. Loss of profit will be of that same order. Each month's delay, therefore, will cost a minimum of Rs. 2.5 million. Surely, then, it is worth paying say Rs. 2.0 million extra to the contractor, which could be the result of placing all the work in his hands, in order to ensure timely completion? Unfortunately this type of payoff is not recognised by the owners in India – and they are not alone. Savings are sought by fragmentation, but this is at the cost of time – and time costs money. Thus experience tells us that the approach is fallacious, that departmental execution will not in fact save money.

It must be realised that nothing can be had for nothing; there is no such thing as a 'free lunch'. Owners are deceived because the costs they incur are hidden. Purchasing costs time, and hence money, whoever does it. With the owner, an expenditure may disappear into his overhead, perhaps not even costed to the project, with the contractor it *must* be paid for directly, as part of the project cost. No one believes for a moment that the owner can operate more efficiently than the contractor, so how is it possible to save money in real terms? Cost engineers have to demonstrate and substantiate these basic facts. Contractors do make profits, but where is the contractor making excessive profits? His margin is a sound investment, because it encourages timely completion.

Korea shows the way

We have already referred to the example of South Korea. Their contractors, armed with know-how gained by the execution of a variety of construction contracts, particularly in the Middle East, supplemented by imported process technology, are now beginning to assume the role of managing contractor. We watched this process all of thirty years ago, then taking place in the United Kingdom. We cite the outcome in relation to one firm in a case study in Chapter 6 (A splendid refinery). Now we see the same thing again in South Korea. The local engineering companies are steadily taking over the role of the foreign, largely Japanese companies, that have been operating there. The miraculous growth of South Korea in recent years has earned striking headlines in the international press. Typical headlines are:

From rags to riches
A second Japan
Changwon: a Korean Pittsburgh

Such achievement is not the result of chance, nor good luck alone. There are two major factors playing a significant role: strict discipline and hard work as a team. Starting from scratch barely five years ago, Korea won some $9 billion of construction work in the Middle East in 1978. This is nearly three times the volume secured by British contractors in that area. As a result, Korea is one of the few countries, either developed or developing, that has achieved a positive trade balance with the OPEC countries. Korean workers, it appears, need very little supervision, their wages are low and their productivity high. Is it any wonder, then, that they are progressively displacing American, British and Japanese contractors in the Middle East?

This growing experience of Korean contractors abroad has brought its 'fall-out' at home. As we noted earlier, Korean Engineering are quite likely to be the managing contractor for the next petrochemical complex in Korea, being planned in 1981. A nuclear power plant, which can take from ten to fifteen years to bring to completion in the USA, is completed in South Korea in five years. They certainly seem fully conscious of the money value of time. As a result of these short construction periods, nuclear power in Korea already provides nearly half of the energy they derive from oil. If the present trend continues, encouraged by the growing cost and problems associated with oil, energy in Korea may well be far cheaper than energy in the USA by the late eighties. Then history is likely to be repeated, with Korea emerging as a 'second Japan'. At their present rate of growth, the Koreans could attain Britain's present per capita income in the course of the eighties, and that enjoyed by Japan in the early nineties. It would then have joined the league of developed nations. How has this been achieved? The specific situation, such as the work in the Middle East, has played a part, but hard work and discipline must be fundamental, because the only significant resource in South Korea is – men!

Where do we go from here?

The theme of this chapter has been the present state of the art of project cost control in the developing countries. We have selected a few random examples from the multitude that are available, and thus we have arbitrarily highlighted certain projects in Saudi Arabia, India and South Korea. Quite obviously, we tend to select in relation to our own personal experience, and one of us has been personally concerned with these particular countries over the years, rather than with the other developing countries. We say this to show you why we have chosen the examples that we have, seeking to make the point that it is by no means our intention or objective to denigrate any particular country or company. We want to *learn from past mistakes*. We can only do that if we find a few mistakes and look at them fairly closely.

Of the examples we have chosen, we could say that Saudi Arabia does not have to worry about cost: there is money in plenty, thanks to petro-dollars. But how long will that last? We are reminded of the years immediately after the Second World War, when costs were so uncertain, and contractors did most of their work on a 'cost plus' basis. Both management and personnel developed what we called the 'cost-plus habit' and when times became more competitive and lump-sum tenders were made, it was most difficult to adjust. Habits of thinking had to be transformed, and that is most difficult. So Saudi Arabia ought to become cost conscious now. India is very conscious of the need, is seriously concerned at the ineffectiveness of cost control in relation to so many major projects, but the lesson still needs to be learnt. It *can* be learnt and it *must* be learnt, for mere survival. That it *can* be done is amply demonstrated by South Korea, also a developing country, but now well on its way to being a developed country. What are the lessons to be learnt?

Time is money
Departmental execution is *not* cheap
Team effort is a *must* (huddling!)
Discipline pays off
There is no substitute for hard work

Further, all this must grow of its own accord. The transfer of the latest in technology to the midst of one of the oldest civilisations is *no* solution. It only creates problems where before there were none, and that at fantastic cost. Please listen.

References

1   Leese, M.G. (Mond Division, ICI Ltd), 'Effective Cost Engineering of Chemical Plants', a paper presented to the Association of Cost Engineers (Northwest Branch), UK, February 1980.

2   Ronald Robinson (ed.), *Industrialisation in Developing Countries*, Cambridge University Overseas Studies Committee, Cambridge, 1965.

3   Schumacher, E.F., *Small is beautiful*, Blond & Briggs Ltd., London, 1973.

4   Patton, F.S., 'Energy – social and political aspects', *The Cost Engineer* (UK) 19 (1), 1980, pp. 8–21.

5   Ashworth, J., 'Renewable energy for the world's poor', *Technology Review*, 82, pp. 42–49, November 1979.

6   Kocher, N.K. & Marcell, R., 'Ethylene from ethanol – the economics are improved', *Chemical Engineering*, 87 (28 January 1980), pp. 80–81.

7   Simplicimus, J., 'Cost overruns – the Third World project problem that won't go away', *Modern Asia,* 52, Feb/March, 1979.

8   O'Brien, R.B., Article in the London *Daily Telegraph* of 30
     October 1979 with the headline 'Saudi's space age hospital
     "inhuman" says doctor'.
9   Kusnur, V.R., 'Kalinadi project delays doubles cost',
     Economic Times (India), p. 9, 19 December 1979.

PART TWO

MAKE FAILURE BRING SUCCESS

4 Heavy water makes heavy weather

It is not often that a process plant is built that does not work at all. As we have said already, of the various factors that enter in, the design is the most likely to be the most reliable of all the factors involved. But it can happen and it has happened. Our case study from Canada begins like that. We are going to see what happened when the Glace Bay Heavy Water Plant was built. But before considering the project itself, let us first see why anybody should ever wish to manufacture what is called 'heavy water': deuterium (D_2O) to the chemist.

Using nuclear power, there are three major routes to the production of electricity. In all three the neutrons produced in the fission process and required to maintain the chain of fission reactions are slowed down in a medium of light atoms called a moderator. In this context the three basic routes that have been developed are:

1 Enriched uranium with water as coolant and moderator. This approach is in use in the USA, France, Japan, West Germany, Sweden and some other countries;
2 Natural uranium with gas as coolant and graphite as the moderator. This approach was adopted in the United Kingdom, and initially by France;
3 Natural uranium with heavy water as the coolant and moderator.

Canada chose the third system, for a combination of technical and economic reasons.

If we take a brief look at the economic aspects, we see that it is a question of what might be called 'raw material' costs. Taking 1972 as our base year for costing, natural uranium fuel elements were

51

then about $45 per kilo, whereas the enriched uranium fuel elements were some five times dearer, at about $220 per kilo. This meant that for a power station of normal size, with say four 500 MW generating sets, operating at about 80% of maximum load, the normal cost of the fuel, using natural uranium rods, would be about $12 million per year and about half what it would be using the enriched rods. So here is a means to a very substantial saving in operating cost, and there is no need to purchase the politically sensitive enriched uranium. On the other hand, the heavy water that has to be used as moderator and coolant with natural uranium is far more expensive than ordinary water. In 1972 it cost some $90 per kilo on the international market. However, the bulk requirement is a one-time purchase, to fill up the plant; after that the only make-up required is for losses due to leaks, which can still come to a lot of money. Leakage on such a unit might be some 16 tons a year, costing $1.5 million. This annual saving in running cost – nearly $10 million per year at 1972 prices – has to be set off against the initial increase in investment. We have cheaper uranium, but much dearer water. The heavy water required to load up a power plant is about one ton per MW of installed capacity, meaning that the initial cost of the heavy water alone would have been some $180 million, at 1972 prices. We have also to consider the cost of the uranium, the difference in the capital investment for the different types of plant, but having got some idea of the approach, let us not go any deeper into the calculations.

Others have done all the studies, and when the figures are analysed a calculated technical and business risk has to be taken because the optimum in relation to the use of heavy water is by no means clear cut. In any event, for a country of the size and with the resources of Canada, the choices are limited. It would hardly be wise to try out a number of different approaches at the same time. In such a context all the effort is better concentrated on one specific type and that is what Canada decided to do. In retrospect, there is no doubt at all that it was the right decision. As a result of this firm policy, Canada now has more than five *billion* dollars invested in natural uranium heavy-water-type reactors, with their associated power generating units. Plants with a total output of 5 000 MW are already in service and plants giving a further 9 000 MW are under construction or in course of commissioning: a state of affairs that should give much satisfaction to those who made that first decision. Curiously enough, their main problem – and eventually their major headache – proved to be *not* the reactor or its operation, but the provision of an adequate supply of heavy water for the power plants as they were constructed. It was unfortunate that their first venture into the manufacture of heavy water, the major plant at Glace Bay, in Nova Scotia, let them down so badly. It is that plant that we have chosen to study. But first, let us set the proposed production of heavy water at Glace Bay in context (Refs. 1 to 5).

The historical background

To trace the history of the ill fated Glace Bay project we thought we should start right from the beginning, from the time of the discovery of heavy water, or deuterium.

1934   Deuterium discovered by Urey.

1941   Spevack worked with Urey to develop the economic 'GS' process for the production of heavy water commercially. No one knows why it is called the GS process. Possibly it stands for Girdler sulphide.

1950   Decision taken by the US Government to build two large plants to provide heavy water for their plutonium production reactors. One was to be built at Dana, the other at Savannah River.

1952   Dana Plant began operation.

1953   Savannah River plant began operation.

1956   Misunderstanding between Spevack and the Atomic Energy Commission led to a claim suit with respect to the use of the Spevack patents. The outcome was to save the US government nearly $2 billion, by reducing the cost of heavy water from some $450 to $60 per kilo.

1963   Construction started on a heavy water plant at Glace Bay in Canada, based on the Spevack process. Its purpose: to create a stockpile of heavy water for the Canadian nuclear power programme. The initial estimated cost was $33 million, with a construction schedule of about 3½ years. The production cost was estimated to be some $40 per kilo, in contrast to the then US market price of $65 per kilo.

   Glace Bay plant was to be owned 49% by Spevack, 51% by the government of Nova Scotia. Burn & Roe of New Jersey in the USA were to carry out the detailed process and engineering design, while Brown & Root, a Canadian company, were the construction contractors. This latter appointment was much against the wishes of Spevack, who wanted Burn & Roe to be responsible for construction as well.

1966   Spevack set up the Deuterium Corporation of New York to offer technology for the manufacture of heavy water.

1967   Glace Bay plant commissioned on 1 May. Sea water was the raw material for the heavy water, not fresh water as had been used at Dana and Savannah River. But the plant never got into production. It had operating problems and problems with heavy corrosion. Cost to date $83 million, since it was also decided to build two 200 ton per annum units, instead of the one decided on in 1963, which was going to cost $33 million.

The plant was being started up and shut down repeatedly, and there were problems of corrosion due to stagnant sea water in the process coolers. Although plant commissioning was done with fresh water within the process equipment, there was no substitute for sea water cooling.

1969   Problems overwhelming, the stituation desperate. $107 million had now been spent, with no solution in sight. A DuPont study recommended a two-year rehabilitation programme, costing some $30 million, but its major findings were refuted by Burn & Roe. (We examine both reports in some detail later.)

1970   Government sanctioned $42 million for plant rehabilitation.

1971   Total cost had now amounted to $150 million. Plant was leased by the Nova Scotia government to Atomic Energy of Canada Limited at no fee. There was a $95 million grant for plant rehabilitation.

1972   Canada had to purchase 1 400 tons of heavy water from the USA to meet the immediate requirements of their nuclear power programme.

We shall end our historical review here and complete the story later. The final outcome is quite fascinating, as you will see, but where are we so far? Simply expressed, the plant failed on commissioning and never went into proper operation. Scheduled to start up in July 1966, construction was finalised in 1968 and the attempts to get the plant into operation were finally abandoned in 1969. Having two parallel process streams of identical size, problems encountered in starting up the first stream were 'solved', in the first instance, by vandalising the second stream plant. For instance, heat exchanger bundles were transferred as an emergency maintenance measure but rapid corrosion continued and the problems merely multiplied.

The DuPont Study Group report

The evaluation and assessment of the Glace Bay Heavy Water Plant by the DuPont Study Group was contained in an exhaustive report which was completed in 1969 and then released to the press. It ran, as published by the press, to some 20,000 words, the press deletions being relatively minor. Questions of secrecy do not appear to have played a significant role, because the account remained fairly detailed. It is instructive, we feel, to quote a few extracts from the report to get an impression of what actually happened to the plant.

DuPont was chosen to make the study because they were the prime contractors to the Atomic Energy Commission in the USA for their heavy water plants. The Glace Bay plant was first designed to produce 200 tons of deuterium per year, but a second stream was later added, making the proposed production 400 tons per year. Although the plant was scheduled to start up in 1966, it was not charged until November 1968, and a period of proper, steady operation never occurred. A succession of equipment failures –heat exchanger tubes, pumps and compressors – brought operation to a full stop by March 1969, and it was then decided that the plant was inoperable. It was at this point that it was decided to seek the advice of DuPont. The report from DuPont can be summarised under three main headings: the proposed modifications, the time factor and the cost factor.

Modifications and repairs

Major modifications and repairs would be required, necessitated by the inadequacies in the design, compounded by the consequent equipment failures. With only one month's field work the conclusions in the report must be considered tentative, but they definitely asserted that a manufacturing organisation with the appropriate experience should be employed for the redesign and subsequent startup. The sieve trays in the columns needed review, the design calculations should be verified, the rate of gas circulation should be reduced, although this would reduce the rate of production of deuterium. Major redesign was also required in the feed and effluent systems. In particular, the emergency H_2S discharge should be thoroughly restudied. The present exhaust, near ground level, was hazardous and there was no low point in the emergency lines to the flare in which liquid could collect. The compressor and turbine setup was also criticised. The plant was congested, sealing was inadequate, there were excessive piping stresses and process upsets. Over 800 butterfly valves, up to 48 inches in diameter, were installed. Many had failed, and must be replaced, or if repaired would require modification.

The process is essentially one of recycling and upgrading of the water to increase the concentration of product, in a series of stages. This series of stages forms a cascade in which the water is increased in concentration, so far as deuterium is concerned, in a series of steps, each higher step being of smaller size. Thus the higher stages cost much less per stage, but contain the majority of the D_2O inventory in the plant. As a result, water distillation is preferred for these higher stages because of its simplicity, reliability and negligible leakage potential. The report nevertheless recommended that the fourth and fifth stages be abandoned, rather than replace them with distillation units. Corrosion by the chlorides in seawater is insidious, they said, and trouble can arise in the most unexpected places; they recommended using fresh water instead of seawater, eliminating many of the special materials. Plant operation and safety were also reviewed. Hydrogen sulphide at high pressures was considered hazardous, and the large compressors should be relocated. The process is very complex, requiring detailed planning with written operating procedures and a carefully staged startup.

The estimate of time

It was considered that it would take anything up to two years to rehabilitate the plant, from the time the work was authorised. Apart from the redesign, procurement and delivery period in general, certain items, such as the turbines, would take at least 18 months to arrive. Time could be saved but at cost, for example by procurement without competition. Time also had to be balanced against cost and risk. For instance, the existing recirculators could be rehabilitated in order to achieve an earlier startup of half the plant. Time could possibly be saved if there was an intensive design effort and construction analysis so that sound decisions could be made on the feasibility of repair as opposed to replacement.

The estimate of cost

A tentative figure of $30 million was put forward, but this figure was hedged about with all sorts of provisos. There was a vast range of possible alternatives, and no decisions could be taken until the detailed design studies had been completed. And each decision taken would affect cost materially. The point was made, with reference to the estimate built up by DuPont, that the deletion of an item would not necessarily reduce cost; extra cost might then be incurred in another quarter. Further, the estimates were based on a normal working week of 50 hours. If massive overtime was authorised to speed up the work, this would have a substantial impact on cost. It had to be remembered, too, that the estimates were by no means the result of detailed design studies, and detailed examination of the plant could uncover further work, and hence cost. Two major assumptions had been made in the estimate: that the plant would continue to use seawater and that there would be no work on the fourth and fifth stages. It would be at least eight months before a detailed cost estimate could be prepared in which some confidence could be placed.

In our resumé of the DuPont Study Group report the detail has been given so that you can have some idea of the problems that can be encountered when a process does not work, for whatever reason. This example is most useful because it is so all embracing – almost everything went wrong that could go wrong. When we say that, let us not forget that there were plants already in operation in the USA to provide a fund of experience. We think that this picture will be a great help to those faced with similar problems, even if their magnitude is not so great. As we said, it is rare for a plant to be inoperable on startup, but there are many plants which on startup cannot be brought up to more than 50% design capacity, for reasons such as we have met here. If the cost engineer can but appreciate how vulnerable his estimates of cost and time are likely to be at that moment, and impress management with that fact, his function will have been performed. These are *our* comments, the lessons *we* are now drawing, but at the time there were others who also commented on the DuPont report.

Burn & Roe's comments on the DuPont report

You know who Burn & Roe are. They are the company that Spevack, whose company had a 49% interest in this plant in the early days, had appointed for process and detailed engineering. They were the real target of all the criticism. What did Burn & Roe have to say?

The report, they said, was only DuPont's opinion, given without full consideration of the circumstances and influenced by their own standards and background experience. The cost and the time schedule did not appear to be the primary considerations in their study, so the time and cost conclusions could be in serious error. The report, as presented, tended to place all the parties, and especially Deuterium of Canada Limited (DCL) in a grossly unfair light. Without an exhaustive, technically qualified commentary on each of the points made, the report will only create unwarranted alarm and confusion. The plant can produce heavy water in far less time, and for much less money, than had been suggested in the report. The study group had not pursued alternatives which would allow production of the income-producing heavy water to begin on an interim basis, with alterations and modifications to follow. A major part of the report, they added, deals with situations and alternatives that had already been considered by DCL, and the decisions taken, now criticised, were dictated by the necessity of saving time or reducing the initial investment. In many cases, decisions had been taken in the face of objections made by Burn & Roe, but without, it was thought, harm being done to the basic function of production, or safety. All the decisions taken were first the subject of extensive review and discussion by DCL prior to finalisation. Criticism of DCL, they said, was implicit throughout the report and many of the suggestions made by the study group had already been earmarked for implementation once the necessary funds had been generated. They thought that the additional information available from them was needed for study concurrent with the DuPont report and that decisions based upon incomplete information would but be a disservice to the project and all those associated with it.

Burn & Roe asserted that there were many points on which they were in strong disagreement, which they summarised as follows:

1 Burn & Roe were not consulted. As a result the design intent and purpose were not thoroughly understood nor properly evaluated;
2 An understanding of the basic design criteria is of prime importance. There was no adequate investigation of the background information and its implications;
3 The report did not have as its objective the manufacture of a commercial product in the shortest possible time, and for the least possible further expenditure;
4 The estimates of time and cost were challenged. The plant could be operable in far less time, and for a much lower cost than had been estimated;
5 Every effort should be made to operate all stages of the plant and to utilise fully the production economies inherent in the design;
6 The plant was complex, and required skilled and experienced, competent staff;
7 The scrapping of the existing compressors and their substitution by a different system would not be necessary. The compressors had been supplied by a reputable and qualified Canadian manufacturer under performance guarantees and every effort

should be made to permit the system to function as designed;
8   The report recommended replacement of the sieve trays, but
    the tray design followed well established design practice,
    developed in cooperation with an eminent consultant.

Burn & Roe asserted that the plant was essentially sound in design,
and could be made to produce heavy water sooner and at much less
additional cost. They were prepared to discuss their own recommendations in detail, which they felt were in the best interest of
the successful completion of a plant that was so essential not only
to Canada but to the world at large.
   What actually happened?

Rehabilitation or reconstruction

We do not know which of these words better describes what
actually happened to this plant. The work, however we describe it,
was authorised by the new company, Atomic Energy of Canada
Limited (AECL) in 1971. If it had done nothing else, the DuPont
report had made it very clear that major work was necessary to
bring the plant into production as a reliable source of heavy water.
There had been considerable damage to the plant, and the tray
design was inadequate. A major decision was taken, to use fresh
water instead of sea water. In addition, while the basic GS system
was to be retained, the design would be modified in accordance
with a new process design developed by Dr V.R. Thayer and later
patented (Ref. 6). The plant was completely dismantled and
inspected thoroughly to establish which items could be re-used,
with or without repair.

The basic restrictions

The new approach was bounded by a number of restrictions, some
existing, some imposed. One fundamental principle was that the
new design should be 'forced' or adapted to utilise the existing
equipment to the maximum possible extent. Further, the original
plant had been built at the apex of a triangle of land surrounded by
water with no room for expansion. In addition, equipment siting
was determined by the location of the ten large towers (see Figure
4.1), the location of the buildings, the location of the effluent
cooling channel and the need to find space on a restricted site for
the expansion loops in the large diameter piping. Not only had all

Figure 4.1 The Glace Bay installation prior to rehabilitation
An aerial view of the Glace Bay Heavy Water Plant at Cape Breton, Nova Scotia.
The plant as illustrated was designed to use salt water. The salt water intake and
discharge can be seen as indentations along the shore line. (Photograph by courtesy
of Atomic Energy of Canada Limited.)

equipment to be reused wherever possible, but no item could be
rejected without specific approval. Once the requirements had been
identified, then tenders were to be secured both for the new
equipment and for equipment modification.

A design problem

It was decided to abandon the original flowsheet (Ref. 7) and a new
and simpler flowsheet was developed to optimise production from
the existing tower volume. A clean sweep approach was taken, all
piping being dismantled and all the original items of equipment,
such as towers, heat exchangers, pumps, electrical equipment and
instruments left to form one large inventory of components from

which the designers had to draw as the new design was developed. The main GS towers were reused, but all the internal trays and other fittings had to be replaced. Great care was taken to match each tower with the most appropriate duty. One should not forget that the new flowsheet was based on the patent of Dr. V.R. Thayer, a concept as yet not employed on any other heavy water plant. A multitude of problems in design were met and overcome, and for those facing what we call 'revamp' work they make most interesting reading (Ref. 8). We thought, however, that you might find it more interesting if we highlighted only one feature on the re-habilitated plant – a rather outstanding one!

The flare stack

The existing flare stack was badly corroded and was found to be undersized for the new duties which would now arise. This old stack was demolished and replaced by two new stacks, one 6 inches in diameter, the other 48 inches, both 400 feet (122 metres) high. Two stacks were considered necessary, one to handle routine purging, the other to handle the very large volumes of gas that would have to be released in an emergency. (What curious problems have to be overcome!) Here, there was no problem in the stack design as such, but obstruction lights had to be installed at the top of the stack, since it was a high structure. This is a Department of Transport regulation, but with this particular stack there would have to have been a costly plant shutdown to maintain or replace the light bulbs. Various alternatives were considered and discussed with the Department of Transport. The solution finally adopted was to illuminate the upper third of the stack – floodlight it, in effect – from ground level. A Xenon-type lighting fixture was used for this purpose. This has a high light output, so that an extremely narrow beam is projected, lighting the top of the stack even on a foggy night.

The rehabilitated plant was commissioned on 15 June 1976, exactly a decade after the scheduled date, with AECL announcing that the Glace Bay plant had successfully produced its first drum of product. This ended a thirteen-year struggle, and is an outstanding example of persistence in the face of what were almost over-whelming odds. That was only a new beginning, not the end of the story. This was true, even of the flare. Yet another flare system has now been installed and commissioned (Ref. 9). Figure 4.2 gives a general view of the plant as it was in February 1980 and the very newest flare stack also 400 feet (122 metres) high can be seen at the left on the photograph. The old flare stack, the same height, is on

Figure 4.2 Closeup of the process units at Glace Bay
Here we can see the GS towers, with the new flare structure on the extreme left, and
the old flare on the far right. No one seems to know with authority where the name
'GS' for the process towers came from. (Photograph by courtesy of Atomic Energy
of Canada Limited.)

the extreme right. The new system has two flares, one providing an
environmentally acceptable discharge of the very small quantities of
H_2S and other gases vented from the purge tower. The larger stack
is used to discharge and burn safely and rapidly the H_2S from any
of the GS towers in the event of an emergency warranting that sort
of action.

The saga continues

We have to remember that the Glace Bay plant was originally
designed to produce some 400 tons of heavy water per year. When
it was finally started up in 1976 the actual production rate was far
less than this: some 70 tons in 1976 and 60 tons in 1977. There was

GLACE BAY HEAVY WATER PLANT PRODUCTION SUMMARY	
Year	Production tons (Mg) per annum
1976	70
1977	60
1978	210
1979	233
1980	249
1981	240

Figure for 1981 is a forecast, and is marginally lower than 1980 because of a shutdown planned in the course of the year.

Figure 4.3 Production summary – Glace Bay heavy water plant
This table shows the progress being made over the years in increasing the output of heavy water.

still a long way to go.

Once started up, the plant presented a rather different type of challenge than it had before. Till startup, it had been a design and construction challenge: now it had turned into a technical challenge. The technologists made their studies and were so successful that production has now risen to more than 200 tons per year. Their goal is 300 tons per year. The progress being made is illustrated in Figure 4.3. The areas so far successfully dealt with are:

1 *Plant capacity*
    Increase in tower efficiency by changes in the trays, made in late 1977. The next stage in this process is due to be completed in 1981;
2 *Process control*
    Close cooperation between the engineers and the plant operators, working together as an operations analysis team, to improve the day-to-day operation of the plant;
3 *Plant availability*
    Development of repair and maintenance technology into effective maintenance procedures, with sound inspection. The result has been that the monthly availability of the plant has been stepped up to in excess of 90%.

The need for this approach, which is very intensive in character, is perhaps best appreciated when it is realised that a unique flow-sheet was developed for this particular plant. The rehabilitated plant features a combination of a first and second stage in a single unit, supported by two satellite booster towers, with direct steam injection and individual strippers for each tower system. This particular setup also moves the concentrated D_2O from stage to stage in the liquid phase as compared with the other Canadian plants, which are all of the 'gas-feed forward' type. The result is that operation procedures are unique, meaning experience cannot be transferred from other plants. Another problem is the persistent instability experienced once flow rates are brought above some 85% of the design rate. There is a suspicion that deleterious organic compounds are selectively concentrated in certain parts of the system and thus either initiate or contribute to this instability. It is factors such as these that make the day-to-day operation of the plant at high output rates so difficult. The measure of their achievement against such odds is well demonstrated by results, such as those tabled in Figure 4.3.

Persistence always pays

When the historical background to this project was reviewed earlier in the chapter, it was seen that the Glace Bay Heavy Water Plant was originally conceived in 1963 when Deuterium of Canada Limited submitted a proposal for the supply of heavy water to the Canadian Nuclear Reactor programme on the basis of a 49:51 ownership between the Nova Scotia government and Spevack. In the following five years, Spevack had difficulty in raising his share of the finance required, and the project had labour management difficulties that were finally the subject of a Royal Commission. The cost estimates kept escalating and then, to cap it all, there were profound technical problems when the plant was started up. In 1969 the Nova Scotia government, who had by then become the sole owner of the plant, abandoned the attempts to commission the plant, and initiated the series of studies to which we have already referred, with a view to rehabilitating the plant. Responsibility for the plant then passed from the provincial government to Atomic Energy of Canada Limited, who awarded the rehabilitation contract to Canatom-MHG.

Thanks to a most thorough post mortem and the comprehensive design and construction effort by Canatom-MHG, backed by the persistence that had first been displayed by the owners, the plant was rehabilitated and started production of heavy water in mid-1976. The wisdom of the approach adopted, involving redesign under a number of major constraints, can certainly be questioned. It might well have been cheaper to scrap the entire plant and start afresh, but this is something we can never know. As a cost engineer should realise only too well, where alternatives are involved we only ever know the cost of the alternative we adopt – never the cost of the other routes we might have taken.

Nevertheless the plant was rebuilt and it is now in full operation. We give you a view of the rehabilitated plant from the air, in Figure 4.4. In a way, we have perpetuated in this photograph one outstanding memento of all the upheaval that occurred over those traumatic years. The existing towers were utilised, preserving the

Figure 4.4 The Glace Bay installation following rehabilitation
The plant now uses fresh water with a recirculating system, and the seven-unit cooling tower in that system stands out clearly in our aerial view. (Photograph by courtesy of Atomic Energy of Canada Limited.)

outward form of the plant from a distance, but on the left is a bank of seven cooling towers. These were built when the plant went over to fresh water cooling, and of course that water had to be conserved.

The heavy water supply and demand situation has changed markedly in the last few years. Owing to lack of growth in demand, two 800 MW power stations originally scheduled for startup in 1981 have now been 'mothballed'. Demand to 1990 is now forecast to be less than 20 000 MW. Thus, in the early eighties Canada will have a total production capacity 2 400 Mg/a from nuclear power stations which can be expanded very rapidly to 4 000 Mg/a in response to a rise in the demand forecasts.

Faulty human engineering

It has been an interesting history. A proven process fails to work. Cost control conspicuous by its absence! The initial project estimate $33 million, but when $107 million had been spent, there was still not a drop of heavy water to be had. Of course, that initial estimate was for a single 200 tons per year plant, while the final cost related to two such units, and over the years escalation also took its toll. The final expenditure was some $150 million. Further, many of the costs over $100 million were capitalised commissioning costs and the interest on the construction costs. These are the very real penalties incurred by the failure of the plant to produce, but they do not reflect the real capital investment in plant and equipment.

There was a monumental lack of communication throughout that first phase starting at the very beginning with the process engineering. The experience available from the Savannah River and Dana Plants in the USA was ignored. It seems as though the presence of the inventor of the process was a handicap – a liability rather than an asset. Perhaps he was convinced that he knew all the answers. He insisted on a flowsheet which was from a process engineering point of view technically very inelegant. It was also extremely complex and the plant that resulted very difficult to get into operation and maintain in a stable condition. The DuPont study may sound extremely critical, but they were indeed faced with a plant design that was very close to being inoperable.

Things did go wrong. They always do. For instance, the Canadian company, Deuterium of Canada Limited, did not accept the inventor, Spevack's, recommendation as to the construction contractor. The construction contract was awarded to Brown & Root, a Canadian company, rather than to Burn & Roe, who were doing the detailed engineering. But was that *so* important? No doubt it added a complication, and possibly a degree of bitterness, but it did not affect the process. Finance also became a problem. A year before the scheduled completion date Spevack was unable to raise the rest of the money he required and as a result the Nova Scotia government finally purchased his interest, paying him compensation in lieu of the technical services and know how that had been made available by him. This was an adverse development, but we have never known the financial wheelings and dealings behind the scenes to affect construction in the field seriously. The plant should still have produced heavy water on time.

When we consider the steps taken to deal with the situation when it had developed although the plant still would not start up, a complete state of disorientation seems to be disclosed. We suspect that this was largely due to understaffing on the operations and maintenance side. Up to about a year before commissioning began, DCL had only two or three engineers in their employ and they did not seem to make any extensive use of consultants. What they had was what we call a 'large train plant', but operating experience was completely lacking. There was a significant underestimate of the manpower requirements and the personnel facilities required for startup and operation. These deficiencies were identified during commissioning and have been substantially rectified since. Additional facilities have included: a heavy equipment repair shop, an insulation/sheet metal shop, a carpenter-painter shop, a major expansion of the tradesmen's locker room, a lunchroom-cafeteria and office space for a majority of the plant staff. Overall about 35 000 square feet of permanent enclosed work and storage space was originally provided and all these extras added some 75 000 square feet more. Apart from other factors, such as availability of resources, the timely provision of such facilities is very important in that it has a substantial impact on morale, productivity and quality of work, all of which together determine whether the job gets done successfully.

When the people on the site started to grapple with the situation that confronted them, a complete fiasco resulted. DuPont were indeed called in, but their terms of reference appear to have been quite loose, and their report sounds rather like that of a sanitary inspector called in to inspect the plumbing. Everything was wrong with everything, drastic and expensive measures were recommended, stopping just short of scrapping the entire plant and starting again – calling for decisions that must have appalled those immediately involved. All in all, there was a lack of consultation, a failure in teamwork, a shortage of resources for operation and maintenance and complete failure in communication. And this with a project of national significance. The failure of Glace Bay to produce threatened the entire nuclear programme of Canada. The needed heavy water had to be purchased at much higher prices from the United States, and since that was not immediately available, the research and experimental reactors in Canada were shut down for periods of about a year in order to supply enough heavy water for the first station, Pickering Station, to be started up without delay. In retrospect, with all these further consequences of delay, the real cost of Glace Bay must have been far greater than that initial cost of getting the plant on stream.

The lessons to be learnt

We think we have been learning lessons all the while, as we have recounted this traumatic story, but the final outcome is a real tribute to those involved in the work of rehabilitation. Reports on various aspects of that work, the subsequent operation of the plant and the steps taken steadily to increase production have been the subject of a series of informative papers that have, unfortunately, had quite a limited circulation. These papers have been presented to the Annual Conferences of the Canadian Nuclear Association and in magazines such as *Nuclear Energy*. But the problems encountered and overcome are of interest to all, not only nuclear engineers, and they are well worth reading.

The story has been brought to you. Are *you* prepared to listen, and learn? This is our recurrent theme, and it is indeed vital. Post mortems such as we are conducting should not be for the purpose of seeking scapegoats and assigning blame, but to help first the project in distress and then those who follow after. You will have noticed the reaction of the interested parties following the publication of the DuPont report. They did not listen: they sought only to defend and justify. We have no doubt that there was a failure in human relations, compounded by a real shortage of skilled staff on site when the plant was started up. In addition, it appears that there had been no detailed startup planning – essential for a most complex process.

How? Why? That is all we, as historians, can ask, hoping for some answers. Some answers we have had: those now involved were most helpful in giving us much detailed background (Ref. 10). Many of the answers will never be known, but the purpose of our study is achieved if a few of us can meditate on the story and learn not to make the same mistakes.

References

1 Blake, L., 'Rehabilitation of the Glace Bay Heavy Water Plant', *Nuclear Engineering,* September 1976.
2 Lumb, P.B., 'The Canadian Heavy Water Industry', *Journal of the British Nuclear Energy Society,* 1976, vol. 15, no. 35.
3 Canadian Nuclear Association. Papers presented at the 14th Annual International Conference, Montreal, Canada, June 1974.
4 *Business Week*, 'Hopeful plunge into heavy water'. 23 May 1975, p. 154 onwards.
5 *Business Week*, 'A fortune for a plant that can't produce', 13 December 1969, pp. 58–59.
6 Thayer, V.R., Canadian Patent No. 924080. 'Process and apparatus for enrichment by countercurrent mass transfer'. (Filed 25 May 1970.)
7 Spevack, J.S., United States Patent No. 3,860,698. 'Dual temperature exchange systems for isotopic exchange'. (Filed 22 March 1971.)
8 Blake, L., 'Design problems in rehabilitating the Glace Bay Heavy Water Plant'. Paper presented at the 1976 Annual Convention of the Canadian Nuclear Association in Toronto.
9 MacInnis, R.D., 'Applied technology at the Glace Bay Heavy Water Plant'. Technical Report presented at the 1979 Annual Conference of the Canadian Nuclear Association in Toronto.
10 Private correspondence.
We are grateful for information, data and advice received during the course of 1980 in private communications from Dr. H.K. Rae, Director, Applied Research & Development, at the Chalk River Nuclear Laboratories of Atomic Energy of Canada Limited, Research Company, and also Mr. H.M. van Alstyne, General Manager, Atomic Energy of Canada Limited, Glace Bay, Nova Scotia, Canada.

5 Concorde – a technical triumph, but . . .

It is self-evident that estimating and cost control have no role to play in the cost control of research projects. The end result in not known, nor is the time likely to be taken to get those results known. If these things *were* known then it would not be research any longer. So research budgets are established on an annual, five yearly or some other arbitrary time basis, whereby it is agreed to fund a certain volume of work, in terms of personnel and materials, for a certain time. The expenditure may or may not produce results.

Research moves on into what is called 'development'. The end result of development in the process industries is a process plant, or a factory, producing products. Development is almost as difficult to cost as research and there are some projects which are 'development all the way'. Typical of these are some areas of the aircraft industry, particularly in the UK. Estimators in particular are familiar with what is called the 'learning factor'. The learning factor first came to light in the aircraft industry. The results of learning are frequently encountered in the process industries, when it happens that a number of plants are built one after the other to produce a particular product, such as ammonia, ethylene or fertilisers. Since each plant is somewhat more efficient, the investment costs less per ton of product for each succeeding plant. Both designers and operators 'learn', and their knowledge is applied to the next design. This saving in investment is independent of the saving in investment that might arise through the 'economy of scale', with which we deal in some detail in Chapter 15, when demonstrating that 'small is beautiful'.

In the aircraft industry, becuase of its particular approach to the design and production of aircraft, they went a step further, and actually established a learning *curve*. Airplanes are normally built in batches. While a batch was being built, design was being reviewed and both management and workforce were becoming ever more familiar with the details of construction. Consequently, each subsequent batch of airplanes cost less, per machine, than the previous one. It was found in practice that there was an empirical law, the saving from batch to batch being constant, at around 80% of the previous cost: that is, the machines in each subsequent batch cost 80% of the cost of the previous batch. Thus it was found possible to calculate the cost of the production machines by assuming the learning curve. In the UK, they rarely got as far as mass production in this field; for them for most of the time it was 'learning all the way'.

Cost prediction

When we come to consider cost estimating in the aircraft industry we find that the 'climate' in which the estimating is done is very different from that normally encountered in the process industries, or in normal mass production. We begin with, or in, an area of substantial uncertainty and we have a long time to wait before we reach production. Faced with a lack of descriptive detail and all the uncertainties associated with a distant time horizon, it is not possible to use conventional cost estimating methods. The estimating process becomes 'analytical', relying heavily on the use of highly generalised estimating relationships based on past experience. To stress this perhaps unpalatable fact, the words 'resource' and 'analysis' are often substituted by the estimator for the words 'cost' and 'estimate': we start to speak of resource analysis rather than cost estimating. Another word that often comes to the fore is *prediction*: again this gives a feeling of future possibilities, rather than present facts. If we used the word 'evaluation', rather than prediction, we might be led to believe that we have a sound basis for the figures we are considering, but in fact the basis is very speculative.

A paper on the prediction of design and development costs for civil airplanes (Ref. 1) makes it very clear that estimating in the aircraft industry is still an inexact science. We are told that after 35 years of modern aircraft manufacture too little information is available on past projects to allow estimators to develop methods which would make the job more positive than at present. At least this is honest. To what extent it is a localised comment, relating only to the aircraft industry in the UK, we are not in a position to assess. In the UK, then, there is some attempt being made to share and pool data by standardising on terminology and the content of the various sections of an estimate. A working party report was made under the auspices of the A.E.C.M.P. with the title 'Definition of an aircraft cost terminology for use in aircraft pricing'. Continuing use of such a standard list can indeed be of great help in the transfer of data. It also helps in the assessment of historical data since the parameters are known and enables the estimator to develop for daily use data in which he can have a degree of confidence.

The problems of cost estimating in relation to new aircraft are accentuated in the United Kingdom by the nature of the industry. Between 1945 and 1976 a total of some 175 *different* types of aircraft have been built of which only 90 or so have got as far as a real production run and of which only seven have had production runs of more than 500. To realise what this means, one has to compare these figures with comparable ones for the USA. There, with about 120 different types, 24 000 planes have been built. Of a total of some 4700 operating civil aircraft, nearly 3000 have been built by one company, Boeing. Further, that company, at the end of 1979, had nearly 800 aircraft on their order book – a different world from the UK. Clearly the aircraft industry in the UK operates under a substantial handicap in a competitive world, if only because of its size relative to the US aircraft industry. The task of the UK cost engineer is made much more difficult, as we have just seen.

What *is* the problem of the cost control engineer? The final cost of an aircraft is intimately linked with what are called the design and development costs (D&D). These costs are part of the total launching cost of an aircraft. The launching cost itself is made up, roughly, as follows:

Production education:	32%
Design & development:	34%
Jigs and tools:	24%

This total initial cost has to be recovered, and has therefore to be spread over the cost of the aircraft that are made and sold once it goes into production. Since these costs can be a substantial proportion of what we might call the repetitive costs of production, a careful assessment is required of the potential market. If the market is over estimated, such costs may well never be fully recovered.

Still looking at the UK, there have only been about 20 new civil aircraft projects in that country since 1945. There is accordingly a lack of experience on which to build, particularly when one remembers that a number of different companies are involved, who are reluctant to share their data, for obvious reasons. Indeed, except for Concorde, the last new civil airliner in the UK was certificated in 1965, so it is most difficult for estimators and cost engineers to assess the impact of what might be called the 'changing scene' on cost – and it has, unfortunately for them, been changing very rapidly. Factors that result in change over time, which can only really be measured in the event include, in particular, productivity of the workforce and price escalation. Yet cost estimates are demanded and prepared. Unfortunately, it is fashionable today to assume that any figures that you can get hold of are better than none. Estimates can be produced by starting with a series of assumptions and then proceeding to calculate. To the uninitiated, such estimates can appear, on the surface, to have all the soundness and authority of a detailed calculation. This happened with the early estimates of cost for Concorde. The initial costs were given in a report issued by the Supersonic Transport Aircraft Committee in 1959. The estimated cost of the necessary research and development, including the building of six planes (one prototype and five production models), was quoted in that report as £95 million. This report was never made public, but *The Sunday Times* reporters who investigated claimed that the figures were simply invented within the Royal Aircraft Establishment at Farnborough, which had a vested interest, since it was seeking to maintain its technical prestige through the project.

The aircraft industry

The aircraft industry has long been a pawn in the hands of the politicians and is now more and more becoming a sort of football for the environmentalists. It has lessons for other industries, particularly the chemical and process industries, because, as we saw earlier (Chapter 2) they too are now suffering at the hands of these same two groups. In fact, as we move through our case studies you will see that these two factors continually come to the fore and have a material influence on cost. So far as the aircraft industry is concerned, particularly in the UK, the words of Lord Beeching, while severe, are in all probability largely true:

> The aircraft industry is a sort of Alice in Wonderland world where subsidised engines were put into subsidised airframes, to be operated by subsidised airlines who don't want the wretched things anyway.

These words, though uttered in another context, apply above all to the Concorde project, first launched in the early sixties. The Concorde project was a politicial animal right from its conception. To learn a few lessons about project cost control, particularly in development projects, we propose to look at the Concorde project in some detail.

Supersonic versus subsonic

Supersonic flight is common with military aircraft. What is supersonic flight? The speed of sound is about 660 miles per hour: the actual speed of sound depends upon the density of air, and hence on the height one is above ground level. This speed of 660 miles per hour is called Mach 1. Civil aircraft cruise below the speed of sound and are *subsonic*, while supersonic speeds are those *above* the speed of sound: that is, they are Mach 1 and above. In the late fifties the possibility of a supersonic civil aircraft began to be mooted. By the end of that decade independent design studies in both France and Britain had led to similar conclusions on the viability of a supersonic civil aircraft. They were talking about an airplane with a speed of about Mach 2, or 1350 miles per hour. Such an airplane would more than halve the time to cross the Atlantic, for instance. These studies led, in 1962, to the British and French governments agreeing to share – on the basis of equal responsibility and equal shares – the costs, the design, the development, the production work and the proceeds of the sales of such a projected supersonic aircraft for civil duties. The subsequent history of this project has almost become a legend. From that time on it was never out of the headlines of the world's press for very long. The history of the project, and the airplane that resulted, finally called Concorde, after a lot of debate and a strong desire by the British to call it Concord, is all set out in Figure 5.1. Figure 5.2 sets out to scale the time involved, so that we can have some idea as to the relationship between its development and production. To show that Concorde was no exception when considered as a development project, although all the world thinks it was, Figure 5.2 compares its progress over the years with that of the Advanced Gas-cooled Reactor (AGR), also a UK project. The total period from the beginning of development to completion can be divided into four phases:

Phase	*Type of effort*
1	Mainly research and development

CONCORDE - A BRIEF HISTORY

1956	Start of preliminary research in Europe on a civil airplane for supersonic flights.
1959 to 1961	Independent design studies being carried out both in France and Britain, bringing similar conclusions.
1962	British and French governments agree to share costs, design, development and production work on the basis of equal responsibility.
1965	Design and development programme begins.
1969	In March the maiden flights of the first two prototypes, one built in France, the other in the UK. Two more are built and used for testing.
1973	End of this year brings flight of the first 'production' Concorde.
1975	Certificate of airworthiness granted by both the British and French authorities.
1976	In January the first scheduled passenger service, London to Bahrein (British Airways) and Paris to Rio de Janeiro (Air France).
1977	In January, US certificate of airworthiness. By July, a commercial service from both London and Paris to New York. Time 3 hours 45 minutes, half that taken by subsonic jets.
1979	Fears expressed of effect on ozone layer in the stratosphere have proved unfounded. January saw the inauguration of a service between London and Singapore, first started in December 1977 but discontinued after three flights.
1980	Flying full, but losing millions. Much talk, but little real progress. Assembly line closes.
1981	House of Commons (UK). Industry and Trade Committee proposes operation be abandoned in view of operating deficit, but British Airways carry on.

Figure 5.1 Concorde – a brief history
This table highlights the major stages in the progress of the Concorde project.

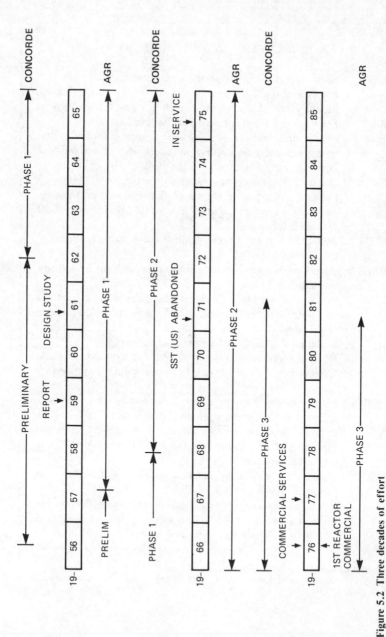

Figure 5.2 Three decades of effort
The progress of both Concorde and the AGR are shown, divided into the three phases described in the text (With acknowledgements to Henderson – Ref. 2.)

2   Mainly construction, but D & D
         continue
3   Operation: first income
4   Profit: income exceeds expenditure

You will see these phases delineated in Figure 5.2, except that in neither of our examples are the projects anywhere near Phase 4, even though it is now some 20 years since the projects were first initiated and 25 years after the first studies were tabled. This is the time it takes, it seems, when a true development project is being progressed, breaking new ground in the technological field.

It is very clear from this study that advanced technology and cost economics do not mix. A characteristic feature of economic planning is that more is said to be known about the future than about either the present or the past. We are continually being offered excellent, detailed statistics about the future, but when we call for past facts and figures, we find, more often than not, that the data presented is:

* inadequate
* poorly recorded
* little used
* handled superficially
  and uncritically

When dealing with advanced technology, which cannot by its very nature have any historic data on which to rest, it becomes very much a case of the 'blind leading the blind'. But if we take heed of the past, we are less blind than we were. A fundamental principle of both estimating and cost control techniques is that the past is analysed carefully, in detail, in order to make estimates of either cost or time, relating to the future. It is now possible to do that for a development project. When a new one comes along, is the past examined and a forecast made of perhaps 20 years before the 'pay-off comes'? Will those early estimates be multiplied by four in order to use that past experience? We doubt it very much indeed, but we are exhorting *you* to do just that when *you* have a development project in hand. The scale may be very different, but the principles are precisely the same.

With Concorde, the one party, the Treasury, who had all the historical data on cost overruns with development projects was never given the opportunity to make a detailed cost appraisal. The Treasury view, expressed in 1971 concluded:

> One remembers cost escalation in the military concept field which have been considerable and one will always be sceptical about this ... these

things are very difficult to do and the original estimates tend to be wrong.

The Treasury had some idea as to 'how wrong', but who would have accepted their experience factor had they been allowed to apply it? No one. 'No', they would have said, 'we shall do better this time'. But no-one does. So remember the development factor when preparing an estimate that breaks new ground of any sort. Remember, too, that the factor can vary from the basic estimate two to eight times!

The learning curve

The concept of the *learning curve* originated in the aircraft industry. But what of the industry itself? Was the data available, other than in the cost records of the Treasury? Let us first translate the Concorde cost history into a few concrete figures. A number of books have been written about the project, with various cost figures scattered through the text. In addition, the Central Office of Information (COI), a government office in the UK, published consolidated data on Concorde in 1979 (see Ref. 3). This particular document gives information on the development, technical characteristics, testing, production, sales and operation of Concorde and even discusses its future development. From it we learn that, as compared with that first estimate in 1959 of £95 million, the total development cost has been some £1 140 million, that production costs to the end of 1978 were some £700 million, while receipts from sales were £350 million.

If we analyse the financial history of Concorde we can develop a table showing the relationship of the various estimates made over the years. This has been done in Figure 5.3 where it can be seen that the final cost was more than four times the original 'official' estimate. More importantly, the estimates of cost rose *with* the event, not *before* the event. So far as time is concerned, all this took place over some fifteen years, originally estimated to be six years. The same picture of escalating estimates is set on the time scale in Figure 5.4. Looking at these figures, we must not forget the effect of escalation. By the time the project was brought to a close costs had escalated some *four* times. Without making a detailed analysis, this means that about half of the total final cost increase was due to inflation. In addition, one has to remember that the costing basis was altered drastically during the development of the project. For instance, the Olympus engine, intended for Concorde,

BRITAIN – THE CONCORDE OVERRUN

Original estimate = 100

SPENT	COST OF REMAINING WORK	REVISED ESTIMATE
100	150	250
150	120	270
200	140	340
250	150	400
300	120	420

Figure 5.3 Britain – the Concorde overrun
This table demonstrates the way in which the estimate climbed as the work progressed.

was also intended to power another airplane as well, the TSR-2 – a military aircraft. But the TSR-2 project was cancelled and all subsequent development costs on the engine had to be borne solely by the Concorde project.

When we consider the cost history and take into account factors such as have been mentioned – escalation and changes in costing policy – the work of the estimators was not so terrible as would appear at first. If a factor for development that we could safely apply to future development projects were sought, a factor of two, applied to the first estimates, would be far more appropriate than four – perhaps only 50% more, if the costing basis had not been altered. Possibly the greatest lesson for the cost engineer, at this point, is that political decisions are entirely outside the scope of his estimate but can nevertheless play a powerful role. Part of his monitoring function, then, is to watch and measure the influence of political decisions. Once again, he cannot alter them, but he *can* warn management in good time.

The results of delay

The first wildly optimistic forecasts made, that Concorde would be in service by 1970, were doomed from the start. In fact, the first production airplane flew in 1973, and regular services were first operated in 1976. In effect, the commercial availability of Concorde was delayed by some five years, largely due to design and technical problems. By the time it was ready for sale, we had the familiar syndrome in such a situation: the potential buyers had gone elsewhere. This is one of those qualitative effects we keep on

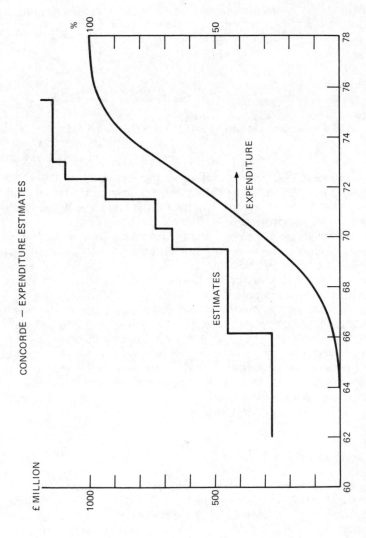

Figure 5.4 Concorde – expenditure versus estimates
Here we see the growth of the cost estimate over time, as the expenditure followed the classic S-curve, familiar to all cost engineers.

talking about. The major US airlines were by then already committed to buying the Jumbo jets being produced in quantity by the US aircraft manufacturers. In addition the oil crisis, which exploded in 1972/1973, added a major and very serious dimension to the equation because Concorde consumes about four times as much fuel when crossing the Atlantic as a Boeing 747. The economics of flying Concorde are therefore much more sensitive to the escalating cost of fuel than those of subsonic aircraft, and this is emphasised when fuel costs are rising out of proportion to other costs. Looking back to Figure 2.6 (Chapter 2) you will see that during the period under discussion, the seventies, fuel costs *trebled*, while prices in general *doubled*.

Air traffic also increased substantially over those same years, and more than was originally forecast, an increase largely owing to tourists attracted by the new low fares. Such individuals are obviously never going to pay first-class fare plus a 20% surcharge, which is the cost of saving some four hours when flying the Atlantic by Concorde. The reverse is in fact the position. They are prepared to wait 24 hours, at the airport, if necessary, to get a cheap flight. The market is still very limited. Despite this, the trans-Atlantic load factor has been quite good. With the overall load factor varying between 70% and 80%, Concorde has been achieving 65%, but very few hours are being flown, relative to all the other flights.

Once the airplane was available for service, the problems were by no means over. It was only after the president of France had personally intervened, making a direct approach to the president of the United States, that a limited number of flights were allowed to land in the USA for a test period. There were a series of legal battles in the USA over landing rights. Everywhere concern was expressed at the thought of Concorde over-flying – yet no one gave a thought to military aircraft, equally capable of breaking the sound barrier, and causing sonic booms. Over the past few years there has been a significant growth in public acceptance of Concorde, but the opponents still outnumber those who are prepared to see the plane fly – at least so far as vociferousness is concerned.

By 1979 the Europe-Washington link had been extended to Dallas in Texas, but Concorde was limited to flying at subsonic speeds (maximum 0.95 Mach) over the USA. This same year also saw the resumption of the London to Singapore service, first started in 1977 but then discontinued after about three flights because of objections by the Malaysian government. Those who first con-templated supersonic flight all of 25 years ago, never dreamt that this type of opposition would ever be encountered. The growth of the environmental lobby is another feature of the seventies, which the cost engineer ignores at his peril.

The Concorde programme has now been 'wound up'. The last five unsold airplanes have been allocated to the two operating companies, British Airways and Air France, but neither can afford to buy or to operate them. Of the total of sixteen that have been built, BA own five, Air France four and two were used for testing and will not be sold. An editorial in *The New York Times* late in 1979 notes the economic and technical problems that have been encountered and points out that not one airplane has been sold in a normal commercial fashion. In their view the Americans acted very wisely in abandoning their own SST project in 1971, even though by then they had spent more than a billion dollars on development. Really? Look at that sum again. The function of the cost engineer, among other things, is to look for value for money. That COI report (Ref. 3 again) tells us that total expenditure was £1 140 million plus £700 million, less £350 million receipts. Net outlay was £1 490 million. For that they have 14 operational aircraft. For one-third of that outlay, £500 million, the Americans got – nothing! Is this, then, the end of the story?

A technical triumph

We have a lot to say about 'quantitative' and 'qualitative' effects in this book, chiefly because it is the qualitative effects, those that cannot be costed, that are ignored. Most of the time, in equations, when totting up profit and loss, particularly for a project that has overrun in time or cost, these qualitative effects are negative, even if they cannot be evaluated. This time, however, with Concorde, there are a number of *positive* qualitative effects. A great deal had been accomplished after that 25 years of effort. The Concorde project was the largest technological project ever undertaken in western Europe, and it *was* a technical success. Although expensive, it was pioneering research at the very frontiers of human capability. From the point of view of the UK it was a matter for pride. The outline of Concorde (Figure 5.5) is familiar to millions, if not hundreds of millions all over the world. It is a 'new shape' in the sky; it is 'as beautiful as it is novel'; it is 'typical of the best the UK can offer'. These were the phrases used as the technicians and the politicians enthused over Concorde. Indeed, according to the politicians, it is just the kind of project the UK ought to undertake, if it is to maintain its position as one of the world's leading industrial nations. As a demonstration of collaboration, it was

Figure 5.5 The Concorde airplane
The characteristic profile of the Concorde airplane, known the world over. This silhouette is recognised immediately by millions; no other aircraft has gained a similar notoriety. (Montage reproduced by permission of The Editor, *The Cost Engineer,* UK.)

almost as remarkable. Two countries, speaking different languages, with varying technical traditions and procedures, came together with success.

This praise is not only home grown. The view from India is very similar (Ref. 4). To quote:

> Concorde made aviation history on 21 January 1976, with the London to Bahrein run. They can be proud of this record having been achieved with every conceivable and inconceivable hurdle. New Yorkers have now accepted the aircraft so much that BA wants to have two flights a day ... the pregnant question: has Concorde come to stay?

But it was not all praise. Others spoke of 'technical success, but commercial failure'. It is true that there never was a realistic estimate, that there was no cost control, that the actual cost of development was perhaps nearly five times the original estimate when all the costs were in. It is true that there was no serious attempt at a market survey – 'it will sell itself' they said. All these omissions carry lessons for the cost engineer. Yet others spoke of the waste, the profligate use of national resources. It may well be true, they said, that the research and development effort opened up new vistas, brought new knowledge, proved new products. But the same sum of money would have been sufficient to pay for the entire research programmes of all British universities for ten years or more. Such comparisons are only odious. They get us nowhere. Progress was made with Concorde, once the project was under way, because they *had* to get results. They *had* to find solutions to the problems confronting them. They were under commercial pressures, and it is these that bring results. Truly a prestige project, but nevertheless a project that has brought many related benefits, what is sometimes called the 'spin off'.

Yes, there is no doubt that to get Concorde to fly the world's passenger routes was a supreme achievement by any standard. It was the world's first major international collaborative venture. It pioneered international technological innovation and industrial collaboration on the grand scale, while restoring to Europe undisputed leadership in the most advanced field of commercial aircraft development. There can be, and there probably are, a great many indirect benefits to society at large that will continue to flow from this new plateau of technology and international commercial cooperation. The lessons are there, if we will only listen.

However, a report (Ref. 5) prepared by the House of Commons (UK) Industry and Trade Committee has urged a review by an independent consultant of the continuing cost of Concorde. The Committee took the view that the entire Concorde operation should be abandoned if the government could not find anyone other than the taxpayer to finance the current operating deficit. Meanwhile, there are fourteen services weekly being operated between London and New York by British Airways. They are said to be highly popular with American businessmen who willingly pay the normal subsonic first-class fare plus the 20% surcharge. British Airways itself remains enthusiastic about Concorde despite much adverse criticism, epitomised in one caustic headline: 'Flying high, losing millions'. By mid-1982 another House of Commons Parliamentary Committee was urging that a date be fixed for Concorde's funeral, being sceptical of the claim that it would be cheaper to keep the plane flying until 1987 than to scrap it.

In retrospect, Concorde may be seen as the price that Britain and France have paid to keep some of their most powerful and critical defence contractors fully stretched. In effect, it is a price they paid for national security.

References

1   Harrold, K.G. and Nicol, S.I.R. (Hawker Siddeley Aviation Limited), 'The prediction of design and development costs of civil airliners', a paper presented at the Royal Aeronautical Society Management Studies Group symposium on 'Cost Prediction', March 1977.

2   Henderson, P.D., 'Two British errors: their probable size and some possible lessons', *Oxford Economic Papers*. July 1977, vol. 29, pp. 159–205.

3   Central Office of Information (CIO – London). Publication No. SN. 6032, revised April 1979.

4   *Economic Times* (India). 'Concorde four years young', 18 February 1980.

5   *The Financial Times,* London, 15 April 1981, pp. 7 and 34.

6   A splendid refinery

Once again, we are going to look back at the sixties and then turn to survey the state of affairs today, at the dawn of the eighties. This time we hope that we shall be able to let you see not only a problem of the sixties, but one that was surmounted by those involved over the ensuing years. They, at least *did* listen! Our recurring theme is that while cost overruns and time overruns are all too common, they need not be. Steps can be taken to prevent them. However, once there is cost overrun, or time overrun or both (and the last is the most usual case) – these two run hand in hand – the worst thing to do is simply record the fact, and then file it away as a bad job and forget it. Something should be done about it. Further, we should let others into our secrets, so that they can take positive action.

Although nothing can help the project that has gone 'sour', filing it away will not help either. If a proper post mortem can be carried out the information garnered might well help with future projects. Our research throughout has been along these lines: we are seeking to carry out a post mortem. This requires a detailed review of the project, particularly in relation to what went wrong, and why! In retrospect, could what went wrong have been avoided or was it inevitable? If it could have been avoided, then what are the steps we ought to take to avoid it happening again? All this is of value only if we are prepared to listen. Otherwise, we shall go on making the same old mistakes and most probably some new ones as well, with the result that more and more of our projects get deeper and deeper into the mire. The end result is: failure of the company, and bankruptcy. We have seen this happen too and we shall bring such a case to your attention in the following chapter. One failed project is enough, as we shall see, to wipe out a company. But that last, disastrous failure does not stand alone. There was a history behind it, a history that we can learn from. However, the case that we are now going to consider is very different. This time we really can talk about 'turning failure into success'. The lessons were learnt.

The beginning of our story

We are going to look at a refinery project, at the work of designing and constructing an oil refinery. Obviously our story must begin with the crude oil that refinery is going to process. One of the major US oil companies, the Continental Oil Corporation (Conoco) discovered vast resources of low sulphur crude in Libya in 1958. Under the import quota system then prevailing in the USA, this low-cost Libyan crude could not be brought back to the USA to be processed there. This meant that Conoco had the choice of either selling it to their competitors, the other oil majors, or processing it themselves in Europe. As a first step towards a European venture, Conoco set up their European headquarters in London in 1960. They established, somewhat belatedly compared with their competitors, a number of marketing outlets. They introduced a new name to the UK retail petrol market – Jet petrol. Arrangements were made for processing their 'sweet' Libyan crude through other refiners but these proved unsatisfactory. This was the background against which the decision was taken to build a refinery overseas, in Europe; this was the conception that led to the birth of the Conoco Humber Refinery. This refinery was to be the first wholly Conoco-owned operating plant outside the USA. While Conoco may well have had substantial experience of building refineries in the USA, they had none in Europe, let alone in the UK. This is a very significant fact in the light of all that followed. We shall see, shortly, what impact it had both on the owner, Conoco and the contractor selected to design and build the refinery.

At about this same time, a report by the Process Plant Export Committee in the UK had highlighted the basic weakness of the British process plant industry: there was a substantial lack of knowledge in the industry concerning the design and construction of oil-refining and petrochemical plants. This meant that they were unable to break into the monopoly enjoyed by their American counterparts in this field. The Committee therefore recommended the consolidation of the engineering contractors into stronger groups, a recommendation that assumed even greater importance after the disaster (for the contractor) of the Humber refinery. But let us not get ahead of our main story.

Conoco decided to build in the UK on Humberside and they got the backing of the UK government, subject to their employing a wholly UK-owned contractor. Power-Gas was one such UK company, and it went all out to secure this particular contract. The company wished to broaden its base and extend itself both technically and managerially to establish satisfactory long-term growth (Refs. 1 and 2). They were particularly encouraged by the fact that, to quote from the records:

> A British company had never built such an animal before, and as we [Power-Gas] were the biggest process engineering Company, we were very anxious to build this one [the Humber refinery]. HMG [Her Majesty's Government] would have done a great deal to encourage Conoco to look for a British contractor.

This contract, therefore, was of great significance both to the US owner and the selected UK contractor. Its execution served as a powerful medium to emphasise, at some cost to both sides, the basic differences in the general management style existing in the two countries.

If for Power-Gas it was a matter of prestige, for Conoco it was nothing more than a routine business deal. As they said:

> Few companies in the world had ever built such a refinery . . . when we gave them [Power-Gas] the job, we did not question their ability to do it. There was no hand-holding: it was purely a business deal.

This despite the fact that for both it was the 'first time'. It was the first time Conoco had built overseas, and it was the first time Power-Gas had ever undertaken a 'grass roots' installation of this type. In their inexperience of British conditions, Conoco insisted on a fixed-price contract. Power-Gas, though knowingly venturing out into the unknown, accepted a fixed-price contract, seeing it as a calculated business risk, worthwhile accepting in view of the entry it would bring them into a field which had hitherto been the monopoly of the US contractors. If they lost out, then that was an entry fee that would still be worth paying. The redeeming feature in the situation was that although there was indeed a very substantial cost and time overrun, the magnitude of which could well have doomed many a lesser (but not necessarily smaller) contractor, Conoco said later of Power-Gas: 'They were very co-operative, sensible *British gentlemen* contractors throughout'. (The italics are ours.) This attitude served to bring the whole exercise to a happy ending, since after the settlement of various claims, while that settlement only recouped some 40% of the total cost overrun, the chairman of Davy-Ashmore, the holding company of Power-Gas, could still announce proudly:

Settlement has been reached at the highest level, after negotiations
lasting several months, in a spirit of mutual understanding and
genuine appreciation of each other's position. An amicable settlement
and a victory for common sense. We are now discussing with Conoco
the possibility of doing further business as soon as the opportunity
arises.

This happy ending is illustrated in concrete terms by the operating
refinery, shown in Figure 6.1. This picture should give you some
idea of the scale of things, a better idea than the amounts of money

Figure 6.1 The Humber refinery
This refinery of Conoco Limited, on Humberside in the United Kingdom, was
designed and built by 'Power-Gas', now the Davy Corporation Limited.
(Photograph reproduced by permission of Conoco Limited, South Humberside,
UK.)

we shall talk about shortly. Since the refinery was completed the value of the pound is less than half what it was then, in real terms, and it is easy to be misled as to the scale of the operation. In all probability this contract was by far the largest contract to be undertaken on a 'lump sum' basis up to that time in the UK.

Let us close this section with a quotation from the chairman's statement recorded in the *Annual Accounts of Davy-Ashmore Limited* about a year after the refinery had been completed:

> We are proud to have built such a splendid refinery in which are embodied some unique features which make it the most modern in Europe. We are proud too that ours was the first British company to have undertaken such a contract.

Historical background

How did they do it? Let us take a brief look at the key steps in the process (Ref. 3).

1958   Conoco discover a vast reserve of low-sulphur crude oil in Libya.

1960   Conoco set up their European headquarters in London.

1964   Conoco plan the Humber refinery.

1966   Invitations to tender for the Humber refinery sent out. Power-Gas were among the qualified bidders.

July: Contract awarded to Power-Gas. A 28-month construction schedule proposed.

August: designs approved and 'nominated' as frozen.

1967   March: design changes still in full spate.

July: mechanical erection begins after a nine months' delay owing to problems in appointing a subcontractor. Wimpey finally appointed.

1968   May: seventeen industrial disputes or stoppages so far. Productivity scheme introduced.

November: the scheduled completion date, but final 'firming' of design is till going on.

1969   January: first published fears of a substantial overrun.

July: the loss expected to be £12 million, seen against the Davy-Ashmore Group's total assets of £17.5 million and net current assets of some £10 million.

August: Sun Alliance (insurers) provide a £4 million guarantee against a loan from IRC, FCI and a group of banks.

September: another labour incentive scheme introduced,

  with extra sums for achieving specific tasks.
1970 March: mechanical completion achieved.

If we look back over this history, two very important aspects stand out: first, that 'frozen design' was never frozen. Change went on long after construction had been started in the field. This has a twofold effect: the costs of the change itself must be borne, as well as those resulting from the disruptive effects of the change on general progress. The other aspect was the labour situation. It is evident that there were no established procedures or techniques for paying for work against effort. Since then a variety of site agreements and bonus schemes have been established throughout the construction industry in the UK (Ref. 4). Were these factors at the root of the trouble?

Was the main culprit the fixed-price contract?

The invitation to bid received from Conoco was a voluminous document and seemed to contain all the information necessary to prepare a quotation, right down to the last detail. We say 'seemed to' because while Power-Gas and others had no hesitation in accepting it as the basis for a fixed-price contract, events proved that the basis was not as solid as had been thought. What was fixed? There was a fixed fee for engineering, together with a 'guaranteed maximum price' for materials and construction. Any underrun on the guaranteed maximum would be shared between the parties. Although there was an air of openness, in fact Power-Gas had quoted a fixed lump sum for the total works.

At the time of the award of the Humber refinery, fixed-price contracts were fairly normal in the USA. Such a contract involves risk, but it should be a calculated and calculable risk and it can bring the contractor a substantial profit – if all goes well. At the other end of the spectrum we have the completely reimbursable contract, when design, procurement, materials and construction are all reimbursable at cost, with agreed fee margins on cost. Under this scheme, the contractor takes no risk, but the owner feels at a disadvantage because there is no incentive for the contractor to work economically in terms of either time or cost.

Power-Gas had no choice. If they wanted to get entry into the exclusive 'club' of refinery contractors, worldwide, they had to fall in line with the ongoing practice in this field. They did. However, according to Conoco, at a later stage, and certainly with hindsight:

> They [Power-Gas] seriously underestimated the size and complexity of
> the job, and that was the root of a number of problems.

But we do not agree. We do not think that an underestimate was
at the root of the problems later encountered. Power-Gas certainly
never said so: they gave entirely different reasons. It is bad practice
to accept a low bid, likely to incur a contractor in loss, but Conoco
had no reason to expect a gross underbid. Power-Gas were the
lowest of four, but they were not 'out of line'. Conoco would not
have accepted their bid in that case.

It is quite possible that Power-Gas did not fully appreciate the
technique involved in preparing a bid of this particular type. One of
us was engaged in preparing a competitive bid and to the best of
our recollection our total for the design on the table was of the
order of £26 million. But equally important is the amount of the
'fixed' element, the fee. This is where the competition really is,
after all. A high estimate of the 'reimbursable' element, is an
estimate of 'what it costs' the owner within the stated ceiling, that
'guaranteed maximum'. The maximum can always include a substantial 'margin for error' which is talked down at a later stage.
After all, says the contractor to the owner, you do not pay my estimate, only what it actually costs. If Power-Gas quoted around £24
million, as they appear to have done, they added nothing as a
margin. Then they indeed took a real risk: a risk the 'maximum
price' form of contract is designed to avoid.

Their low bid, together with their pre-qualifications, won Power-
Gas this prestigious contract. At the post-mortem however,
Conoco said:

> We were hopeful that it could be done by a British contractor for
> public relations purposes, but if they had been outbid, we would not
> have given them the contract. The underbidding aspect only came
> from hindsight.

The possibility that Power-Gas had underbid was only the visible
tip of a great iceberg. The more important part of what was ahead
lay below the surface and was only exposed after the contract was
well underway.

There were frequent and extended design changes made during
the execution of the contract and these proved very expensive in
terms of both time and money. Within a month of the award of the
contract the design was supposed to have been approved and
'frozen', but for several months thereafter numerous design changes
were requested by the client: changes to their own original process
design, embodied in that comprehensive bid document referred to

earlier. These changes were considered to be quite normal by the client, entirely to be expected in a project of such magnitude and provided for in the contractual agreement. True, but change has to be noticed, advised and properly costed if the contractor is going to recover his costs. There is another factor as well; once change exceeds about 10% of the basic contract value, the whole basis of the contract also begins to change. There is no doubt at all that the total changes must have exceeded 20%, perhaps 25%; the evidence for this is in the extra money Conoco eventually agreed to pay. Power-Gas, quite probably, were unaware of the impact of change on cost: indeed, their chairman said as much as the contract was drawing to its close. Process design is a living thing, a concept that grows and changes with time. According to Conoco:

> The changes in design that we requested were made shortly between the original bid pack and the final signing of the contract. There had to be a lot of firming up, which is perfectly conventional. Most of the changes were requested in the first six months, priced and a schedule worked out. After that, the field changes that occurred were less than usual for the size of the job.

We really do not believe it. Changes made while the contract is in the final negotiating stage are most unfair; the contractor is being pressurised to price them low to get the contract. We suspect that by the time the project got into the field Power-Gas were in no state, administratively, to measure field changes and claim them from the client. That, we believe, is why they were 'less than usual'. All this leads to one basic conclusion in the field of cost control: measure change as it occurs, and make sure that the *total cost* of the change is claimed. The owner never believes that total cost, but you have to claim it, and convince him later. Power-Gas were in a very good position to convince the owner because the reimbursable element was open to him – it was a maximum price contract.

As expected, Power-Gas had a very different view. Change and what is euphemistically called 'firming up' continued right up to the time when the project was first scheduled to be complete (November 1968). If this were so, then perhaps Power-Gas were indeed too much the 'English gentlemen', seeking to continue to please the client by keeping quiet. There is no doubt that this was where a halt should have been called, and change of that magnitude called 'breach of contract', allowing the whole affair to be reassessed. As Conoco themselves said later:

> Had we jointly had an assessment of the problems earlier in the project, we could constructively have prevented quite a number of problems of timing and delay.

At this stage it might have been possible to place a sound price and an absolute time limit on further change, and obtain an agreement in good faith. What is very clear is that the owner has a responsibility and will save money if he exerts himself and keeps a close watch on what is happening with the contractor and his subcontractors. He ought to know as soon as, if not before, his contractor is moving into a loss-making situation. In this case, preemptive action might not have solved the problem completely because costs were already charting their own path, but certainly the severity of the situation could have been abated.

There is no doubt at all that quite minor changes in design have a 'ripple' effect and a number of minor changes build up into a 'torrent' so serious that it can hold up the entire engineering and construction effort. After learning this particular lesson, Power-Gas observe: 'Though you can quantify the cost of changes, the full effect of them will never be known'.

Attempts to recover these hidden costs are violently resisted by owners, who demand detailed justification of the cost of a change. But, as we have just said, justification is not possible, not then and there, at any rate. The final cost balance sheet will show the true position but by then it is too late, and who can prove 'what caused what'. Owners would do far better really to 'freeze' their process designs, build the plant and then make changes afterwards if their process engineers remain dissatisfied.

Was the main culprit the fixed price contract? So far nothing wrong has been seen with the contract. Only its execution by the two parties involved.

Misfortune or mismanagement?

There is no doubt that the contractor himself had more than his fair share of problems. Such problems are not entirely unexpected, but in this case it really was true that 'everything that could go wrong *did* go wrong!' One of the first major setbacks was in relation to the mechanical erection subcontract, which was by far the largest of the 30 or so subcontracts that were in prospect. To match and protect their own fixed-price bid – for that is what a guaranteed maximum is – Power-Gas were in the final stages of negotiation with a subcontractor on the basis of a bill of quantities worked out by Power-Gas. That particular contractor went into liquidation. Not only was much valuable time lost in firming up a contract with another contractor, George Wimpey, but the original concept of the contract had been lost, too. Instead of a lump-sum contract for mechanical erection, the contract now concluded was reimbursable, on rates, with a fixed fee.

Other problems also largely outside the control of Power-Gas arose as work in the field progressed. There was exceptionally bad weather through the summer and then winter of 1968. There was a major accident when the crane hoisting one of the coke drums failed, causing loss of life and severe damage. Insurance covered some of the cost, but nothing could compensate for the losses, including inefficient working, while they waited for the replacement drum to arrive. Apart from a great many industrial disputes and stoppages, it was found that the right sort of labour was scarce in the Humberside area, while the idle periods resulting from a variety of holdups, including the major accident, caused frustration and added to labour unrest.

With problems mounting daily and almost everything going wrong, the Power-Gas troubleshooter (specially appointed) became as pessimistic as he could about everything, adopting a system, as he said, 'to determine as far as I possibly could the financial provisions necessary for separate eventualities and to put a time on these eventualities, so that as the dates arrived, they were either reviewed, eliminated or reduced'. At the end Conoco summed it all up with the words: 'They [Power-Gas] took their licking, we took ours and it has all now been consigned to history'. To sum it all up ourselves, the client got a working refinery costing rather more than he had expected, but not so much more than the real economic cost. An additional £4.25 million was paid as their share of the £10.25 million overrun, but the more significant loss was time. They had to wait an extra year before the refinery could go into production.

In a wider context, the Humber refinery contract forced Power-Gas to take a 'cool hard look' – their own words – at themselves and they initiated a major reorganisation and consolidation plan. They most certainly learnt a lesson:

> We built a beautiful refinery and we gained an enormous amount of experience. We have been forced to look at ourselves and, all in all, we are a better company for what we have been through. Everybody in this business gets a 'wild one', and this was ours.

They could well have added: 'But not everybody learns; we did!'

It was good for Britain ...

The owner and the contractor did not always agree with each other.

This was particularly true, when the various claims were being discussed. But they were one in asserting that the Humber refinery was good for Britain. To quote an excerpt from what the contractor said, and quoted by us in full earlier in this chapter:

> A British company had never built such an animal before ... we were very anxious to build this one ... and the government would have done a great deal to encourage ... a British contractor.

On the other hand the owner, through the mouth of the managing director of Conoco, said:

> We believe that the plant will contribute substantially to an improvement in the United Kingdom's balance of payments through increased exports and reduced imports of fuel products, petroleum coke and benzene.

At that time the Humber refinery was the only refinery in the UK producing electro-grade petroleum coke, used in smelting and the manufacture of aluminium and special alloy steels. When in full production, the Humber refinery was expected to effect annual import savings of the order of £6 to £10 million (Refs. 5 and 6).

... but not so good for the contractor

The effect on the contractor of executing this contract has already become apparent from the previous sections of this chapter. A loss of some £12 million was first expected; it was finally about £10.25 million. This was on a single contract, with a company whose profits were running at around £1 million per annum (Ref. 7). It was therefore a terrible blow. The first warning of what was happening was given to the holding company for Power-Gas, Davy-Ashmore Limited, and issued to shareholders in January 1969. But such is the intelligence system of the Stock Exchange, truly a barometer of both a country's and a company's health, that the day before the actual release of the disastrous news the parent company's shares slid from 19 shillings (90 p.) to 6-4½ d (32 p.). The company's most immediate problem was liquidity. Thanks to the Industrial Refinance Corporation (IRC) a £5 million short-term-loan package was set up as 'first aid' to help the company out of its very tight financial position. Also, at the suggestion of the IRC, Simon Engineering, another UK company in the same field, started talks with Davy-Ashmore in order to see whether the two groups could co-operate together to their mutual advantage. A merger between the two groups seemed an obvious possibility. The two groups were roughly the same size in terms of assets, but with its exceptional loss, Davy-Ashmore would be making about half of Simon Engineering's profits.

When featuring the above story, *The Economist* used headlines such as: 'A customer not always right. IRC steps in' (Ref. 8). Three years later, the tune had changed. Now *The Economist* headline was: 'Process engineering. Too simple, Simon' (Ref. 9).

This meant that the negotiations between the two groups had by then come to naught. It was reported that Davy-Ashmore did not want to have anything to do with the bid from Simon Engineering. There was in their view no logic in the merger proposal. When first suggested in 1969 by the IRC, since defunct, it might have had point, but the shake-up following the disaster, as well as the virtually clean sweep of top management, made the merger proposal largely superfluous. There have been changes in the basic structure of the group as well. Previously predominantly a fabrication company, the group emerged from the aftermath as a major designer/contractor operating in the international market. Power-Gas, now known as the Davy Corporation Limited, grew in size till it was comparable to the major American contractors in the field, such as Lummus or Kellogg, offering a wide range of processes. In fact their range of processes was wider than most, covering the entire spectrum from steel works to synthetic fibre factories. The share value, which had plummeted from 19 shillings to less than 7 shillings, rose again to over 16 shillings (81 p.).

The story in headlines

It is interesting to follow the fluctuations in propects of this major British engineering group by reading their chairman's statements from year to year. Relevant excerpts, largely retaining the original wording, as noted below, tell the entire story quite vividly:

1965–66   Davy & United Engineering Co. (a member of the Davy-Ashmore Group) get the Queen's Award to Industry for export achievement. Nearly 50% of the group's total order book is for export. There has been a turn-around in Power-Gas (P-G) affairs due to good management and good engineering: the two requisites for success. P-G will continue to do even better. P-G contributes largely to the global results of the group and results for the current year (1966–67) should be even better.

From now on we shall note in particular the references to Power-Gas rather than the progress of the other companies in the group.

1966–67 Substantial increase in profits, but a work shortage is in prospect. P-G continues to justify the faith of the Directors, with results an all-time record. We have the contract for the new grass roots refinery being built for Continental Oil Co. at Killingholme on the Humber. The contract value is approximately £30 million. P-G France has technical trouble with a large contract.

1968–69 Our entire situation is coloured by the contract for the Humber refinery. The order is for £25 million, we are one year late, the overrun may reach £12 million. There is the problem of liquidity.

1969–70 We have come out of an exceptionally difficult year with our contract obligations honoured, our debts paid and our resources substantially restored. We have a major reorganisation involving high initial expense, but it is possible to foresee profits in the future at a level NOT achieved in the past ten years.

1970–71 We have perhaps our business on sounder foundation and are now proceeding steadily with our planned expansion into a process engineering and contracting organisation of real world status. Concentration of P-G into a single operation in London will bring savings in operating cost of £1 million per year and put the company in a better position to bid for large world projects. We are making selective acquisitions ... Zimmer – synthetic fibre plants ... Wellman-Lord – fertiliser plants ... liquidity has been restored to a healthy level.

1971–72 We have a new, lean and active business. Movement forward has continued throughout the year, with the completion of more profitable and less troublesome contracts. There are considerable direct benefits from the radical reorganisation of the last two years, which largely account for the profit increase ... we have acquired Chemibau (sulphuric acid plants).

1972–73 The industries we serve throughout the world are calling increasingly for our services. We have enjoyed a good year with a proper reward for our efforts and are set fair for another good year. Davy-PG wins

Queen's Award to Industry for the second successive year for export achievement in process plant. Davy International becomes group name, with a new symbol.

1973-74 A record order book, but bank borrowing rising. Process plant industry world-wide is still booming and some 85% of Davy's work is abroad.

1974-75 Still trying ...

1975-76 The immediate outlook is good and we aim to continue the progress of recent years. The balance sheet is again strengthened and liquidity improved. Our projects have a long cycle time, hence short term prospects are influenced by the efforts of the past several years. Adaptability, skill and keen application of management remain the key to success.

1976-77 We have new levels of performance, size and strength. This has been an active year and the new year (1977-78) will be no less so. We have a good order rate, improved profits and cash flow and two successful mergers. The basis for success – adaptability, management enterprise, keen application – Davy have these in full measure.

1977-78 Every quarter of the world is now a Davy market. The high performance level of recent years has been maintained and we have had a notable success in *large projects*. There has been a change in company structure and organisation to adjust to growth and the mergers. We are well placed for future expansion.

1978-79 Our strength across the world has been enhanced by the merger with McKee. All the engineering and construction companies of the group throughout the world will be known as Davy McKee. This merger has been the most important event of the year. The mainstream activities of the business, engineering and construction, again did extremely well. The manufacturing companies are facing hard, competitive times. Energy will doubtless continue to be the central theme and the main agent for economic change and Davy McKee is at the very centre of these world movements. Companies with sound medium-to-long-term objectives are the most likely to prosper and we consider ourselves amongst them.

As we survey the scene set out above, we see this company's recovery from the disaster of the sixties as nothing short of remarkable. We have a picture of steady growth and several acquisitions, the largest being the US company, McKee, almost comparable in size. These were all by prior agreement, and Davy McKee now stands among the first ten in the engineering contracting field, and this company is certainly the largest outside the USA. Late in 1980 there was a takeover bid from a Dallas-based company. Davy put pressure on the UK government to prevent this happening. The government while desiring to encourage foreign investment could take little comfort in seeing one of its largest exporters becoming part of a little-known US group. In this context Sir John Buckley, the Chairman of Davy McKee, addressing an Institute of Export luncheon meeting told Lord Carrington, then Foreign Secretary, who was also there, and who once served in a cavalry regiment:

> We do not expect the cavalry to come to the rescue, but a suitable gesture by the Government would not be out of place.

This part of the story may be concluded with some information culled from the technical press (Ref. 10). We learn that Davy McKee have safely completed a fertiliser plant said to be worth some $250 million for Occidental Chemicals, on time and within budget. They were responsible for the project from start to finish – for design, procurement and construction and in the field they completed over one million manhours without a lost time accident. There was a novel agreement with the unions designed to increase production, no doubt a continuing echo of their earlier experiences. We *can* learn from experience.

The story in figures

As we have just seen, this major contractor came out of its experience, its disastrous experience, much wiser. There is no doubt that this came about because they *listened*, and *learnt*. By acquisition and expansion, by reorganisation, the Group has grown to be one of the largest in process plant contracting worldwide. The figures that demonstrate this, from 1964 onwards, when the Humber Refinery was still but a gleam in Conoco's eye, tell their own story. Look at them: Figure 6.2. No further comment is needed. The figures speak for themselves!

	Sales	Profit before tax	Order book*	Forward order load*	Dividend pence per share	No. of employees
		£ million				
1964–65	32	0.80	...	...	2.8	...
1965–66	33	0.60	...	...	2.8	...
1966–67	59	2.30	...	...	3.1	...
1967–68	50	2.00	...	...	3.1	...
1968–69	53	-3.80	...	...	...	...
1969–70	79	0.80	...	...	1.0	...
1970–71	73	1.46	...	...	1.3	7269
1971–72	75	2.30	...	...	1.9	5729
1972–73	121	4.15	300	...	5.0	7870
1973–74	143	4.43	360	...	5.1	7810
1974–75	181	5.96	670	355	5.4	8643
1975–76	306	10.40	733	360	6.2	8809
1976–77	329	18.80	1157	457	4.9	9498
1977–78	387	25.40	1240	750	5.5	14901
1978–79	611	26.10	1688	1006	6.7	17782
1979–80	752	15.90	1810	1073	6.7	20380
1980–81	671	18.70	1910	1036	6.7	18791

THE DAVY GROUP STORY – IN FIGURES

* As at 30 June. Financial year is April/March.

Notes (1) The Davy-McKee merger came in November 1978.

(2) The 1978–79 results include some 4 months of operation with McKee. Davy and McKee complement one another both technically and geographically.

Figure 6.2 The Davy Group story – in figures
This table, presenting data abstracted from the published accounts of the Group over the years, illustrates their remarkable growth in a worldwide, highly competitive business. Despite the gaps in the table, the trend is very clear indeed.

The owner learnt a lesson too

We have seen that the contractor suffered much from this 'disastrous' contract. It took him some years to recover and, even though he *did* recover, and far more than that, suffered a heavy financial loss. But what of the owner, Conoco? There was suffering there, too – and perhaps even more. In cold financial terms almost certainly more. Apart from the extra direct cost, there was also the even greater loss of revenue from the delay in completion of the refinery by nearly eighteen months. The Humber refinery was designed for low-sulphur Libyan crude, but it can also cope with North Sea crude, since that is also a low-sulphur crude. In 1976, Conoco set out to undertake production from the Murchison Field, in the North Sea. Did they apply their US 'know-how'?

This time, based in the UK, having had experience of construction work there, they could apply the lessons that they had learnt from that experience. No flying start this time. Before initiating planning on the Murchison project they took stock of the problems, the very serious problems, that had been faced by previous companies operating in that area. To learn from past mistakes, not only their own but those of others, and in order not to repeat them, a complete study of the earlier projects was undertaken and data compiled. This was, in effect, a 'book of errors'. Its actual title was: 'Application of North Sea experience to Murchison Project planning' (Ref. 10). The major lessons that had been learnt were:

> Do not start the project before completion of design;
> Avoid serious under-estimation of weights of individual equipment for the platform;
> Use a well-knit project team (80 Conoco personnel) working closely and in parallel with the consultants and contractors.

Although there has been the usual catalogue of mishaps with the Murchison project, including a strike and the collapse of a giant crane, and that first lesson was most certainly not fully applied, nevertheless production is confidently expected in the second half of 1980, on schedule.

To conclude, in this case both the contractor and the owner came out well, and wiser, following upon their experience with the Humber Refinery project. That outcome represents the ideal for which we are looking, and from which we should all learn. Our case history demonstrates that it is indeed possible for corporations, and people, to learn from their own mistakes. We want to take that one step further, so as to learn from the mistakes of others.

References

1   Annual Reports, including Chairman's Statements, first of Davy-Ashmore Limited, and then the Davy Corporation Limited, over the years 1964–82.

2   Private communication from Sir John Buckley, Chairman, Davy Corporation Limited, dated 29 November 1979.
3   Brown, W.F., 'Conoco invests £50 million in new British refinery', *Chemical Processing,* 1968 vol. 15, April, pp. 52–56
4   *European Chemical News,* 17 November 1980, p. 5, Construction News.
5   Lyons, P. 'Humberside joins the big 'uns', *Petroleum Review,* 1971, vol. 25, August, pp. 285–288.
6   Overal, J. 'Conoco's Humber Refinery', *Petroleum Review,* 1969 vol. 23, December, pp. 333–336
7   Mansell, C. 'How Davy-Ashmore dived', *Management Today,* 1970, December, pp. 74–83
8   *The Economist,* 'A customer is always right', 2 August 1969, p. 687
9   *The Economist,* 'Process engineering. Too simple, Simon', 16 December 1972, pp. 111–112
10   *The Financial Times,* 'Murchison Field Platform', 1979, A 4-page supplement, 17 September

7 The Algerian LNG project

We are all familiar with the fact that crude petroleum is found in places such as the Middle East, far removed from the industrialised countries where it is in demand for fuel and for the manufacture of a wide range of petrochemicals. The transport of crude oil across the oceans of the world has thus become a factor of crucial importance to the economic prosperity of a great many countries. Not only crude oil, but also petroleum gas, or natural gas as it is more commonly called, has been found in tremendous quantities along with the crude oil in some of these places. Natural gas is a product of ever-increasing importance in the fuel economy of the world and it also has to be transported long distances from source to the user. In order to achieve the economic transportation of natural gas across the oceans, it has first to be liquified in order to reduce its volume. This need has resulted in the development and construction of liquified natural gas plants at locations where the natural gas has been found, but requires transport overseas to bring it to the user. The natural gas is liquified by cooling to very low temperatures. It then has to be transported at these low temperatures in specially designed tankers.

One such installation is the Algerian liquified natural gas plant built at Arzew, which came on stream in February 1978. The plant, known as LNG-1, is a six-train unit, and is Arzew's first major facility. At the time that it was completed it was heralded as 'the world's largest liquified natural gas (LNG) project' (See Ref. 1). We propose to look at the history of the development and construction of this plant in some detail and we shall start our study by looking at a design and construction contractor known worldwide as Chemico.

Chemico

The Chemical Construction Corporation (Chemico) of the USA experienced phenomenal growth during the first two decades after the Second World War. As a result they qualified as a select member of what is known in the construction industry worldwide as the Top Ten league. This is in the process plant area. The ranking varied from year to year, and even the lead position changed hands quite often, for the construction industry, by its very nature, is a very erratic business. Sometimes a firm is extremely busy, at others it finds it hard to get enough work to keep its employees fully occupied. Contractors try very hard to establish an even, regular workload but they rarely succeed.

The assets of a construction contractor are almost entirely in men, with just a few machines – office equipment and construction plant. This great strength in manpower and lack of physical assets creates an inherent weakness in the industry. A contractor can be pursuing contracts worth billions of dollars, yet his own assets are minimal. The financial risks incurred, therefore, can be enormous in relation to the financial strength of the company itself. As a result, even one major contract, if it goes 'sour', can destroy a contractor, blotting him out of existence. We have already considered in Chapter 6 (A splendid refinery) a case where such a fate threatened a contractor in this field but as you saw, they survived, grew and prospered. At that time they had strength in areas other than contracting: they also built heavy industrial equipment. That contractor listened, and learnt a lesson. Now we come to a contractor who was complacent, who seemed indifferent to his experience and so failed to learn. Then disaster is at the door.

The early warning signals were ignored

During the sixties Chemico were involved in the construction of the Trombay Fertiliser Plant, a tragic story with which we deal in some detail in Chapter 8. Their record on that occasion was one of which they could hardly be proud. Admittedly there were faults on both sides – there usually are. The contract between the two parties was faulty, leading inevitably to misunderstanding and dispute. Where owner and contractor share responsibility for closely integrated elements of construction, problems will always arise, since an ideal condition has been created for 'passing the buck', as the Americans say. While this phrase is American in origin, the game is universal, and no doubt there is an equivalent term in all languages.

The outcome, with respect to Trombay I, was that a plant scheduled for completion in 1963 was completed three years later, with
a 50% overrun on cost. As if this were not enough, production was
well below design capacity, due to defects in the process engineering and the equipment, and the usage of both raw materials
and power was above the agreed specification. Naturally the owner
suffered heavily, both financially and politically. The nation
suffered, owing to the shortfall of home-produced fertiliser, which
had to be made good with expensive imports. There were arbitration disputes and legal battles between the owner and Chemico, one
result of which was full-page advertisements in the international
press, each party to the dispute blaming the other in public in this
way.

In Chapter 8 we see how all this affected the owner; at this time
we want to see how it affected the contractor. He seems to go 'scot
free'. We say 'seems' because that is only in the immediate context
of the Trombay plant. The reputation he then gained must have
followed him wherever he went after that, unless there was a drastic
reversal in his approach to such projects. Did they change their
ways? It would seem not because we meet Chemico again in Algeria
where earlier patterns of work culminated in this final disaster and
they dropped out of the running.

From beginning to end

Let us try to get an historical perspective on the Algerian LNG
project, in order to see how it proved the death-knell of a giant
among the international process plant contractors. That story
begins in 1972 and ends in 1976, so far as Chemico is concerned. It
took till 1979 actually to complete the plant and bring it on stream,
the work being taken over by another contractor, Bechtel, called in
to 'rescue' the project, a role they have fulfilled more than once.
The sequence of events:

March 1972   The USA Government authorises the first long-
                  term import of LNG into the USA, a 20-year
                  contract. This is designed to ease the shortage of
                  gas in the Northeastern states.

March 1973   EXIM and other banks approve a $402 million
                  financial package for the construction of a series
                  of projects to enable the import of 1 billion cubic
                  feet *per day* of LNG from Algeria. There are
                  plans to construct a pipeline, a fleet of LNG

tankers, and a liquefaction plant. The liquefaction plant is proposed to meet a 1.75 *trillion*
cubic feet annual demand now expected. There
are agreements with various British, French,
West German, Belgian and US firms.

April 1973   The Transcontinental Pipeline Corporation files
an application with the US authorities for the
import of 375 million cubic feet of Algerian
LNG per day, beginning in 1977. The El Paso
National Gas Company announces that work
will begin immediately on the construction of the
facilities necessary for the import of Algerian
LNG into the USA. Chemico are awarded a contract to build a plant for the liquefaction of one
billion cubic feet per day, at an estimated total
cost of $350 million. Work is to start in May
1973, the plant being scheduled for completion
in April 1976, reaching full production capacity
by mid-1977.

September 1973   Chemico, a unit of General Tire & Rubber Co's
Aerojet General Corporation is a member of a
consortium to which Sonatrach, the Algerian
national oil and gas company, has awarded a
contract, worth some $850 million, to build the
world's largest plant for the liquefaction of
natural gas.

November 1975   Sonatrach cancels the $327 million contract with
Chemico to build the natural gas liquefaction
plant at Arzew in Algeria because of they say,
'The contractor's total incompetence and poor
performance'. The project is already running
seven months behind schedule and Sonatrach are
under contract, with heavy penalties for delay,
for the supply of LNG to the El Paso National
Gas Company.

January 1976   Sonatrach concludes a multi-million dollar
contract on a cost-plus basis with the Bechtel
International Corporation (Bechtel) for the completion of the Arzew LNG plant.

May 1976   The US Securities & Exchange Commission announces that Chemico may not have properly ac-

	counted for some $15 million paid in connection with the building of the LNG plant in Algeria.
July 1976	Sonatrach sues the General Tire & Rubber Company for $45 million, alleging that three of its subsidiaries improperly used 'payoffs' in securing the contracts at Arzew.
February 1977	The Algerians are very concerned about their relationships abroad, particularly in view of the cost overruns and the failure of US companies to meet their commitments. There is also concern at the US Federal Power Commission's slowness in acting on the application for the LNG import contract. They also fear an 'Americanisation' of their culture.
July 1979	The Arzew LNG project finally completed by Bechtel. Total cost?

We are very sure that no one – we repeat, no one – knows the answer to that last question!

Why was the contract with Chemico cancelled?

Reputable contractors pride themselves on the fact that much of the work they have in hand at any time is repeat business from satisfied customers. In a recent advertisement a major West German contractor operating internationally declared that of their total current workload, which amounted to a few billion deutschmarks, more than 60% was repeat orders from satisfied customers. This is the best bonus from good workmanship that any contractor can ever hope for, and constitutes a far more powerful inducement towards proper performance than any clause in the contract. Nevertheless let us consider those clauses.

Construction contracts quite often provide for what are called bonus/penalty clauses, which have to be equitable relative to both parties, the contractor and the owner. For instance, the contractor can be paid a bonus for completion earlier than the schedule agreed, while failure to complete on time would then incur a penalty. At best, from the point of view of either party, these can be only token amounts, since they usually never exceed 10% of the contract value. Quite often they are limited to 10% of the fee element – that is, the cost of the work done by the contractor himself, excluding the cost of materials and construction that he handles through other suppliers and contractors. The precise details and terms will vary from case to case. There is no standard, but all such clauses must allow for a number of very relevant factors. The situation is fraught with 'ifs and buts'. For instance, if it can be demonstrated that delay in completion is due directly or indirectly to non-performance by the owner in some area, then the penalty cannot be enforced. That would be unfair. The impact of a failure in performance by the owner on the work of the contractor is most difficult to determine, making negotiations on the amount of either penalty or bonus, prolonged and time-consuming.

Even when a bonus or penalty is incurred, the amount involved is never more than nominal. A penalty in itself is never a deterrent to the contractor, if he is forced into a position where delay is occurring. It will always be cheaper to let things take their course, rather than to spend effort, and hence money, trying to retrieve the position. By the same token bonus is rarely a true incentive, since the cost of a crash programme designed to save time will always be far greater than any prospective bonus. The most effective encouragement for the contractor remains his 'good name' with that particular owner, so that he can secure further contracts from him. Once an owner is dissatisfied with the performance of a contractor, his name will not even appear on the short list of contractors invited to tender. These are the facts of life and reflect a sound commercial approach by the owner. A contract completed smoothly, on time and to the complete satisfaction of the owner can even result in the contractor getting a blanket follow-up contract, without the owner even asking for competitive bids. This is also sound commercial practice, since it can save months: the months taken up with the preparation of a detailed, formal enquiry, the pre-qualification of bidders, waiting for offers to come in and then evaluating them. Such a procedure can easily take six months, even longer if the design work is in the preliminary stages, since design work has to be done to get sufficient detail to enable sensible offers to be prepared. With a blanket order work on detailed design and project development can proceed in parallel, so that a saving of up to twelve months in the total project schedule can be achieved. An approach of this sort assumes that there is complete faith and a situation of mutual confidence between contractor and owner – a state of affairs developed by their satisfactory co–operation on the previous contract. They already 'understand one another's language', as we say. So much conflict is created by sheer misunderstanding: misunderstanding of terminology, specifications and practices.

We have dwelt on this aspect at some length because of its impli-

cations in relation to the Algerian LNG project. The initial contract
let to Chemico was to be one in a series. The first installation for
the liquefaction of the gas was known as LNG-1, but there was to
be over the years LNG-2, LNG-3 and so on. Once experience has
been gained, the second and the third projects become that much
easier for the contractor and hence more profitable. A huge
quantity of LNG was to be exported to the USA and other
countries and this was no secret. Chemico were very fortunate to
secure the very first of these contracts. Had they performed well
they would have been in an extremely strong position with regard to
the follow-up contracts. They would have had a material advantage
over any other contractor because of their 'know-how' in relation
to conditions in Algeria as they affected construction work,
conditions by no means the easiest in the world. Their initial
contract of some $350 million could well have swelled to billions of
dollars by way of follow-up contracts.

There is really no doubt at all about this. It has already been
mentioned that Bechtel were called in to rescue this project in
January 1976, after the initial contract with Chemico had been
cancelled. Bechtel undoubtedly did a good job of work because
even before that first project had been completed by them their
Canadian company had been awarded a further contract worth
$550 million for the development of the gas fields at Rhourde en
Nous in Algeria. This was followed in January 1979 by the award
of a further contract, said to be worth $1 150 million to Bechtel for
the construction of a LPG pipeline between Hassi R'Mei and the
Port of Arzew. We are sure that the end of this string of contracts
for Bechtel from this one owner is nowhere in sight!

To return to Chemico and their misfortunes. Having failed at
Arzew, they were not even invited to bid for another similar
liquefaction plant in Algeria. They say that troubles never come
singly, and this seems to be true for Chemico for at this same time
they were also in difficulty with several of their US projects. What
went wrong? For one thing, Chemico changed hands several times,
and at every change of ownership its management style was
modified to conform to the whims of its new principal. The Aerojet
General Corporation, a subsidiary of the General Tire & Rubber
Company, was seeking to diversify and bought Chemico early in
1973 for the sum of about $20 million. At this time Chemico had
annual sales of the order of $100 million, together with an
'excellent record on profits', although it had suffered a modest loss
in 1972. When taken over by Aerojet, Chemico had a considerable
backlog of work, a substantial part of which was the Arzew
contract, which had recently been signed. This was almost certainly

the largest single contract ever to be undertaken by that company.
What happened next? Following the Aerojet management philosophy as developed by its president, Chemico was split into several
autonomous divisions, according to its major lines of business. An
Aerojet vice-president was installed as the chief executive, but he
was soon replaced when he failed to produce results. This course of
action completely demoralised the senior staff within Chemico who
also felt that the formation of a series of 'little companies' not only
increased overheads substantially but also reduced effectiveness.
Many of these senior executives finally left in disgust, while others
were asked to leave. What is most significant in this context, and
very serious in relation to the Arzew contract, was that the nucleus
project team, initially some 25 people, soon broke up and most of
its members left Chemico. In the light of such failure in
management, is it any wonder that the contract was mishandled
too? Independent observers in the chemical and process plant field
saw the prospective decline of Chemico not only in Algeria but
elsewhere, on the heels of its takeover by Aerojet. The Arzew plant
had been planned to export 1 billion cubic feet of natural gas per
day to the USA within a certain time and it soon become clear to
everybody that the plant could not go on stream until late 1977,
nearly eighteen months later than the original target date, to which
the Algerian government was bound by contract. Is it any wonder
that the contract was cancelled?

It must be realised that cancellation is the very last resort for the
owner because inevitably he will lose many months while a new
contractor establishes himself. But the step was taken in this case.
According to Sonatrach, the owner company, 'Chemico never
completely engaged in the project'. They also said that it was quite
clear that the contractor never put adequate personnel and equipment on the project. There were other factors, too, the effect of
which had not been appreciated when the plans were laid. For
instance, the Algerian formalities with respect to customs clearance
also retarded the progress of the project quite materially. There was
frequent labour unrest. These difficulties, or ones similar to them,
are to be met on every project, but who was there to surmount
them? Management was failing; the result a 'failed project'. What
else could one expect?

It is also probable that the project was underbid by Chemico.
The contract was on the basis of a fixed fee and a ceiling price for
the materials and construction. There was a modest escalation
clause, but the selling price, was soon found to be too low. The
contract had looked good when it was signed, but fearing a very
substantial cost overrun, the contractor opted for cancellation

rather than attempting to complete the contract and incur heavy losses. When contracts run into trouble – and this is by no means rare – it is usually possible for a settlement to be negotiated that is reasonably just to both parties. This can only be achieved if the contractor is serious in his approach and intends to make a sincere effort to complete the project to the satisfaction of the owner. The completion of the Conoco Refinery, which we discussed in Chapter 6, where the contractor was also faced with financial loss of some magnitude, is a good example in this respect. With Chemico it was different. Owing to an almost 100% turnover in the senior management, none of the new management team had been involved in the contract negotiation. As a result, they would have no commitment to creating success out of failure. It was never 'their fault'.

What is the sum of the matter? There was a difficult contract, the biggest the company had ever undertaken, for construction in a difficult and expensive location. There was a major change in management owing to the acquisition. There was an attempt to apply management practice from an aerospace company, apparently quite successful in that field, to a process plant contractor. The result was the demoralisation of management, with all that flowed from that fact. The result was ineffective project management, cost overruns, with finally contractor and owner not even on talking terms. The construction schedule eventually doubled. In these few words we have depicted the doom not only of the project but also of the contractor. In 1975 Aerojet acknowledged that they had trouble with the Arzew contract and with some other process plant contracts in the USA. However, they said, 'other contracts are being completed satisfactorily'. Maybe, but they were not sufficient to keep the company in business.

How did Bechtel succeed where Chemico failed?

The simplest answer to this question is in the words of the project manager who ran the Arzew Project for Bechtel, and what his colleagues have to say about him. We have emphasised time and again the importance of the role of the project manager in the successful completion of any project (Ref. 2). First see what his superiors and colleagues had to say about this particular project manager.

> If he (the project manager) has to write a letter to the client in which some points may be disputed, he first takes the proposed letter to the client unsigned, gets his reaction to it, and then sends it to him . . . He's tactful and diplomatic . . .

Bechtel took this particular project over from Chemico early in 1976, a project then running some eighteen months behind schedule. It is, very obviously, extremely difficult to pick up a project in progress, with no certainty as to the scope of the work still to be done. For precisely this reason the award to Bechtel had to be on a 'cost-plus' basis. Once the terms had been agreed, the contract awarded and the scope determined, the work was taken up in all earnestness. To quote again:

> It took someone like this project manager to bring it all together and to co-ordinate ... He did it, with the result that Arzew came in under the budget and essentially on schedule.

That must have been a new budget and a revised schedule. Such statements tend to mislead the onlooker, ignorant of the history behind them. However, they have justification. The person who recruited this particular project manager goes on to say of him, in relation to the project he was involved in immediately prior to Arzew:

> That job was on schedule and the client was very happy ... the bottom line is that he is a quality person. He's orientated towards doing a good job and in the course of doing so he exhibits a winning, persuasive manner.

What does his vice-president have to say about him?

> He looks at the big picture and doesn't become mired in details or lose sight of overall goals.

Thus the view of the 'outsiders', those who were watching the project manager at work. What does he himself have to say? How does *he* see his role, his function, and philosophise about his work?

> The role of a project manager is essentially to keep an objective view of the whole project – its trends, problems and activities – from an informed viewpoint ... It is important that the project manager does not become, for example, the engineering manager or the construction manager on the project but stands back and ensures that engineering and construction are performed and properly managed.

Though working long hours, much of his time was spent meeting and talking with the client to make sure that his needs were being met. According to the project manager, communications are vital:

> As the size and significance of the projects increase, coupled with their technical complexity, the need grows to have increased dialogue and understanding between a client and contractor if both are to contribute what is needed to bring large projects to successful conclusions.

His recipe for defusing tension and the pressures that build up on every major project is most significant:

> It's necessary to ensure that the actions taken are based on good information and on frank and open exchange of ideas and data relating to the issues ... In my experience the need to provide people with time to think before precipitating action is an important function of the project manager. That has to be coupled with making sure that analysis of the circumstances is as complete and as objective as possible. Thus the project manager must firmly control discussions and actions in these circumstances.

Projects abroad – not in one's own country – which have an 'alien' environment, need very special care:

> In handling projects overseas, there is a constant need to bear in mind how the environment, the society and its religion and customs will impact on the working of the project. For example, while many people speak English, it's *not* their mother tongue, and there's a need to use mutually understood vocabulary and avoid idioms.

When working for an international process plant construction contractor, the staff are likely to be sent anywhere in the world to a project. The project manager is fully aware of this. His view:

> In joining Bechtel, along with everyone else we have had to learn to be prepared, like the Bedouin, to be nomadic and to fold our tent at frequent intervals.

And his family? They did not merely accept this situation gracefully; they made the most of it.

> Our daughters both benefited tremendously by the experience of camp life with its mixed community and activities together with the school and its visits to places of interest, such as the Roman ruins at Tipasa, the site of the ancient harbour and associated community, and the old port and fossil fields at Mostagenam.

We have quoted at length, if only to show you that this human detail is the proper background to a successful project. A sound approach at work, a contented family in the background, a satisfied client – these are the basic elements to success with any project. All these elements were undoubtedly lacking with the previous contractor, from whom Bechtel took over. How do we know all this detail? We are quoting from a Bechtel Brief. These are published for the employees and friends of the Bechtel Group and the issue from which we have quoted (Ref. 1) deals with Bechtel's project managers.

The thin line between politics and business

Throughout modern history, big business and corruption have unfortunately been intimately connected. For example, many of the present philanthropic organisations throughout the world were founded with capital not necessarily obtained via legitimate, honest business. This statement is made as a matter of fact, since this is not the place to enter into the moral and ethical issues involved, but it is the background to yet another aspect of the construction of the 'world's largest LNG installation'.

The Algerian contract first entered with Chemico also figured as part of a major suit by the US Securities & Exchange Commission (SEC) against Chemico's parent company, General Tire & Rubber Company in mid-1976. A brief reference was made to it earlier; let us now look at the circumstances in a little more detail, since they also played a role in the disaster. The action was part of a post-Watergate drive to expose questionable corporate payments. It happened to cover the broadest array of charges that the SEC had brought against any Company. General Tire & Rubber Company agreed to settle the suit without admitting or denying any of the charges that had been brought. Here is a short list of the charges that were made:

1   Illegal and improper payments 'in excess of several million dollars' for political campaigns since the early sixties.
2   A payment of $500 000 to a consultant in Morocco (shared with three cabinet level ministers) with the object of obtaining a tire plant expansion, and so a monopoly in this field in the area. The payment was made through 'overbilling'.
3   Illegal payments in Chile to directors and consultants through a reduction in the profits taken. These were to obtain a price increase and also to maintain their monopoly in Chile.
4   Payment to a consultant in Romania to obtain approval for the building of a plant there.
5   A $300 000 'nominal' payment to government officials and others in Mexico to obtain certain favours.
6   A payment of $150 000 from 1971–73 to 'get off the Arab black list'.
7   No proper accounts maintained by Chemico, its subsidiary, of a total of $15 *million* paid in connection with the obtaining of the Algerian contract. (This is the contract we have been reviewing.)
8   Numerous gratuities and other benefits to military officers and civilian employees of executive agencies in the USA with whom it had contracts.

How were these payments made? The story goes that it was done by over-invoicing, recording losses on profits, 'slush funds' in Mexico, and cash 'doled out' by the president of General Tire & Rubber Company from a wall safe kept in his office.

To what avail, so far as Chemico were concerned? No doubt their poor performance elsewhere was either suppressed or ignored, but their poor performance on this job could *not* be ignored. Despite everything, they lost the contract and were eliminated from the process plant contracting industry. Since the debacle in Algeria we have never found a reference in the technical press to Chemico securing a contract in this field. In fact, they came to our attention again after some three years in a news item (Ref. 3) saying that the Russian government was going to Geneva for arbitration in respect of ammonia plants built by Chemico in the USSR. It appears that Chemico were seeking relief from performance guarantees because of, as they assert, a bad job of plant installation by the Russians. However, Chemico are reported as saying that they themselves had no knowledge of these arbitration plans. It is true, they said, that several contractual obligations were still outstanding, and they were trying to resolve these through talks with the Russians.

There we must leave Chemico.

Algerian fuel and US technology

. Following the failure by Chemico, Bechtel completed the plant with success – success being measured primarily by having a 'satisfied customer'. In Algeria it is by no means 'roses all the way'. There is a growing economic interdependence between Algeria and the USA. The United States depends upon Algeria for natural gas and some oil, while Algeria depends upon the USA for technical expertise in expanding their facilities and also for their foreign exchange requirements.

Up to now we have been looking at but one corner of the activity that has been going on in Algeria. Early in 1977, shortly after Bechtel entered the field there, there were said to be a total of 70 American contractors working in Algeria, with a workload of some $6 billion. They have been involved in building not only gas liquefaction plants, but also electronic plants, irrigation projects, in the setting up of scientific institutes and a multitude of feasibility studies. The US businessmen working in and with Algeria complain of problems with the customs, state bureaucracy, congested ports, inadequate transport and the desperate lack of skilled workmen.

Educational facilities, especially for ex-patriate children, are meagre, living costs very high. Yet, in spite of all, US firms and their employees seem to thrive on Algerian assignments.

On the other hand, government officials and others in Algeria do not like the excessive dependence on the American contractors, consultants and particularly the multi-nationals, such as the General Tire & Rubber Company, the company who bought Chemico. Relations with such companies are said to be 'hardly idyllic'. Talking about the performance of American firms, the Algerian presidential economic counsellor said: 'targets are not being met, costs are overrun and we have very little control . . .'. He places the blame for such happenings squarely on the Americans, adding bitterly that the multi-nationals and some American companies are 'walking out after they have got enough money.' The counsellor was also bitter about what he called 'foot dragging' by the FPC in approving five contracts for the import of a total of 1.2 trillion cubic feet of liquefied natural gas from Algeria every year. In view of the inordinate delays, Algeria had opened negotiations with other potential customers in Italy, Spain, France, Germany and Switzerland. Yet another fear expressed by the Algerians relates to the adverse influence they feel the American social pattern may have on their own life style.

Turning to the construction field, we find that the three natural gas processing plants built at Arzew, which is in eastern Algeria, were contracted to the Bechtel Corporation, Foster Wheeler and Pullman Kellogg – three 'majors' in the construction industry. Stone & Webster, another major, had a contract for a gas treatment plant. Amoco International are exploring for crude in the Sahara, while the Dravo Corporation have a joint venture with the Algerian National Mining Company to exploit lead and zinc mines. There is thus a very large involvement and a substantial stake between the two countries – Algeria and the USA. It portends well for continuous collaboration over a long period and can be to the benefit of both. A 'sour' contract, such as that entered into by Chemico, can quickly mar such relations and soon put progress into reverse. Building up confidence and trust is a slow, long and time-consuming process; breaking it down can be fast and sure, leaving no time or opportunity to stop the slide.

Shall we now point the moral?

Failure to listen and learn spells disaster

Our present story started, and has now ended, in Algeria, but in a way it really started nearly ten years earlier in India, at Trombay, thousands of miles from Algeria. It was the same contractor, but a different project, with a very different client. Yes, there were lots of differences, but there were also many similarities. The Trombay project (See Chapter 8) was completed some three years late, and cost 60% more than the first budget. When complete, it failed to perform in accordance with expectations. It could not be brought up to design capacity, and the raw material and energy requirements were higher than had been specified. The result: a dissatisfied customer, a sick plant, a lot of arguments and litigation. None of this did the contractor any good at all, nor the owner, nor the plant – nor the relations between the two countries!

A decade later, we find history repeating itself. Only the setting is very different. The Arzew LNG project is some ten times as large in value (in current dollars, although not in constant dollars). The construction period was first set at eighteen months, but some six months before the scheduled completion date the plant was said to be twelve to eighteen months behind schedule. The project was going so badly that the contract had to be cancelled, or the contractor opted for cancellation. We shall never know, but the overrun was clearly going to exceed the original value of the contract, so he would opt out if he could. When the contract was awarded to another contractor – Bechtel – the balance of the work took a further eighteen months to complete, exactly the same time that the whole project was to have taken in the first place. We are not surprised, for Bechtel were as good as starting from scratch or perhaps worse. It is extraordinarily difficult and time-consuming to 'pick up the pieces'. We gave you another example of that in Chapter 4, the case of the Glace Bay Heavy Water Plant; you will see that the effect on time is very similar. Since this second contract was on a cost-plus basis, the total cost was never published, but we have no doubt that the total cost originally estimated doubled, at the very least.

Why did the owner take the drastic step of cancelling his contract with Chemico? He was under very considerable pressure from external sources. The plant was of crucial importance. To quote (Ref. 4):

> By any standard LNG-1 is of absolutely vital importance – not only to Algeria in terms of new and permanent sources of revenue, but to the world's financial community which has provided the immense amounts of capital needed for development and construction of LNG facilities, and to the regions in the eastern and southeastern United States, which are facing a natural gas shortage of increasingly critical dimensions.

The plant was inaugurated on 21 February 1978 by His Excellency President Houari Boumedienne and other high-ranking officials. At the same time, the startup of construction on LNG-2 was commemorated with the commissioning of the opening of the port of Arzew El Djedid. To ship the LNG a fleet of nine 125 000 cubic metre LNG carriers was standing by. Each shipload yields 2.6 billion cubic metres of natural gas when regasified. So the penalties for delay were enormous.

How did Bechtel succeed where Chemico had failed? Chemico in its day was a reputable international process plant construction contractor. All contractors make mistakes, but those who make good are the ones who learn from their mistakes. They listen to the voice of experience. Davy Power-Gas certainly did. We told their story in Chapter 6. There is no doubt at all that Bechtel have learnt from theirs! Apart from the technical aspects of cost control, we think we have, with this case study, demonstrated that there is the much more important and far more difficult task of human relations within the project team, and also in the relations with the client's project team. This is the key to success. It is instructive to see, as we have done, the way Bechtel went about it. They recognise the importance of the role of the project manager to the extent of highlighting his activities in a Bechtel Brief. But the project manager does not, cannot, stand alone. He heads a *team*. 'I am proud of our Bechtel people at Arzew', said chairman S.D. Bechtel Jr. 'They can take great satisfaction in knowing they have done an outstanding job in helping Algeria develop this vital natural gas resource.'

References

1   Bechtel Brief, October 1979, 'Bechtel's Project Managers: Roger Elton directed the world's largest LNG project' Bechtel Briefs are published monthly by the Public Relations Department, Bechtel, PO Box 3965, San Francisco, CA 94119, USA.
2   Kharbanda, O.P., Stallworthy, E.A., and Williams, L.F., *Project Cost Control in Action*, particularly Chapter 11, 'Proper project management'. Gower, Aldershot, 1980.
3   *Chemical Week,* New York, 20 February 1980.
4   Bechtel Brief, March 1978, 'Algeria's new LNG Plant – fuel for U.S. homes and industries'. For publication details, see Ref. 1 above.

PART THREE

DARE WE TELL THE STORY?

8 The Trombay fertiliser plant complex

We saw earlier, in Chapter 3, that most of the major fertiliser plant projects in India, particularly those in the public sector, have suffered substantial overruns in both time and cost. In both Figures 3.2 and 3.4 we listed phases in the development of the Trombay Complex among our examples. Now the time has come to take a specific project in this area for an in-depth study and we have chosen the Trombay Complex. Our reasons for this are:

> The series of projects is well documented;
> The Owner *listened*, but did not learn;
> The major contractor *failed to listen*, and failed

The owner was the erstwhile Fertiliser Corporation of India (FCI) with more than a dozen fertiliser projects scattered throughout India. In April 1978 the FCI was split into five separate autonomous companies as part of a decentralisation process. The objective of this reorganisation was to improve the decision making and hence the working of the various operations. The division made was based upon either feedstock, location or function, and the outcome is set out in Figure 8.1

Ten troubled years

The history of the Trombay site begins in 1954 and we think it will help to understanding the picture better if the various phases in the development of that site are set out in chronological order.

1954   A committee suggest the Trombay location, based on the availability of gases from nearby refineries.

PRODUCTION COMPANIES	UNITS
Fertiliser Corporation of India (FCI)	Gorakhpur, Korba, Sindri, Talchar, Ramagundam
Hindustan Fertiliser Corporation (HFC)	Barauni, Durgapur, Haldia, Namrup
National Fertiliser Limited (NFL)	Bhatinda, Nangal, Panipat
Rashtriya Chemicals and Fertilisers (RCF)	Trombay, Thal
DESIGN AND ENGINEERING	
Fertiliser Planning & Development (India) Limited (FPDIL)	

Figure 8.1 The Fertiliser Corporation of India
The table sets out the five separate autonomous companies into which the FCI was divided in 1978.

1957   Initiation of project authorities. Negotiating committees recommend basing production on refinery gases and/or liquid fuels. Products to be ammonia, urea and double salt.

1959   Year opened with technical feasibility report recommending the production of urea and nitrophosphate. Later in the year report accepted and government clearance received. Global tenders invited, although source of foreign exchange not then known.

1960   Tenders received in June. In August foreign exchange via a US aid loan, so retenders from USA only, resulting in offers some 15% higher than previously. By end of year doubts expressed regarding the suitability of citrate soluble nitrophosphate for Indian soil conditions.

So we come to the first lessons to be learnt. Untied credits are much preferred if one is to receive the most competitive bids and in any case the source of the credit should have been established before any tenders were invited. The change in specification that then followed is an obvious 'open door' for the contractor so far as price is concerned.

1966   Trombay I, producing ammonia, urea, nitric acid, sulphuric acid and nitrophosphate commissioned, but there is a very low capacity build-up, even a year later (1967).

Through the sixties and early seventies several other projects were begun, together with the expansion of the initial units, termed Trombay II, III, IV and V, and completed. Thus, fifteen years on from those first ten troubled years, we can read in the technical press (March 1980):

> RCF's Trombay plant achieved new production records last month with nitrogen fertiliser and phosphate output at 13 400 tonnes and 8 090 tonnes respectively. RCF also created a new delivery record during January. The total amount of product handled equalled 130 000 tonnes, which included some 63 000 tonnes of fertilisers.'

How did they get there? Let us begin by following the course of Trombay I.

Trombay I

The project known as Trombay I was first scheduled for completion in 1963 but, as we have just seen, was finally commissioned in 1966. Costs rose as well, and not only because of inflation. The first estimates were Rs. 247 million, while the final cost was Rs. 378 million. This is the overall picture. There were in fact a total of six separate plant units and the commissioning schedule for these was constantly slipping, as illustrated in Figure 8.2. Once the plant had been completed, it could not be brought up to capacity. More than a year later some 60% of design output was all that could be achieved with any of the plants, as further illustrated by Figure 8.3. The delay in completion was attributed to factors such as:

> Diversion of equipment to other ports, owing to congestion at Bombay, with the loss of some packages;

	COMMISSIONING SCHEDULE				
	Original	Rev. 1	Rev. 2	Rev. 3	
DATE OF SCHEDULE	6–60	9–60	2–62	7–64	Actual
PRODUCT:					
Ammonia	11–63	1–64	4–64	10–64	10–65
Urea	11–63	1–64	4–64	10–64	10–65
Nitric acid	11–63	1–64	4–64	12–64	10–65
Sulphuric acid	–	11–63	6–64	2–65	1–66
Nitrophosphate	11–63	5–64	8–64	2–65	11–65
Methanol	–	–	–	11–65	10–66

Figure 8.2 Commissioning schedule – Trombay I
The table shows a total slippage of some three years in the commissioning programme. The project took six years, when elsewhere it would have taken some three to four years at the most.

PRODUCT	Rated capacity '000 t/year	Production as percentage of rated capacity 66–67 %	67–68 %	Major causes
PLANT CAPACITY				
Ammonia	116	50	57	Technical defects
Urea	99	54	58	Non-availability of ammonia
Nitrophosphate:				
– sulphonitric	330	–	–	Process not used
– carbonitric	270	26	59	under capacity
Nitric acid	106	26	38	Lower nitro-phosphate
Sulphuric acid	66	13	12	Failure of the SN process
Methanol	30	16	32	Serious defect in catalyst

Figure 8.3 Capacity utilisation – Trombay I
This table sets out the capacity utilisation on the several plants in Trombay I when the project was first commissioned, and then a year later.

The change made in the production pattern;
Delays in construction due to a heavy monsoon;
Contractual disputes with plant suppliers.

According to a thorough post mortem that was undertaken, the delays have been 'systematically studied and detailed reports prepared in order to avoid such delays in the execution of major projects'. Of even greater significance was the failure to produce, once in operation. For a cost of 50% more than first indicated, they got a plant running at 60% design capacity. So the real increase in cost was far more. To that initial overrun should be added all the costs required to bring the plants up to design capacity. However, let us look at some of those reports in a little more detail and see what *was* learnt.

The post mortem

An audit prepared in 1968 revealed and emphasised the following facts:

1   In the contract with the main contractor (Chemico of the US) there was no penalty clause for delay.
2   Claims for $820 000 and Rs. 2.6 million against the contractor on various counts were withdrawn as 'bargaining points'.
3   Nitrophosphate manufacture using the sulphonitric process failed. Thus the sum of Rs. 1.2 million paid as licence fee was wasted. A further consequence was that the sulphuric acid plant, costing Rs. 8.5 million, could not be fully utilised.
4   Nitrophosphate manufacture by the carbonitric process was only partially successful.
5   There was low production, leading to higher production costs per ton, due to defects in the engineering design. The poor design also resulted in excessive consumption of raw materials and power.

Parallel with this, the Committee on Public Undertakings also made a report. They were concerned more with the administrative aspects, and their report mentioned:

1   A number of procedural and functional lapses on the part of management.
2   The government took no serious note of these lapses.
3   Defects in the agreements led to high financial losses, apart from poor production on the plants.
4   The contractor selected had neither the capacity nor the experience to handle large contracts of this type.

Yet another commission (the Bedi Commission) was appointed in 1969, and required to report within three months. That deadline was extended from time to time, and ten years later the report had still not been issued. In July 1978 it was stated that the report could not be finalised because the nitrophosphate plant, built by the Chemical & Industrial Corporation, now IDI Management Incorporated, was the subject of a dispute under international arbitration. On the basis of this, FCI obtained a stay order from the courts against examination by the Bedi Commission. The evidence in respect of the arbitration proceedings has now long since been completed, but the award has not been announced since FCI have not paid the arbitration fees.

The specific issues framed earlier by the Trombay Fertiliser Committee of Enquiry embodied the following questions:

1   Did the managing director act entirely in the interest of FCI so far as the main agreement with Chemico, dated 22 March 1961,

and a supplementary agreement dated 27 June 1965, were concerned?

2 Was the dropping of the claim of Rs. 5.75 million against Chemico right?

3 Were the delays in the execution of the civil works and erection of equipment by FCI, or the delays in the supply of drawings and equipment by Chemico, the root reasons for the plants not being ready for initial operation before the supplementary agreement was entered into, and who was at fault?

4 There was no penalty clause for delay in the supplying of drawings and equipment by Chemico, thus enabling Chemico to leave FCI in the lurch. Was this intentional, and if so, by whom?

5 Is a 5% retention sum sufficient to ensure guarantees being met?

6 Why were the general manager and the financial director of FCI not associated with the negotiations with Chemico in June 1965?

7 Why was the record of these discussions not submitted to the Board and the Government?

The trend of the above questions is very evident, and we do not need to elaborate here. In addition, some basic failures in the contractual arrangements instituted by FCI, going right back to 1961, were also noted by the Committee of Enquiry:

> When the original enquiry failed to attract a sufficiently wide response from US contractors (being an aid project, this was the limitation), no fresh tenders were called;
> There was no spares contract with the main contractor;
> There was no feedstock contract;
> No action was taken against Chemico following their admitted 'over-invoicing' in order to secure larger payments against shipment.

The weaknesses in the contractual arrangements led to a series of disputes with the contractor. For instance, FCI were to provide compressor foundations to the Chemico design. However, Chemico declared themselves not satisfied with the workmanship and demanded that some parts be demolished and rebuilt. Chemico also expressed doubts about the lean concrete on which the compressor foundations were built. This led to Chemico expressing a desire to relinquish responsibility for running the machinery unless they could be satisfied that the foundations were safe. These disputes delayed the project for many months. An expert committee from the Central Water & Power Commission examined this issue, so far as the technical aspects were concerned, and declared that the foundations were quite safe. The Committee concluded that much unnecessary controversy could have been avoided by mutual discussion prior to starting the foundation work.

Our own comment is that all this discloses the basic weakness in the contractual arrangements between owner and contractor: related works divided when they should all have been in one hand – that of the contractor. Then he has no one to blame but himself, and if the penalties for failure are appropriate he has some incentive to perform. It is also clear that apart from the many irregularities in the arrangements with the contractor, there was a complete lack of communication and co-ordination between the various departments within FCI, and between FCI and the government, who were ultimately responsible. Is it any wonder, then, that apart from the very considerable cost and time overruns that had to be met, the contractor involved, Chemico, got away 'scot free', leaving what ought to have been his responsibilities behind him, while the owner, FCI, had a 'sick unit' from its very inception. So what happened next?

The rehabilitation of Trombay

It is not difficult to guess. More money had to be spent. The four major units, making ammonia, urea, nitrophosphate and methanol, were all producing very much below their rated capacity, as we saw from Figure 8.3. This was due to poor design, equipment deficiencies and operating problems. Do not forget that the 'rated capacities' should have been achieved from the start. Now steps were being taken to remedy the position but experience had still not brought the lesson home. Means to be taken to rehabilitate the plants were considered by a number of committees. To list some of the results of these committees:

June 1967	A departmental committee recommended several measures for de-bottlenecking in order to reach the rated capacities. Estimated cost: Rs. 8.7 million.
July 1967	These recommendations reviewed and ratified by another technical committee, being endorsed with some slight modifications.
August 1967	Board approval given for Rs. 10 million for plant replacements and modifications, together with another Rs. 15 million for a new phosphoric acid plant.

December 1967   Further review by a two-member team from the TVA. They found that the ammonia output, maximum 75%, was a design limitation, with low quality feedstock. They recommended the installation of a naphtha reformer and additional filters to prevent stoppages in the heat exchangers on the air plant. With the methanol plant, where the maximum attainable was 60%, they endorsed the proposal to install a naphtha distillation column, with redesign of the reformers.

February 1968   Estimated cost for a 100 t/day reformer and the redesign Rs. 9.3 million, with a foreign exchange component of Rs. 3.65 million.

April 1968   A committee sits to evaluate the above three findings.

Finally, action is taken, and by 1971 there is a distinct improvement in ammonia production. But at what cost? A further 10% has been invested, and we are now getting to where we first said we were going to be. But what about the loss of production over the years? Who pays for that, in terms of lost profits on the investment? The owner, of course!

The methanol plant

If you look back to Figure 8.2 you will see that along the way a methanol plant was introduced. This phase of the development was known as TROMBAY II and it ran a very similar course to TROMBAY I, but with another American contractor. Let us see whether a lesson can be learnt by reciting the history.

December 1962   The methanol plant project was approved by the Board.

February 1964   A turnkey contract was awarded to the Girdler Corporation for a 100 tons/day plant, at a cost of $6.04 million. The plant to be commissioned fourteen months from the effective date of the contract, September 1964. So scheduled commissioning date was November 1965.

December 1965   Erection completed.

October 1966   Plant commissioned.

March 1967   Performance guarantee tests. These were made fifteen months after completion of erection, instead of the normal six months. There were serious apprehensions concerning the reformer catalyst, which should have had a life of one year but was disintegrating after a few weeks.

May 1967 — Established that the catalyst was not of the contracted quality. Plant completely shutdown in April, and restarted in May, but there were still repeated breakdowns.

July 1967 — The owner, FCI, takes legal possession of the plant, without prejudice and at the contractor's risk and cost, in order to get the plant right. The owner runs the plant with new catalyst, and achieves 55% throughout but the reformer tubes fail.

December 1967 — It is decided to take legal action against Girdler. The FCI chairman is on record as saying that, just as with the nitrophosphate plant, so with this plant: the contractor had no experience of the type and size of plant being designed.
An Indian arbitrator awards in favour of Girdler.

October 1974 — FCI file a petition in the Delhi High Court against the arbitrator's award.

A sorry history. Once again we see the employment of a contractor lacking the necessary experience, associated with a weak contract that lets him escape without penalty. Even if there had been some penalty, that would have been no compensation for the owner's loss of production over the years. Before the contract was let, the owner was in command. Then was the time to investigate the capability of the contractors and to ensure that a watertight contract was placed. This might have been done if the fruits of the previous, similar unhappy experiences had been applied quickly enough. Another solution is to buy such experience by employing a consultant to vet the contractor and the form of contract.

Phosphoric acid

The next major step, a few years later, and while the management was still wrestling with the problems associated with Trombay I and II, was the decision to build a phosphoric acid plant. The objective was to replace the import of diammonium phosphate with the import of raw sulphur. This, it was said, would result in savings of some Rs. 4.0 million a year in foreign exchange. At the same time, the sulphuric acid plant, made redundant through the change in type of nitrophosphate, could be brought into use. Let us see whether this adventure fared any better, by following, once again, the history of the plant.

August 1967	Decision taken to build a 100 tons/day phosphoric acid plant at an estimated cost of Rs. 15.0 million, having a foreign exchange component of Rs. 5.4 million.
August 1968	Project approved by the government of India. Tenders for the imported equipment invited from Germany, Japan, the USA and the UK.
January 1969	Project entrusted to the planning and development division of FCI, stipulating the Nissan or NPK hemihydrate process.
November 1970	Agreement made with International Ore & Fertiliser Company for the NPK process, licences being approved by the government of India.
January 1971	Revised estimate: total cost now Rs. 32.2 million (just about double the 1967 figure).
January 1976	Revised estimate, now Rs. 50.4 million. Government approval to the expenditure still awaited.

At this time, the reason for the increase in the estimate was analysed. The analysis is quite interesting. Thus:

Changes in scope:	Rs. 9.6 million
Inadequate provisions in earlier estimates:	Rs. 7.1 million
Price escalation and financing costs:	Rs. 18.4 million

The plant was finally completed in March 1978 at an actual cost of Rs. 49.6 million, within the estimate made some two years earlier. We take this as solid evidence of 'learning', but what a slow process it has been.

The planning can now be examined as set out in Figure 8.4. When the plant was started up in March 1978 it could not be brought up to the planned capacity. Since the deficiencies could not be rectified within one year of startup, International Ore's obligations ceased. With a plant rated at 30 000 tons per year, they were only achieving some 17 000 tons, and the deficiency was made good by continuing imports of diammonium phosphate, thus defeating the very purpose for which the plant was built. The lower production than rated was due almost entirely to equipment failure, not to design sizing. To let you see the problems of the maintenance

---

**TROMBAY PHOSPHORIC ACID PLANT
PROJECTED COMPLETION**

DATE OF ESTIMATE   COMPLETION DATE

September 1970   June 1973
January 1973   June 1974
–   March 1978*

* Plant started up, but planned capacity not being achieved.

Figure 8.4 Projected completion – Trombay phosphoric acid plant
As time went on, the completion date was still further delayed.

teams, trying to keep the plant running, we will mention a few of the failures they had to deal with:

Repeated leakage on the dilute sulphuric acid supply line;
Failure of the rubber lining in the concentrated-acid section;
Failure of fluorine scrubber circulation pump;
Failure of carbonate heat exchanger, fume exhaust fan, gear box bearings;
Low capacity of a bucket elevator.

Now we come face to face with real life: a plant in operation and full of problems. The liquids and gases being handled were difficult and high-quality equipment was needed to ensure operating reliability. In the course of the initial guarantee runs, it was established that:

The low production was *not* due to the system concept or the design, which was the Nissan responsibility.
The plant capacity and specific consumption guarantees were met with one exception: sulphuric acid consumption was slightly (1%) higher than guarantee.

We see another case where responsibility was divided over a number of different parties, due to the 'departmental execution' approach discussed in detail in Chapter 3 – Does departmental execution save money? Quite clearly it does not. The only way to secure adequate safeguards against non-performance is to place complete responsibility in one hand.

Trombay IV

The story goes on and on: A catalogue of indecision and split responsibilities. Although each phase echoes the one before, there is merit in repeating the story yet once more. The basis of Trombay IV was a detailed project report prepared in 1969, proposing that imported ammonia be used to produce a complex fertiliser (20:20:10), carrying 60% of water soluble P_2O_5. Let us follow the history of Phase IV from there:

July 1970	Project approved, using the Stamicarbon process. Estimated cost Rs. 435 million, with a foreign exchange component of Rs. 100 million.
November 1970	Licence agreement concluded with Stamicarbon.
October 1971	Revised cost estimate of Rs. 577 million, with a foreign exchange element of Rs. 164 million.
November 1971	Application to the World Bank for financing drew the following comments: complex project, high capital cost, with a low nutrient product. It would be better, they were told, to increase the utilisation of the existing NPK and urea plants.

As a result of the comments from the World Bank, a revised scheme was formulated, with an estimated cost of Rs. 375 million and a foreign exchange element of Rs. 138 million. We reiterate the amount of foreign exchange required because this was a very significant element in the cost of a project at that time – and still is. Is there a project? Not yet. Due to uncertainties regarding the supply of ammonia from world sources the project was reassessed on the basis of ammonia from indigenous sources. The result:

November 1973	Two schemes formulated, Trombay IV, with an estimated cost of Rs. 440 million (foreign exchange Rs. 190 million), with completion a year later of Trombay V, with new plants for both ammonia and urea. Estimated cost Rs. 1140 million (foreign exchange Rs. 278 million).
June 1974	The World Bank sanctions $33 million for Trombay IV, production by April, 1977.
January 1975	The firms selected: Bamag/UHDE for the nitric acid plant, and Powergas/UHDE for the nitrophosphate plant.
March 1975	Tenders re-invited, and final choice now Davy-Powergas for the nitric acid plant, and UHDE for the nitrophosphate plant.
November 1975	Revised estimate of Rs. 763 million for Trombay IV. The increase attributed to: change of scope Rs. 64 million, change in exchange rates and

	escalation Rs. 158 million and increase in financing charges and customs duties Rs. 100 million.
January 1979	Plants (Trombay IV) in production.

Looking back, it took nine years to reach that point: commercial production. That is the day when the plants begin to pay back in relation to the investment that has been made over the years. Our history mentioned Stamicarbon. The design fee of Rs. 0.9 million paid to them had to be written off, following the change in process which we noted. The ammonia terminal facilities were delayed because the concrete foundations were late. They had remained the responsibility of the owner. The owner had to face costs for disruption and delay claimed by the contractor which he himself had originated. It is the same old story, isn't it? Divided responsibility once again, and the consequent losses, all borne by the owner, and hence later, by the product and the consumer.

De-bottlenecking schemes

This story could go on and on, but repetition is tedious. In addition to the major schemes which we have reviewed, a number of smaller de-bottlenecking schemes were studied, some of which went ahead eventually. De-bottlenecking is a way to secure a major increase in production for a marginal increase in investment, but if it is to increase profits it has to work correctly. There was a supplementary gasification scheme, for instance, with an additional reformer furnace, first estimated to cost some Rs. 23 million, and finally costing Rs. 35 million, which nevertheless failed to bring the increase in production that had been anticipated. The urea plant was studied, and Technip paid a fee of Rs. 0.14 million for a scheme that was estimated to cost some Rs. 13 million. That scheme was dropped when Trombay V was approved, in September 1974. And so we could go on. But we believe the point has been made. The lessons for the cost engineer are there in plenty. We see the frustations of government control and intervention; we see the importance of proper, comprehensive and sound contractual conditions; we see how vital it is to purchase from reliable and experienced suppliers, even if that costs more initially. The Indian scene is beset by the continuing need to minimise on foreign exchange, a fact which places the local supplier, whatever his quality, in a dominant position. But what about the owner, both in India and elsewhere. What is the lesson there?

Did FCI listen then and learn now?

As a result of the feedback from the experience gained at Trombay, and with other fertiliser projects in India, certain recommendations were made in 1965 by the Committee on Public Undertakings: the Lok Sabha Secretariat. The actions, if any, arising from these recommendations were reviewed in 1969 and we cannot do better than quote from these two reports. The action that followed the recommendation is described in the form of a reply from the government.

Recommendation
   It takes some six to seven years to erect and commission a fertiliser plant. This long duration brings substantial additional expenditure in departmental charges alone ...
Reply
   With the experience now gained, it should be possible to commission the new plants within a period of three to four years.
Recommendation
   Every day's delay increases the capital cost and there is an associated loss of production. This is of the order of half a million rupees per day and serious attempts should be made to reduce the time taken for erection and commissioning.
Reply
   Noted. Suitable instructions have been issued to the Fertiliser Corporation.
Recommendation
   There is a need for the setting up of cost reduction units on big projects where construction accounts for a substantial proportion of the expenditure. Immediate steps should be taken to organise such a unit on all the projects of the Corporation.
Reply
   . . . .?

Did these recommendations, embodying some very basic points, really have any effect? Were future projects really helped as a consequence? We think not, judging by what has happened since then. Subsequent projects have suffered almost as badly as the early ones: just scan the list in Figure 3.2 once again. It is indeed a pity that having pinpointed the causes of the delays and even recommended a course of action designed to mitigate the situation, there seems to have been no positive action. Almost every project continues to be burdened with substantial unnecessary expense as a result of overruns in time. One of the more recent reports, published in 1978, had a three-page section headed 'Cost control', but alas, project construction is excluded from its scope. The section deals in fact with a system of process costing that will allow the cost of production of the various end products and intermediate products to be established. The subjects dealt with are 'standard costing', 'actual costs', 'profitability', 'material management' and 'inventory control'. Project cost control, which was at the heart of the problem, does not even get a mention.

Now readers, wherever you are, and whoever you are, will *you* listen and learn?

Further reading

The following Reports were referred to in the development of this Chapter and the information so gained incorporated in the text:

Fertiliser Corporation of India, 'Annual Reports.'
Government of India, Committee on Public Undertakings.
Lok Sabha Reports from 1965 to 1975.
Government of India, Ministry of Chemicals and Fertilisers, 'Annual Reports'.
Government of India, Lok Sabha: 'Questions and answers. 1976 to 1979'.

9 Nuclear power plants tell their own story

When we looked at the alarming development of 'regulation' in the USA in Chapter 2 we took a brief look at the nuclear power industry and *its* regulations. Let us now examine the design and construction of the nuclear power plants themselves as they have developed over the years, influenced by these same regulations, from the point of view of the cost control engineer.

In the early fifties, when the nuclear power plant programme first got under way, both in the United States and elsewhere, the specifications that were drawn up were far too onerous. The reason for this was quite clear. There was a desire to ensure absolutely safe operation, at a time when not one industrial plant had even been built. As a result, all the early plants which were built had substantial cost and time overruns. No one appreciated the impact of the regulations, the new design standards, the details of the new specifications, until they began to build. Manufacturers and contractors, naturally enough, refused to commit themselves to lump-sum prices, and so there were very many 'open doors'. The closest the industry had come to the type of control now demanded was in the aircraft industry, with its strict control of materials, and all the certification that went with it. Now a new factor had been added: what was called 'clean conditions', particularly in construction. The cost impact was enormous; how necessary the strictness was, an open question. As a result, everyone suffered: owner, vendor and construction contractor. Vendors, in particular, thought the extremely rigorous specifications not only unnecessary but unachievable. Accordingly, they only gave lip-service to these requirements, finding out too late that every word in the fine print was going to be enforced.

Surprise, surprise!

In those early days, one of us was associated with the design and construction of what we believe was the first industrial nuclear power station, Calder Hall, built in the United Kingdom for the Central Electricity Generating Board, so we saw all this happen at first hand. Later, as the technology spread abroad, and reached the developing countries, the other was intimately associated, in the late sixties and early seventies, with the nuclear power programme in a developing country, India.

In the second stage of her nuclear power programme, India standardised on the CANDU type reactor, using a natural uranium fuel, with heavy water as a moderator and coolant. This particular design is the basis for most of the nuclear power programme in Canada. As the programme in India was implemented, the first of a series of reactors was imported from Canada, with the intention of manufacturing the subsequent reactors in the series locally, in India. This was in pursuit of the continuing policy of minimising overseas costs, building up self-reliance. Quotations were requested, and an Indian manufacturer quoted what he thought was a 'very safe' price. A little later, one of us happened to visit Canada and were able to meet the chief engineer of the Canadian firm who had manufactured the first reactor imported into India. This was an informal meeting at a social function and in due course the conversation turned to the 'lighter things of life' – work. The chief engineer was asked 'How on earth do you estimate the cost of a nuclear reactor for the first time?' The answer he gave is of interest to every estimator, every cost control engineer involved in a development project; and we have already had a lot to say about development projects of various types. This chief engineer scratched his head and said, 'Very simple! You estimate what you see on the drawings in the normal fashion, add a little more than the normal margin and – double the price.' Oh dear, we thought, the Indian manufacturer has forgotten – better, did not know of – that last, simple step. No wonder the Indian manufacturer lost heavily on his first contract to build a nuclear reactor. But we have learnt the first lesson when entering the unknown. We have told you before and now we tell you again: development projects cost from two to four times the basic estimate. Never forget that. Always ask yourself, as you start out: is this a development project? For us, at least? In the developing countries, almost every project is a development project; they are doing so many many things for the first time. Also, the contractors who go out are often working there for the first time, and have to learn that local experience *cannot* be imported. It has to be learnt.

The developed countries possibly did a little better than the developing countries in the first round of construction of nuclear power plants, but not much. For instance, one of the earlier nuclear reactors built in the USA was scheduled to be delivered within four years at a cost of some $55 million. It was actually completed several years later with an *overrun* of $100 million. Even later, at the end of the sixties, we remember a small nuclear facility being built by 'newcomers' and estimated at some $12 million, still over-runing by 150%. How are we going to get first the estimators and then management, to accept and allow for the 'development factor'? Will they ever learn? We shall return to that theme in our closing chapter.

History speaks for itself

The new technology involved in the construction of nuclear power stations has brought its own special technical problems. But that is not all. As we have seen already, in Chapter 2, this particular field has been further plagued by far more serious problems relating to the environment, problems created once more by people and politics. Technical problems, once solved, stay solved, but this second type of problem is, as it were, a growing living thing. Problems multiply. Let us take a brief look at the history of nuclear power stations and see how the problems multiplied and grew over time. We shall follow that history in the USA.

April 1970   Government revised a decision to close a nuclear power plant in the State of Washington. A power supply problem was posed by an economy step. Resumption must await move by Congress.

May 1970   The two largest, costliest nuclear complexes in the south initiated. Cost, $1 billion; capacity 3.6 million kwh; the contractor, Westinghouse Electric; the owner, Carolina Power & Light Company.

December 1970   The Atomic Energy Commision (AEC) will allow work on fifteen nuclear power projects to continue, but three are halted.Work on 26 sites has been affected.

January 1973   The Pacific Gas & Electric Company's $800 million project halted due to geological and environmental problems.

March 1973	The South Carolina Electric Company given a permit from the AEC for the construction of their previously announced $340 million, 900 mw nuclear power plant in Fairfield County, S.C.
June 1973	Ralph Nader (see Chapter 2) sought to close down nuclear plants, through the Friends of the Earth group. A lawsuit was entered saying 20 power stations were unsafe and the AEC was charged with a 'gross breach' of its obligations.
August 1973	The AEC directed ten nuclear power plants to reduce output, fearing overheating. All these reactors were supplied by General Electric.
September 1973	The Palisadec nuclear power plant to be shut down for 90 days in order to prevent leaks.
October 1973	Virginia Electric and Power Company ordered by the AEC to show cause why it should be permitted to continue the construction of two nuclear generating units, on which it would have spent some $460 million by the end of the year.

We are at the end of 1973. The blows have come thick, and fast, and heavy, have they not?

August 1974	There is controversy over the safety of nuclear power plants despite recent reports that a person has a far greater chance of being killed in a hurricane, or by lightning, than by a nuclear power plant accident.
October 1974	The environment and nuclear power critic David Coney declared: Unless the reliability of nuclear power plants increases substantially, utilities and the public may well pay more than $100 billion over the next fifteen years for nuclear power generating capacity that just won't produce electricity.
January 1975	Suspension of construction work on the nuclear power plant of the Cleveland Electric Illuminating Company. The NRC ordered the operators of 23 nuclear power plants to close them down for inspection of their backup emergency cooling systems.
May 1975	GAO said that their fast breeder nuclear reactor programme, already faced with a $9 billion cost overrun, could cost the government another $1.7

billion to make it commercially competitive with other energy sources. (Don't forget: a billion is 1000 million in this book.)

A court refuses to rehear on its decision to bar construction of a $400 million nuclear power plant proposed by Northern Indiana Public Service Company.

August 1975   A petition by some 2000 scientists presented to Congress and the White House seeking to cut back the programmes for nuclear power plants on the grounds that they are unsafe.

November 1975   The Philadelphia Electric Company closed down its Peach Bottom Unit 2 nuclear reactor for 35 days, to correct vibration problems in certain monitoring devices.

February 1976   A big plant to recycle nuclear fuel hit by delays and cost escalation. Have we a 'white elephant'? The owner, Allied Chemical Corporation, blames safety rules. The plutonium worries their foes.

News breaks of the Royal Dutch Shell Group losses on their nuclear reactor manufacturing programme through General Atomic. Their gas cooled reactor project ends in fiscal debacle; total loss estimated at $1 billion!

. What we have just described happened to a multi-national company. The contagion spreads, with countries other than the USA itself affected by the campaign there against nuclear power.

March 1978   Three environmental groups ask the NRC to hear their pleas for the stoppage of some 20 tons of nuclear fuel to be exported to India.

April 1976   The Soviet Union cancels a contract for a $1.6 billion plant being negotiated with Kraftwerk Union AG of West Germany.

December 1976   The fallout from the nuclear explosion in China could, it is said, cause an additional four thyroid cancers in the USA.

Then the governmental experts quarrel among themselves. Thus:

June 1976   The EPA asserted that a major nuclear power plant accident could kill two to ten times more people than earlier estimated by the NRC (Nuclear Regulatory Commission).

February 1977	NRC again suspended construction permit granted Public Services Company of New Hampshire.
	The Supreme Court agreed to review a lower court ruling that could stall several nuclear power plants.
February 1978	New uncertainty over the Seabrook, New Hampshire nuclear power plant created by a Federal Appeals Court decision that voids the EPA's previous approval of the plant.
July 1978	The US House of Representatives US, inviting a veto showdown with President Carter, rejected by 187 to 142 a compromise that would have prevented completion of the Clinch River breeder reactor project in Tennessee.
March 1979	The fate of the 'on-off' Seabrook nuclear power station became blurred again over the weekend. The NRC ordered five large nuclear power plants to close indefinitely because they were built with too little protection against damage by earthquakes.

So the story goes on, and on. Why have we dwelt at such length on the history of a few of the many nuclear plants and all the turmoil of opinion that surrounds them? We want to drive home the point, above all, that anything – even a good thing – can be overdone. It is not until a series of such events over the years is set out that one really see what is happening. Global figures – the number of plants shut down, the losses, and so on, make a small impact on the mind. A little detailed history paints a far more powerful picture.

What has really happened? Thanks to the foresight of scientists and engineers over the past three decades or so nuclear power is now undoubtedly practical, safe and economical. Since the 'oil crisis' of 1973 and its aftermath it has become really economic in competition with that other main source of energy. Yet, thanks to people playing politics we are being so kind to ourselves that nuclear power plants are being *killed by kindness* – the title we gave to Chapter 2, where we saw the same thing happening to all new construction in the USA.

TVA turns a challenge into an opportunity

The Tennessee Valley Authority (TVA) published plans to construct a series of seven nuclear electric power plants, starting in 1966. There would be seventeen units, each with a reactor, with a total installed capacity of some 22 000 MW, the total estimated cost then being $15 billion. These plants are listed in Figure 9.1. This was and is the largest commitment of this kind by a single power generating authority anywhere in the world. In common with all the other utility companies in the USA, the TVA found to their misfortune that many of their early assumptions were but myths. For instance:

> Building a nuclear power facility is *not* the same as building a conventional power plant;
> Previous concepts on safety and environmental protection just did not apply;
> Codes, regulations and design guidelines had to be almost completely rewritten;

The learning process was slow but sure, and proved very expensive. At about the time of the TVA's entry into the field, the first feedback from the early turnkey projects was highly favourable. The first commitment entered into by the TVA was an order for two 1100 MW units in June 1966 for Browns Ferry Station, followed by a third about a year later. This action virtually coincided with

THE TVA NUCLEAR POWER STATIONS
COST AND TIME OVERRUNS

	Cost estimate – $/kw		Completion time – months		
	Original	January 1980	Original	Latest	Factor
Browns Ferry	113 (1967)	263	46	81	1.75
Sequoyah	138 (1968)	598	47	117	2.50
Watts Bar	200 (1969)	581	55	78	1.40
Bellefonte	271 (1970)	770	55	63	1.15
Hartsville	274 (1971)	1127	54	71	1.30
Phipps Bend	615 (1974)	1146	62	67	1.10
Yellow Creek	731 (1974)	1082	66	72	1.09

Figure 9.1 The TVA nuclear power stations
This table sets out the overrun in both cost and time experienced and being experienced by the TVA with respect to their nuclear power station programme. The latest estimate of cost assumes completion of the programme by the late eighties, but it has now been set back by a further ten years. (Data reproduced by kind permission of the TVA.)

the discovery of the huge losses that were being suffered by the equipment manufacturers, particularly those committed to fixed-price contracts. These losses were occasioned, as we have already seen, by the increasingly stringent regulatory requirements, the increased scope of work, earlier not seen, and severe delays in the delivery of materials. The last was again primarily due to the need to comply in detail with the new regulations. This growing complexity was clearly reflected in the huge growth of the various elements that go to make up such plants. We have illustrated this already in Chapter 2 (see Figure 2.4) together with the way in which the regulations multiplied (see Figure 2.3). The growth in the regulations had to be reflected in the standards and specifications governing engineering and construction and these also grew phenomenally – from about 50 in 1965 to more than 1,700 by 1978. Compliance with these standards has become a project in itself, with a separate task force for the purpose (Ref. 1).

As a result of these factors, which unfortunately all worked in the same direction so far as cost and time were concerned, not only those first three units at Browns Ferry, but all the other nuclear power stations proposed by the TVA were threatened with substantial cost overruns. Four of these have still to be started and the programme will not now be completed until the late nineties because of a fall-off in the anticipated demand for electric power in the area. The photograph, Figure 9.2, shows the Bellefonte Station in the course of construction. The photograph was taken at the beginning of 1979, the plant being due for completion by the end of that year.

It should be remembered that the wide discrepancy shown in the table in Figure 9.1 is not wholly due to the growing complexity of the regulations. Inflation played havoc, too – and is playing still more havoc now (1982). The USA had long been accustomed to a slow, regular movement in the escalation index of some 2–3% per year, but in the late sixties it approached 10%, and in the early seventies hit double figures, following the oil crisis in late 1973. As illustrated in Figure 9.3, inflation affected the TVA, as it did all the rest of the world. The problem is very pronouned when we look at the plants being built by the TVA. They had long lead times – more than nine years from the granting of the first certificate – with construction itself spanning some five years. As may be seen from Figure 9.3, in the crucial five years for the TVA, from 1975 to 1980, costs in the USA rose by some 50%, instead of the 15–20% that had been expected.

All this had its effect not only on the power companies themselves, but on all their suppliers and contractors. In addition to a

Figure 9.2 Bellefonte nuclear power station
This photograph shows the TVA Bellefonte power station in course of construction
(Feburary 1979). Compare with Fig. 9.5 showing a completed station. (Photograph
by courtesy of the TVA.)

great increase in the degree and detail of inspection, there was a
great volume of documentation that had to be rigorously processed. The papers became just as important as the items of equipment themselves. In addition, there was a degree of new technology
that also stretched the time schedules and further increased the
cost. This unparalleled experience resulted in what might be called
'over-reaction' so far as the TVA's suppliers were concerned,
affecting their ongoing construction programme following Browns
Ferry. The steel shortages of the early seventies compounded the
problem and in many cases suppliers just refused to bid unless the
steel supply was first set up by the Authority. This combination of
adverse factors was no help at all, either to the TVA or to the power
plant industry in general. There was a substantial slow-down in the
tempo of the industry, and all projects under construction were

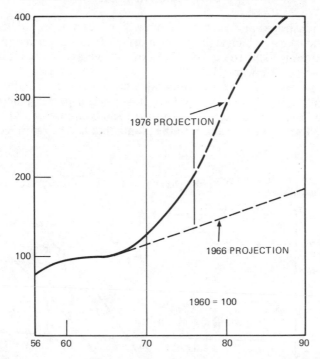

Figure 9.3 Inflation in the USA
This graph compares the projected inflation when the first estimates were made by
TVA in 1966, with the actuality up to 1976. A very different prospect is in view for
the eighties. (Data reproduced by kind permission of the TVA.)

considerably delayed, while potential projects were shelved. The
specific effect on the TVA programme can be seen in Figure 9.1, by
comparing the original and the latest estimates of time and cost.

In spite of this catalogue of problems, the nuclear alternative still
appears to be the best choice. It is to be hoped that the lessons of
the past twenty years will not have all been in vain. There is at long
last a growing sense of realism. It is slowly being recognised that
there *is* a limit to regulations, standards and controls. Regulation
cannot bring perfection. When we look at the TVA, we find that
they have indeed applied their experience and operated with
realism, within the constraints that they have had imposed upon
them. All in all, their performance has been very much better than
average, but they still had to pay the price. Nevertheless, the TVA
did very well when their results are compared with that of the
power generating industry (called utilities in the USA) in general.

This is illustrated in Figure 9.4, from which it can be seen that their investment cost, which is the governing cost factor in nuclear power generation, is likely to be some 75% of the average in the industry, reckoned per kilowatt (Ref. 2).

The passage of time has thus allowed us to see that the bold decision of the TVA in 1965 in favour of nuclear power generation was a wise one, of benefit both to their local community and to the nation. They have safe and reliable plants that can be operated at a

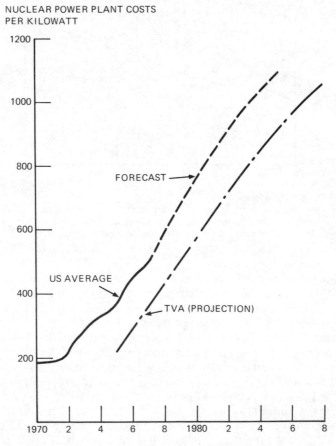

Figure 9.4 Electric power costs (nuclear stations) in the USA
This graph compares the cost of generating electricity using nuclear power plants, in the USA, with the specific situation enjoyed by the TVA. Their bold programme has brought a clear cost advantage. (Data reproduced by kind permission of the TVA.)

reasonable cost, and a competitive price for electricity gives sub-stantial economic advantage to their customers. To conclude our look at the TVA, Figure 9.5 shows one of the latest plants to be completed and brought into use – the Sequoyah Station. Now you can really see what costs some several billion dollars a time to build.

Probabilistic cost estimating

The recurrent and substantial overruns experienced in the nuclear power plant construction industry in the USA and elsewhere have added a new dimension to project cost constrol and, more parti-cularly, to project estimating. Never forget that once a project is 'off the ground' and work has started in earnest, the series of re-estimates that have to be made are an important part of the

Figure 9.5 A completed nuclear power station
The TVA Sequoyah Nuclear Power Plant, substantially completed in 1979. (Photograph by courtesy of the TVA.)

function of the cost engineer. He has to forecast the trend: he has to tell management where they are going so far as cost is concerned. Both estimators and cost engineers have been attempting to find ways and means of defining and measuring the scope of the problem with which they have been faced. Earlier we mentioned a neat 'rule of thumb' – double the figure first thought of! But that is far too rough and ready an approach. And who knows, perhaps our multiplier should be three or four, rather than two. The objective is to forecast final cost as early as possible: preferably, before we even start. Unfortunately there are political as well as estimating hurdles to be overcome. The estimator cannot use 'broad brush' factors; he has to provide a satisfactory demonstration to his management of probable cost since they have to vote the money and fund the project.

In order to cope with this problem, insight is sought into the areas of greatest cost uncertainty, then the various factors are weighted that might cause the cost to vary significantly from the original estimate, provided it has been prepared in accordance with the standard techniques. There have been a number of papers and articles on techniques designed to define and quantify the variables involved, and the term 'probabilistic cost estimating' has come into use to describe this particular approach.

With nuclear power plants costing anything from one to three billion dollars; with construction spread over some ten years; the cause of the overrun eventually found arises from a sequence of events over that ten-year 'life' of the project itself, prior to the plant coming into operation. These uncertainties multiply, if only because of the time they have to appear, and at one time they used to be covered by a single line at the bottom of the estimate: contingency. But we cannot have a contingency of 100 or 150%. It would be ironic indeed for an estimator to spend months of effort, in conjunction with the design engineers, to arrive at a detailed cost estimate, only to add anything from 100% upwards at the bottom line. The problem is: the addition is clearly necessary, but how can it be demonstrated to management? An answer is sought by listing and quantifying the elements of uncertainty, and then evaluating the chance, or probability, that the final cost will fall within certain limits. The approach can and should be applied to all the major cost elements, one by one, including the engineering, purchase of equipment and construction. It has to be clearly understood that 'probabilistic cost estimating' (PCE) does not attempt to predict the *final* cost, but the final cost as seen at a particular point in time, while assessing the trend visible at that time. It is, therefore, an *instant* estimate. Tomorrow, something could happen

– and often does – to make its provisions null and void.

How does it work? PCE must identify and try to quantify cost risks such as:

Effect of design change on equipment and construction;
Uncertainties in relation to licensing regulations;
Project scheduling and manpower loading uncertainties.

These various risks, or uncertainties, and any others that can be thought of, have to be evaluated, through discussion, from the viewpoint of the various agencies involved, such as:

Specialist plant suppliers
Standard equipment vendors
Engineering contractor
Construction companies
Utility owner
Governmental authorities

The estimate has to be examined item by item from these several viewpoints, and the risk quantified in discussion, and with the assistance of the experts in the particular field. Where possible, in areas of significant risk, such as in relation to new regulations, a concensus of opinion from a number of experts in the field should be taken, if possible. All these opinions are then consolidated, and cost parameters set, generally as illustrated in the table in Figure 9.6. Assuming the figures tabled to be representative of a nuclear power plant, such as we were discussing earlier, let us say that the estimate was prepared in 1970. At that time, they saw a 99% probability that the plant could cost some 40% more than the detailed estimate then made. It was actually completed in1979 for $2500 million, or nearly 70% more than first estimated. You will notice that this is close to the situation demonstrated by the Phipps Bend Station in Figure 9.1, but that most of the TVA stations finished up costing more than twice the original estimate – even more than four times in one case. If this approach does nothing else, it should awaken management to the fact that they are dealing with an estimate, and an estimate with a very wide margin of error, at that. If only that one point is made clearly, then the PCE will have served its purpose. Another aspect is that this approach highlights the critical cost areas, helping to provide 'warning signals'. It is always possible, perhaps by speeding up work in those areas, to migitate against the growing cost. Forewarned is fore-armed!

Let us not be carried away by the jargon and the complexities of risk analysis, as involved in PCE. Instead, let us appreciate the key

COST ESTIMATE – PROBABILITY STUDY
YEAR – 1970

SECTION	COST ESTIMATE $x million	ANTICIPATED COST $x million	PROBABILITY RANGE	
			1% $x million	99% $x million
Cooling systems:	450	490	390	560
Reactor vessel:	300	340	280	375
Fuel handling equipment:	150	190	110	270
Reactor core:	255	300	250	350
Turbogenerators, switchgear & transformers:	150	160	150	170
System engineering	75	90	75	145
Project Engineering	120	140	120	250
TOTALS:	1500	1710	1375	2120
Ratio:	100	114	92	141
Actual Cost:				2500 (167)

Figure 9.6 A cost estimate – probability study
An assessment of cost probability in relation to a nuclear power plant. The analysis is realistic, although the specific cost breakdown cannot be taken as typical.

point, that risk and uncertainty must be broken down into as many separate elements as possible and then evaluated for risk, one by one. This technique is to be contrasted with the earlier 'conventional' approach of adding as the last line, a single 'contingency percentage', a figure which may have no rationale except feel and feedback from the past. As we have seen so often with our case studies, the past is no guide when new ground is being broken. If the previous project overran, and they usually do, then we will merely repeat the error. But we can learn from our past failures. We can, for instance, learn from the history now available to us in relation to the construction of nuclear power plants. We can see the way it goes; we can estimate, therefore, the way it is likely to go in the future. It is possible to learn from experience; that is why we have dwelt at length on the work and the efforts of the Tennessee Valley Authority. A study of their successive efforts demonstrates that they are learning; the next generation of plants will, we are sure, be more closely estimated. It is true that PCE, one of the techniques developed to overcome the initial ignorance, is almost trying to quantify the unquantifiable. At least it encourages a scientific and methodical approach to the problem.

While risk by its very nature can be said to be unquantifiable because once we *really* quantify it, the risk has gone; yet we can *know* what we are talking about, and compare risk with risk. Some factors in an estimate are clearly much more uncertain than others. Experts closely involved in a project can say with a measure of certainty: that risk is twice (or half) *that* risk. This is the road that PCE takes, and if expert opinion is used intelligently, we will certainly have something far more reliable that a 'fat' contingency, which may well not be as 'fat' as it looks, and the approach will also inspire management with a degree of confidence in the figures they are assessing.

What is the moral?

There is no doubt at all that in the present situation, almost worldwide, and particularly in the USA, with the cost of energy from the more common sources, such as petroleum, natural gas and coal, continually rising, nuclear power generation is no longer an option, but a necessity. Few people realise just how far it has already gone in the USA. In 1980 there was a total of 192 nuclear power stations in various stages of construction, concentrated largely in the eastern States. When we look at the situation worldwide, we see that nuclear power has established a foothold in at least 44 countries. By mid-1978 some 22 countries had licensed a total of 220 reactors, having a total capacity of some 100,000 MW. A further 320 reactors are under construction or on order, worldwide. The investment required is massive, and as costs rise the electricity generating companies shy away from such heavy investment, but they come back again. Their money is going to be locked up for some ten years, the time it takes to license and construct, but if not nuclear power, what then? It is indeed a murky picture full of uncertainty and beset by emotion. There is one sure fact: never again will energy be either cheap or easy to get. We have two extreme views on nuclear power generation. The 'Friends of the Earth' say that 'nuclear energy is dying', but an economist says that 'the vigorous development of nuclear power is not a matter of choice, but of necessity'.

What is certain is that the construction of nuclear power plants will be with us for a long time to come. Keeping costs under control and within budget is never easy. In the newer fields, of which nuclear power plant construction is typical, it is even more difficult. There is a new dimension, in terms of the regulatory and environmental considerations, whose cost impact must be evaluated. We are even moving on from nuclear power to newer fields, such as the production of liquid fuels and chemicals from solid fuels and here we can expect the final cost, perhaps, to be ten times the original estimate, rather than double, if we are not careful. However tenuous the data, and it is indeed tenuous when we are dealing with new and unproven technology, the capital cost estimate is always the beginning of the story. No-one will proceed without an estimate of cost, and once that estimate has been tabled, those charged with the responsibility for design and construction find that they have to live with it.

It is clear that we are reaching the limit, the extreme limit perhaps, in terms of environmental and regulatory considerations. A halt will *have* to be called, otherwise not only nuclear power plants, but all production units, will be out of business. There are already some sound indications that this is in fact happening. There is not, nor never can be, 100% safety. Life itself is most certainly not like that, so how can anything man-made be expected to be any better. Even the approach to 100% safety can only be made at phenomenal cost, so that if attempted, the projects are no longer viable. So then there would only be one route – the simple life. No risk, no progress – nothing! Other routes to energy, such as oil and coal, are finite. New routes and new developments here are indeed coming quickly, but they will still take time. Meanwhile, nuclear energy is here. It can be economic, but a surprising price is having to be paid – a completely unexpected price – in terms of regulations and environmental considerations. A sleeping dog has been woken up and now we cannot stop him barking. The repercussions are being felt throughout manufacturing industry.

It is now recognised that energy is basic to all manufacturing industry. The conservation of energy has now become the prime motivator in the design and construction of process plants of whatever kind. This is because energy is a raw material of industry for which there is no substitute. But of course it has its price. When the price was low, it tended to be ignored. Now the price is climbing it can no longer be ignored. Energy must be produced at the lowest possible price, a problem that leads to the consideration of a variety of alternatives. The range of possible alternatives grows as the price climbs. The rising price and the search for alternatives result in more options being available, bringing in their train the consideration of novel processes, such as those now being considered for synthetic fuels from solids. These are inevitably development projects of one kind or another and so we exhort all involved in such projects to remember at all times the special problems of development projects, such as we have highlighted in our frontispiece. We have returned to this theme time and again as we considered our various case histories and our present objective is to make all those associated with the design, development and construction of such projects remember that development inevitably costs money, far more money than one usually even begins to expect.

References

1   Willis, W.F., 'TVA's first ten years of nuclear plant design and construction experience', *Cost Engineering*, 1979, vol. 21, no. 1, January/February.

2   Tennessee Valley Authority. Private communications during May and June, 1980.

10 The non-starters

We are now going to take a brief look at a few projects that will be built – if they are ever built – for political rather than for economic or techno-economic reasons. The projects that we are going to look at fall essentially into two different categories:

> The real non-starters. These are plants which may never be built, such as the Korba Fertiliser Plant, already mentioned in Chapter 3;
> Plants which may well be built, but are built for political reasons and are hopelessly uneconomic. They are non-starters in the sense that they will never make a profit.

We have brought these projects together in this chapter because of their obvious similarities, as outlined above. They all suffer from a lack of decision; there is no planning and no real prospect of financial viability. Project cost control never gets a chance because the only considerations are of a political nature and the plant is going to be built whatever the cost. There are lessons to learn from such examples, if we will but listen.

Will Korba ever be built?

Korba is the location of a proposed coal-based fertiliser plant. Korba is in India, right in the heart of the coal belt at Madhya Pradesh. For countries heavily dependent on imports of oil but with vast coal resources, such as India, the use of coal as a feed-stock for the manufacture of fertilisers makes sound economic sense. The processes are well proven though they were not widely exploited commercially, since the product was more expensive when produced from coal rather than from naphtha (an oil product). At least this used to be the case, but the sharply rising cost of crude oil through the seventies has dramatically changed that picture.

When the plant at Korba was first proposed, the intention was that it should be financed from the private sector. However, once it become clear that its profitability would not bear comparison with that of a plant using a naphtha or gas-oil feedstock, the private sector lost interest, and the project was finally taken over by the public sector, and was to be built through the Fertiliser Corporation of India (FCI). This organisation was charged at that time (late sixties) with the setting up of major nitrogenous fertiliser capacity throughout India, as part of the 'green revolution'. But there was continuous delay and indecision. We have already described this aspect in Chapter 3 (Developing countries are difficult). Look again at Figure 3.3. At the same time as all this was going on, two other coal-based fertiliser plants had been put in hand, one at Ramgundam and the other at Talcher, which have been completed but have since been plagued with serious operational problems.

As we said, although the technology for making fertiliser from coal was well proven it was perhaps not wise to put 'too many eggs in one basket'. It was decided to let the other two projects proceed to completion and to defer Korba until sufficient experience had been gained in respect to the coal technology involved. The end result of this decision was that ten years' work on Korba came to nothing, after an expenditure of some Rs. 300 million. All that was left was a bare construction site and a few items of hardware.

What is the lesson here? We must remember that technology is a 'moving target'. There is seldom any finality and there are always 'improvements' coming up. If one listens too hard to the process engineers, then one is running into desperate danger. The solution is to 'freeze' the technology at a certain point in time and *build*. If one waits for the 'best', one will never build. If one tries to improve once the plant is under way, then those improvements will cost a lot of money. Korba should have been built with all speed, using the available technology. It would then have been a 'pilot plant' and the lessons could have been learnt. Now there are two 'pilot plants' and only history will tell us whether the right decision was made. The two other projects are now complete, though they cost some two to three times the estimated cost. This you can see by referring back to Chapter 3 once again, where they are both listed.

Paper projects in the doldrums

For developing countries, such as India, paper is a necessity next in importance only to food and housing. We have just looked at the influence of political decisions on the fertiliser industry in India.

Now we look at the effect of the political approach to the paper-making industry, so crucial to India's literacy programme. Much of the paper produced in India has been produced by private industry, but since industry could not cope with the cyclical shortages that had been occurring from time to time, the government of India decided to take a hand in 1970. They set up a public corporation, Hindustan Paper Corporation. The objective was to set up new pulp, paper and newsprint mills. The company had an authorised capital of Rs. 1500 million and by April of 1979 there had been a total investment of some Rs. 1050 million. The major projects undertaken, with their location, proposed capacity and estimated cost, are set out in Figure 10.1. The total capacity of the four plants detailed was to be some 317,000 tons/year, but the situation as it has actually developed is very different from what had been anticipated. None of the projects has, as yet, gone into production, though Nagaland is nearly ready (April 1982) for commissioning. But non-availability of raw materials and power may delay the achievement of full production (Ref. 1). This has cost not only time but money, adding a further financial burden to costs that were already escalating sharply.

We indicate in Figure. 10.1 a *re*-revised schedule for completion, the latest that has been published, but we doubt very much whether even this schedule has the least chance of success. The total estimated cost of these several projects has now risen to some Rs. 6370 million directly as the result of delay and indecision.

STATUS OF PAPERMAKING PROJECTS – HINDUSTAN PAPER CO.						
			Cost estimate			
		Capacity	Original	Revised	Completion date	
Product	Location	000T/yr.	Rs. mill.	Rs. mill.	1st revision	latest
Newsprint	Kerala	80	829	1519	Oct 1979	1982
Pulp & paper	Nagaland	37	187	837	Dec 1976	1982
Pulp & paper	Nowgong	100	1143	2300	Dec 1980	1983
Pulp & paper	Cachar	100	1140	2300	Dec 1981	1983
	TOTALS:	317	3299	6370		

Figure 10.1 Status of papermaking projects
Here we give details of the four plants under construction by the Hindustan Paper Corporation. The capacity of the first, at Kerala, has been increased to 1200 tons per year, so that the total output is now 4100 tons/year, whilst the latest estimate of cost has gone up to Rs. m. 6,000.

Comparing this figure with the original estimate of Rs. 3299 million, we see a *direct* loss of some Rs. 3000 million. The indirect loss, in terms of loss of output and hence revenue, is estimated at a further Rs. 4000 million per year. The result may well be that from the day they start up, these four plants may be doomed to be 'sick' units, unable to bring a return on the investment that has been made in them. And yet HPC has taken over a private sector sick unit (India Paper & Pulp Company) for rehabilitation.

The indirect loss is far greater than the financial loss from failure to get the plants into operation without undue delay. The shortfall of paper due to the delay in commissioning these four major plants has to be made good by imports. Not only do these come in at much higher international prices but they also contribute to the drain on the country's foreign exchange resources. In 1980 there was said to be a shortfall in India of some 400 000 tons of paper and this is likely to rise by some 50%, to 600 000 tons in three years time. Until the four plants in prospect through HPC are commissioned, the annual expenditure abroad in this context, at some Rs. 7500 per ton, is of the order of Rs. 3 billion, or over some three years – the time they may still have to wait for these plants – a total of some Rs. 10 billion. All this when the oil import bill alone may well use up the *entire* export earnings of India.

This is the cost. What is the cause? Progress seems to have been bogged down right from the start, and the failure to make proper progress so far has been attributed to:

Over-centralised control;
Poor project management;
Delays in placing orders.

These projects have had the 'benefit' of several outside consultants, even though HPC itself has nearly 200 qualified paper techno-logists and engineers on its payroll. There seems to be the possibility of 'too many cooks spoiling the broth'. There is evidence of a complete failure to communicate, either within the organisation, or with the consultants.

One of the plants is for the manufacture of newprint and there the failure to communicate between the consultants and the project group was such that 'they' forgot to order certain requisite cables. This omission alone brought a delay in completion of some 18 to 24 months! With the Nagaland project, a boiler supplied by an Indian manufacturer was found to be defective on arrival at site. It was nevertheless installed – in the face of violent objections from the project team. When, later, the boiler did not work, the tubes had to be replaced, with imported tubes in order to get the necessary quality. Result: *that* project was delayed eighteen months. The two other projects, at Nowgong and Cacher, seem to have suffered even more. Here, the consultants were appointed very late in the day and there were substantial arguments – and hence delays – in the placing of orders for the long-delivery items. On some occasions, the government recommended the appointment of Engineers India to undertake projects on a turnkey basis, much against the wishes of the project team. To crown all, there now appear to be doubts as to the availability of the raw material, wood pulp, since the forest area allotted to HPC by the Assam Government has since been completely denuded of its woodstock. That the Corporation has been without a fulltime managing director and chairman for some time, can hardly have helped in the decision-making process.

We think the lessons to be learnt here are clear for all to see. When a project team is put in charge, it should have the full authority to implement its decisions. Here we have what is in effect one government department being overruled by another desirous of furthering its own special interests. The divided responsibility leads to 'buck-passing', a subject we dealt with earlier. The multiplication of consultants can only result in conflicting advice because there is always more than one acceptable way of doing a job. Once again those involved seem to have no sense of the 'money value of time', so that there is no urgency in their decision making and the projects are in effect left to chart their own course. It then becomes a wonder that the project is ever completed at all! There is warning to us all in this because all over the world governments are taking an increasing interest in commercial enterprises, and delay in decision taking seems to be inherent in government administration wherever you are. So consider very carefully if your project has more than one partner, and make clear who runs the project. Make sure, too, that they have the requisite authority and do not have to refer back at every step. Examine closely the significance of government requirements and involvement, and allow time for all that right at the beginning, so that you are not caught by surprise as the project develops.

Petrochemicals and politics are 'oil and water'

Petrochemicals and politics do not mix! We see this on every side these days, but a classic example must be the $5 billion Bandar Shahpur petrochemical complex being built in Iran. This is a joint venture in which a group of Japanese companies led by Mitsui has a substantial interest. Originally estimated to cost some $0.6 billion, the project cost estimate has been successively revised, first to $2.4 billion, then to $3.5 billion, and now there is talk of $5.0 billion. Some in the know are now calling it the 'most expensive white elephant' in the history of the industry. It has even been suggested that the most sensible thing to do, even now, with the project more than 65% complete, is abandon it, and so stop throwing good money after bad. The reason for this suggestion is that even if the project is carried through to completion, it cannot possibly make a profit for its partners until well into the nineties. The only reason for the Japanese to back and complete the project is their heavy stake and their dire necessity for an entitlement of crude oil, which has now been increased by some 50% to 30 000 barrels/day, as an incentive. This was the fundamental prerequisite for their investment in the first place and so it becomes essential for them to honour their commitment. As a result of the substantial cost overrun, associated with the reluctance of Iran to provide the funds required according to their proportion of the equity in the joint venture, both the Japanese Government and banks have come to the aid of Mitsui by sanctioning additional loans. The overrun has been so substantial that the invested capital in the joint venture has had to be doubled and if the Iranian partner (the National Iranian Oil Company) fails to provide the money required pro-rata to its share, then that share will fall below its original 50%. That in itself could well have political repercussions, seeing that the installation is located in Iran.

The project came to a halt soon after the revolution and the work was resumed eighteen months later, after arrangements had been made for an additional financial package from the Japanese government and the banks. But the Iran-Iraq war threatened the very survival of the project. The site was bombed several times (Ref. 2), both from land and from the sea. The extent of the damage is not fully known but in any case the plant and equipment must have corroded severely during three years of inactivity. Both cost and time for completion are now anybody's guess. Completion in the shortest time would require a large Japanese force, say some 6,000 men including perhaps 2,000 engineers and technicians. However, the Iranian government is insisting on the deployment of Iranian personnel, who must first be trained. This can take a considerable time. Moreover there is a considerable 'culture gap' between the partners.

Now let us look at a few technical details. The joint venture company, Iran Japan Petroleum Company (IJPC) was set up to provide an ethylene capacity of 300 000 tons per year, of which 50% was to be earmarked for export. Iran has a sizeable population, unlike the other oil-producing countries of the Middle East, and there is therefore a growing market for petrochemical products. This is to be compared with the other oil-producers in the area, who while proposing to build similar plants, contemplate exporting almost the total production, since they have a negligible home market.

Another way in which politics is impinging on the progress of the project is in relation to nationalisation. Shortly after the Iranian Revolution four of the smaller American and Japanese joint ventures there were proposed for takeover by 'mutual agreement' by the Iranian National Petrochemical Company. However, IJPC appeared too large and too complex a project for this. In addition, it was as yet unfinished. Iran has since staked her claim for management control of this fifty-fifty partnership project and this must add more delay and further increase the cost.

The project also had political repercussions in Japan, all those thousands of miles away. Mitsui's stake in the project was so large that they persuaded the Japanese government to declare the project a 'national' project. This device entitled them to low interest foreign-aid loans of the money they required to complete. Despite these several devices, uncertainty and delay continues to plague this gigantic project. A senior official of Mitsui is reported to have said: 'Our abacus tells us that we should have pulled out of this mess a long time ago.'

The prime lesson to be learnt from the construction of the Bandur Shahpur Petrochemical Complex is that the one thing that risk analysis can *never* do is take political uncertainties into account. Without the politics there is no reason to believe that the complex would not have been completed reasonably well. With the politics the sensible business thing to do is to 'cut your losses'. Lacking resources in both oil and coal, Japan has so few options. She thought it wise to make substantial investments abroad in order to secure an assured supply of oil. The Iranian project is but one of several that fall into this category.

Ethylene projects galore

The oil producing countries, seeking to achieve a higher 'added value' to their crude oil, have made ambitious plans and are seeking to build petrochemical complexes that will be majors on a world-wide basis in terms of capacity. One way to measure the capacity of such plants is to speak in terms of the ethylene produced. Ethylene is the primary building block these days for petrochemicals, and the size of plant being built worldwide these days is of the order of 300 000 tons per year. With most of the oil producers, the domestic market for petrochemical products, such as plastics, is quite limited, and the bulk of the output of these must therefore go to export. In Figure 10.2 are some of the complexes planned, with details of the feedstock and the capacity of the complexes in terms of ethylene. The only factor that can be said to favour the construction of these plants 'at the well head' as it were is the availability of the feedstock at much below international prices. But that is not to look at the matter clearly because if a certain profit can be made on the feedstock, then only the *increased* profit should be considered when evaluating the merits of a plant using that feedstock. This is one of the internal conflicts within the major oil companies themselves. They set up a chemical company to produce the petrochemicals, and then there is continuous debate as to the cost of the feedstock that is transferred to the chemical company. Should it be at cost, at fuel value, or market value, and so on. The main criterion is not return on investment, but the national cost/benefit and perhaps the desire to 'keep up with the Joneses'.

Another, and most curious aspect of the matter is that since the oil producers lack a broad 'consumer' base, and most of the products have to be exported, markets have to be found. Marketing is made the responsibility of the foreign partners in the joint ventures that have been established. The foreign partner has to

PROPOSED ETHYLENE PROJECTS – MIDDLE EAST			
Country	Location	Capacity in terms of Ethylene '000T/year	Feedstock
Egypt	Alexandria	300	Naphtha
Iraq	Khar-Al-Zubair	130	Ethane
Libya	–	330	Ethane
Saudi Arabia	Al Jubail	1156	Ethane
Saudi Arabia	Yanbu	450	Ethane

Figure 10.2 Proposed ethylene projects in the Middle East
This list of petrochemical plants in the Middle East, under planning, is not necessarily complete. Further details of the Saudi Arabian projects are given in Figure 10.4

bring in the know-how and market the products. The carrot in all this is the supply of crude. Purchase of these products may well be linked to the supply of crude to the country needing that crude and this poses a dilemma. To insure their supply of crude the users are being induced to buy products they make themselves and would prefer to make. Politically the need for crude becomes the over-riding factor, and the profitability of the operation becomes a matter of relative insignificance.

When one considers the matter dispassionately, the profitability of such plants is wholly suspect. Projects in the Middle East, in particular, demand the most comprehensive services and support from outside the area, and such support is extremely expensive. Operators have to be trained, the plant has to be commissioned by experts who are few on the ground. There is the problem of long-term maintenance of the plants if they are to operate efficiently and a host of financial arrangements to be made with respect to the sale of the products. The marketing may be on the basis of barter or 'buy-back', with all the complications that can bring. Even the con-tractors who supply the know-how can be placed in an invidious position because of the political background, having to undertake fixed price contracts with all their inherent risk in locations where there are no local resources.

The end result is that the plants will never make a profit. The cost of constructing a plant in the Middle East is said to be some two-thirds more than for an identical plant in Europe because of the logistic problems. A few years ago (1974) the differential was said to be less, perhaps one-fifth. The increase has come about as a result of the much increased rate of inflation in relation to costs in the Middle East. Easy money brings inflation in its train – we shall see that most clearly when examining the impact of building TAP across Alaska, in Chapter 11. In addition operating costs are higher in the Middle East. Let us consider a steam cracker, using some 1.7 million tons/year of naphtha and producing 500 000 tons/year of propylene, or its equivalent. The cost comparison between Europe and the Middle East is roughly as set out in Figure 10.3. According to a study made some while ago (Ref. 3), if Middle East feed-stock were costed at 25% of its delivered European value – and today's basic cost is far less than that – then it would be cheaper to produce ammonia and fertiliser in the Middle East. But these are primary, bulk products. The picture with polymers, plastics and fibres is very different. The Middle East prices cannot possibly be truly competitive because the higher operating costs of complex plants and the high cost of transport completely neutralise the advantage of using the oil at location. These products only become

STEAM CRACKER – COST ANALYSIS

	Europe	Middle East
Capital Investment		
$ million	2600	3700
Capital & other charges		
$ million per year		
Minimum	55	230
Maximum	155	250
Mean	105	240
Material cost		
$ million per year		
Basic cost	M	M
Extra over	–	500
Labour Cost		
$ million per year		
Basic cost	L	L
Extra over	500	–

NOTE: Since this table is indicative only, precise costs are not stated for materials (M) and labour (L). It is the variance which is of interest.

Figure 10.3 Steam cracker – cost analysis
It will be seen that the extra cost of the raw materials, say naphtha, in Europe is offset by extra cost of labour on location in the Middle East. Thus the overall cost of operation in the Middle East remains unfavourable by some $135 million per annum.

competitive on world markets by pricing the feedstock artificially low as compared with its current market value. In addition, crude oil is by no means the best option as a feedstock. Gas (natural gas or ethane) is more economical than a liquid feedstock such as naphtha. Thus it is only those projects in our list in Figure 10.2 that have the best chance of becoming profitable.

The crux of the problem is not technical, nor economic, nor even political. The basic problem is undoubtedly marketing. The joint-venture partner is required to market or buy practically the entire production from such plants. If this is linked with the crude oil entitlement, then the project may be considered by the foreign partner to be quite attractive. That is why he entered into the arrangement in the first place. Such projects would therefore be set up by traditional producers, but in new locations, thus giving a dramatic shift in the production pattern. There need not be a glut in the market. With a realistic and coldly practical approach, the five million tons/year of ethylene capacity proposed shortly after the 1973 oil crisis may not now exceed some one to one and a half million tons/year. And to that extent, many of the projects may now remain on paper and therefore be non-starters. The point we made earlier is reinforced, petrochemical and politics are like oil and water – they just do not mix.

The Saudi Arabian dream

The petrochemical complex under planning for construction in Saudi Arabia is probably the most ambitious petrochemical project ever. Its magnitude in terms of the total investment and the size of the construction force that will be needed at peak staggers the imagination. Nothing on this scale has been attempted even in highly developed countries – and here we have a developing country.

The idea behind it all seems perfectly sound. There are substantial volumes of gas coming off with the crude oil which has to be flared (burnt) at the moment. This gas could be used as feed for a complex of plants. Such plants were to be a joint venture with companies spread around the globe. The initial offers which were made by the Saudi Arabian government to prospective partners in these joint ventures seemed too good to be true. The basis of the financial arrangements was such that the projects looked quite attractive, though profitability was not the main criterion. The foreign partner was required to contribute a mere 15% of the equity to match that of SABIC (The Saudi Arabian Basic Industries Corporation). The Government of Saudi Arabia would then loan some 60% at a low interest rate and the rest of the investment would come from the banks. The joint venture would enjoy a five-year tax holiday and the partners profits were to be freely repatriable. In addition, and this was a most important 'carrot', there would also be a crude oil entitlement. Initially this was stated as 1000 barrels per day of crude oil for each $1 million of investment by the foreign partner. This has proved to be 'easier said than done', but more of that aspect later.

In Figure 10.4 is set out the scope and magnitude of the joint project currently envisaged for building at Al Jubail. In the five years that it has been under discussion not only the product patterns but also the firms involved have changed. However, the basic concept has remained constant: to create a new city from scratch,

PROPOSED PETROCHEMICAL PLANTS – SAUDI ARABIA

	Shell	Exxon	Dow	Mobil	Mitsubishi consortium	Celanese & Texas Eastern	Taiwan Fertiliser Co.
ect cost ion:	2.0	1.1	–	2.0	–	0.4	–
ned pletion:	1985	1985	1986	1985	1983/5	1985	1983
DUCTS							
lene	650	–	500	450	–	–	–
lene							
chloride	455	–	–	–	–	–	–
nol	280	–	–	–	–	–	–
ene	295	–	–	–	–	–	–
stic	355	–	–	–	–	–	–
E	–	260	90	200	130	–	–
E	–	–	90	90	–	–	–
lene							
ycol	–	–	–	220	300	–	–
nanol	–	–	–	–	600	650	–
	–	–	–	–	–	–	500

tes: 1. All production capacities are in thousands of tons per year, and are approximate only.
2. LDPE = Low density polypropylene
   HDPE = High density polypropylene
3. With respect to the consortium, the ethylene cracker will be a joint venture with Dow, the downstream units with Mitsubishi and others.
4. All the plants are at Al Jubail, except Mobil, which is at Yanbu.
5. All contracts appear to have been concluded. Mobil and Exxon projects seem to have progressed the fastest. The Mobil project also includes a $1.1 billion export refinery.

Figure 10.4 Proposed petrochemical complex at Al Jubail
This is a broad outline of the various plants that are being proposed for the several partners. Once again, the picture is constantly changing.

in the middle of the desert, together with a complete infrastructure. The total investment envisaged at one time was said to be $45 billion, but the final cost is more likely to be some $100 billion. Let us set that proposed cost out in full, so that you can appreciate what we are talking about – $100,000,000,000. It was said this gigantic project would require (and who could possibly dispute it?) a peak construction force of 500 000 – all expatriates. But where can one find 500 000 skilled men who are prepared to go and work in the desert, under the hot sun, for years? This factor alone could well prove its downfall, if the scheme is allowed to go forward as now conceived. There are still *some* things that money cannot buy!

Of course, progress is being made. Work is proceeding on the methanol units and a contract has been signed by a Japanese consortium consisting of Mitsubishi, Mitsui and Sumitomo. A joint venture company styled The Saudi Methanol Company Incorporated has now been formed. Its terms are secret and it is not known whether the final agreement includes an oil entitlement clause, or the possible extent of such a clause, if it is there. The five joint ventures proposed with the US-based firms have also now been signed. We have The Saudi Yanbu Petrochemical Company (YANPET), the Al Jubail Petrochemical Company (KEMYA), the Arabian Petrochemical Company (PETROKEMYA) and the Saudi Petrochemical Company (SADAF). This last is the largest petrochemical project in the Kingdom, a joint venture with Shell, established in 1980. It is planned to go on stream in 1983 at Al Jubail industrial city.

What does the crude oil entitlement 'carrot' actually mean? Why is it so interesting? On the basis of the original formula that was published, if we consider a $2 billion investment, such as Shell were contemplating, their share would be 15%, say $300 million. At 1000 barrels/day per $1 million of investment, the Shell entitlement would be 300 000 barrels/day, but apparently they have been unable to get this agreed. Hence the delay in concluding the agreement. There is also another difficult question: the price to be charged for the gas that would be utilised by the joint venture. This has been escalating in line with current international prices, whereas the original concept was that it had no value, since the alternative was to flare it.

Why are the Saudis hesitating with respect to granting the entitlement? They have plenty of crude. There is now a conflict of interest between the four parties involved, who are SABIC, The Saudi Ministry of Industry, Petromin and The Saudi National Oil Company.

SABIC want the entitlement to be given to induce the overseas investors to join in. The Ministry of Industry are on their side, since they are anxious to encourage foreign investment in Saudi Arabia. Petromin, the national oil marketing company, has other ideas. The granting of such an entitlement would reduce the total supply of crude available to Petromin by as much as 1.5 to 2.0 million barrels/day, a substantial reduction in relation to their operations. Petromin is therefore advocating that the oil entitlement be halved, but at that lower level it may not be attractive enough for the joint venture partners to proceed. In the event of stalemate, the final decision will have to be taken by the Supreme Council for Petroleum in Saudi Arabia. Meanwhile, the negotiations drag on.

As a result of these uncertainties, including the recent oil demand recession worldwide and the delays in decision making, some of the potential investors may well withdraw. A producer company with profitable operations steadily generates cash which must be invested to bring profit promptly. If the funds are diverted to other projects then they will not be available for the Al Jubail complex. Some withdrawals, therefore, cannot be ruled out. In the final analysis, once the carrot becomes much less of a carrot, as now appears to be the case, only those projects with a sound economic base will survive. We wonder whether any of them fall into this category. One interesting point is that although the plans are still largely on paper, $80 million has already been spent on the preliminary engineering studies. *That* is a project in itself! And the insurance premium for the proposed public facilities is stated to be $10 million!

What is the lesson in all this? It is very apparent from the way the situation has developed that the real inducement for foreign companies to participate is the oil entitlement. As such the profitability of the projects, despite the very favourable financial arrangements that have been proposed, is extremely suspect. Saudi Arabia cannot 'go it alone'. A partner is needed, not only to provide the know-how, project management and construction supervision, but also – and even more importantly – the facilities for the marketing of the products. Since present domestic demand is very small the bulk of the output would have to be exported.

The conclusion would appear to be that if a satisfactory oil entitlement cannot be negotiated, then the projects will never mature. Once again, the attempt is being made to mix oil and politics and it just does not work. The projects ought to be viable on their own merits, but we gather that this is not going to be the case. The investment is likely to be up to 70% above that required for a European location, and the financial inducements offered do not seem to offset that initial disadvantage. No oil entitlement, no project, and we have another series of non-starters.

Certainly the credibility gap can be clearly seen. The Saudis feel that the building of grass roots petrochemical complexes in countries without hydrocarbon reserves does not make economic sense. But the joint venture partners may well retort: No market, no complex! Will the twain ever meet? It appears advisable, rather, for the OPEC countries to participate in downstream industries in third (consuming) countries rather than to build very expensive facilities at home. These huge petrochemical complexes in the desert may well become mere 'skeletons' if and when the foreign partner has to pull out for reasons beyond his control. Certainly the recent events in Iran do not bode well for this 'petrochemical dream' of the Middle East countries in general and Saudi Arabia in particular. Could a revolution in Iran have been foreseen in the seventies? Could this be repeated elsewhere in the Middle East? No one can possibly say.

References

1   Centre for Monitoring Indian Economy (Bombay). Various documents and data bank.
2   *Chemical Insight,* various issues up to April 1981. Published by Mike Hyde, 6 West Grove, Greenwich, London, SE10 8QT.
3   Turner, L. and Bedore, J.M., *Middle East Industrialisation,* 1979, Gower, 220pp.

11 People, politics and a pipeline

Our next case study, following on from Chapter 4 and the Glace Bay Heavy Water Plant, is also in the frozen north, in the North American continent. We are going to take a look at the construction of the Trans-Alaska Pipeline – TAP for short. The construction of this particular pipeline became famous, or perhaps we should say notorious, for the trials and tribulations of the people involved in it, who became enveloped in a political 'cloud'. Another might also be added to the three already in our title – publicity! There was far too much publicity surrounding the construction of this particular project. Both the politics and the publicity greatly increased the problems that had to be faced by the people building the pipeline, adding to these problems and magnifying those they already had. Certainly there were problems, but our four Ps – when people are seen as the public – magnified those problems out of all proportion. What were the real problems that had to be faced?

The problems

Of basic consideration was the fact that the pipeline had to be constructed in an area of 'permafrost', in a severe arctic climate, where the ambient temperature ranged from $-62°C$ to $32°C$. The permafrost, in particular, created a number of ecological problems to which was added government involvement. It was 'only a pipeline', planned to be completed in months at a cost of $0.9 billion, but it took years and finally cost $8 billion. The project proved to be the world's biggest ever, technically, managerially and legislatively. The TAP project included the design, engineering and construction of a 48-inch diameter pipeline 1200 km. long, with a 240 km. gas line, a 600 km. road, a bridge over the Yukon river, a number of boosting stations, a marine terminal, a complete communications network and a number of infrastructures. Over 8000 people were employed on the project at its peak of effort. First scheduled for completion in 1972, it was actually started on the ground in 1974.

Everything on this project was on the grand scale, even the mistakes and the crimes. The X-rays of the welds were falsified, resulting in repairs costing $55 million. The project manager for the X-ray contract company died in his flat after taking cyanide. Theft and fraudulent billing was estimated at between $40 and $70 million! Yet the pipeline was completed by mid-1977, a deadline first set in November 1973. There was a tremendous problem in logistics, well illustrated when we talk about the diesel fuel that was needed for construction purposes. Nearly a *million gallons* of diesel fuel was transported, about half by road, and half by air. So, 500,000 gallons of fuel were actually brought on to the various working sites by air.

Pipelines are notoriously difficult to photograph. Most of the time they are underground anyway, so we thought that the best way of giving you some small impression of it all was by providing a photograph of Valdez Terminal. This is at the southern end, and can be seen in Figure 11.1. The snow-clad mountains in the background tell you where you are, although the photograph was taken in summer. The photograph shows the 'end' of the story; how did it all start?

Historical background

Once again it can be very instructive to follow the history of the project chronologically. We shall start at about the time construction *should* have started, but did not. Then we shall see *why* they failed to 'get on with the job' at that time – people and politics were playing a major role:

January 1971	There are hopes of a 1971 start on road construction, *if* an injunction against start of work can be lifted. The US Department of the Interior urges clearance for TAP.
February 1971	The Chairman of the President's Council on Environmental Quality wonders whether a pipeline is the best means of carrying Alaskan oil.

Figure 11.1 Valdez Terminal, Alaska
An aerial view of the Valdez Terminal during construction. (Photograph reproduced by courtesy of Fluor Europe Limited. Fluor were responsible for a range of installations, as outlined in the text.)

	Any hopes of starting in 1971 are killed by the Secretary of the Interior.
March 1971	A new set back. The Defence Department poses a long list of reservations. Progress is further stalled by requests for environmental data. The Canadian government invites the seven major oil companies to discuss the possibility of laying TAP through Canada to the USA. Fisheries & Forest Minister indicates that there is a 90% probability that construction work can start in 1973.
April 1971	The Commerce Secretary strongly endorses TAP.

June 1971   The Interior Secretary is optimistic. The environmental safeguards are considered 'pretty good'.

July 1971   The Federal Court turns down a request from the Justice Department to permit the transfer to Alaska of a suit that has prevented the government issuing permits for construction.

September 1971   Is shipment an alternative? The stalling of TAP sparks an array of ideas, most of them impractical, to protect the environment.

October 1971   The Interior Department seems close to endorsing the TAP plans.

November 1971   The state of Alaska to pursue plans for pipeline control. An estimated $1.5 billion is needed by the seven firms involved in the Alaska project, to build TAP.

December 1971   Controversy over the route from the North Slope to Valdez.

We enter a new year, and the arguments continue unabated.

January 1972   There is fresh controversy over environmental considerations. The original estimate of $0.9 billion is now revised to $2 billion. It could be $3 billion if there is further delay. The conservationists lose their bid for an extra hearing.

February 1972   March 15 is a possible date for the completion of the environmental impact statement.

March 1972   President Nixon's backing for the project is confidently expected.

April 1972   If the Supreme Court gives its ruling this year (1972), construction could start in 1973.

May 1972   The question is raised: is there the possibility of a 'catastrophic crack' in the pipeline, with the danger of huge spills along many miles of the route? President Nixon approves the pipeline, but the injunction still blocks the issuing of construction permits.

June 1972   Proposal for 'emulsifying the oil' to save the ecology. This suggestion is not favoured.

August 1972   The injunction is lifted!

September 1972   Suits by the oil companies to overturn the new laws for Alaska may delay the building of the pipeline.

December 1972   A boom is expected as a consequence of the

$5 billion that is to be spent on a national pipeline.

Another year has passed. A lot has happened, as can be seen, but it is all in the political sphere. Construction seems as far away as ever.

February 1973   A further six-month delay. Start is snarled by the Court ruling, the construction ban being re-instated on appeal by the ecologists.

March 1973   The plan has now been held up for three years. The issue is sent to the Supreme Court and to Congress.

April 1973   The Supreme Court refuses to review the construction ban. Attention then centres on the Senate bill.

July 1973   The Senate give the 'go-ahead'. They have voted the bill that will expedite construction.

August 1973   The House votes to bar further court challenges by the environmentalists and gives its approval for construction to go ahead.

October 1973   Now there is a start date and cost is reviewed. Still very open: perhaps $3.5 billion, but could easily be $4.5 billion.

November 1973   The Senate approves the Bill, and it is sent to the President for signing.

December 1973   The Defence Department proposes a related oil pipeline right across the US, to provide for self-sufficiency.

Another year. From now on the emphasis will lie elsewhere. We are moving out of the higher 'political sphere', and now getting, as it were, down to earth, as you shall see.

January 1974   The environmentalists decline to challenge the permits by the deadline, but assert that they will monitor construction most closely.

February 1974   With the immediate job prospects on TAP dim, the Machinists Union advises that anyone going to Alaska should take fishing rods and plenty of money for an extended vacation.

May 1974   Expecting a flurry of cases during construction of TAP, the National Labor Relations Board opens an office in Anchorage. Working conditions are being explained. This is hardship duty, and construction workers are to get a week's leave every quarter, with paid transportation and

	travel time to rest and recreation sites.
July 1974	The owners agree to double the initial capacity of TAP, and a re-arrangement of the shares for ownership is finalised. TAP is having a profound effect on the economy of Alaska. Pay is skyhigh, and inflation therefore acute.
August 1974	Atlantic Richfield, the lead owner, expects the cost of TAP to exceed $5 billion.
September 1974	The contractors engaged on TAP get an unusual supply priority under the Defence Production Act. The El Paso Company file an application for a $6 billion combination pipeline and ship transportation system to bring natural gas to the US west coast.

Yet another year:

February 1975	The continuous delays are giving rise to nervousness among the investors.
March 1975	The nineteen construction camps along the 800-mile route of the pipeline are said to be 'mighty comfortable'. Action at one location is suspended indefinitely when surveyors find a hole containing a hibernating bear.
May 1975	The existence of the Alaska Pipeline construction highway stirs a new ecology row. Should it be open to the public?
July 1975	For the second time in nine months, the estimated cost is revised. It is now $6.38 billion, but the Alyeska Pipeline Service Company (APSC) says that it still cannot be sure of the final cost. Washington is considering legislation to speed construction of the pipeline.
October 1975	The pipeline itself is now 41% complete, and the 50% mark is expected to be reached next month. A tank is punctured by falling rock and spills some 30 000 gallons of petrol into a Marina near Juneau, Alaska.

At the close of 1975, we are more than half-way with the work of construction in the field. How far is that from completion?

January 1976	The cost estimate further revised to $7 billion. Construction is now scheduled for completion in July 1977.
May 1976	Delays now arising due to technical, rather than

	environmental problems. There are construction holdups. Trouble with the welds could extend that mid-1977 completion date now on the table.
June 1976	The woes multiply because of faulty welding. Bad work appears to be concealed. The X-rays have been falsified to avoid checking buried seams, raising ecology fears.
July 1976	Cost estimate now raised to $7.7 billion. The auditors question the records on pipeline construction flaws. The Transportation Department is considering possible alternatives to X-rays for checking the welds. The APSC Chairman defends the weld audit, and denies any cover-up. An oil pipeline bursts during test at low pressure. The cause is a mystery. Was there excessive pressure due to an operating error? The project is now four weeks behind schedule, but the mid-1977 completion can still be met.
September 1976	Nearing 80% completion. Will there be further weld problems? The government orders repairs on 31 faults, but grants a waiver on three others.
November 1976	Atlantic Richfield sees the opening of TAP on schedule. Oil should go into the line in July 1977.

And it did! TAP was opened on time, but the short-cuts that had been taken had scarred the environment. There were silted and polluted streams, substantial erosion and the worry over tracing leaks. The first estimate of $0.9 billion had now risen to $7.7 billion. Start-up took place without a serious hitch, nine years after that first discovery of oil at Prudhoe Bay. Who will actually benefit? When the line was proposed it was supposed to be the consumers, but things have changed since then. There has been an 'oil crisis', among other things. Although the line is now in operation, the saga is not yet finished.

| July 1977 | TAP is closed for three days beginning 4 July after a nitrogen leak was discovered. There is an explosion on 8 July, killing one worker and injuring five others. This forces closure of TAP for ten days. |
| August 1977 | There is a charge by an Alaska State Service Commission official that $1.5 billion had been 'wasted' during construction, but 'this will prove to be unfounded', reply the owners. TAP is closed for a further three days following an oil leak. |

February 1978   The explosion of July 1977 is still being inves-
                tigated.
March 1978   RCA file suit against APSC for alleged losses in
                building the microwave system.

Even after completion, there are still 'ripples', ripples that are
likely to cost money, so that the final cost of $8 billion is only a
'round figure'. It is interesting to note, as we follow the history,
that although this was a private venture, not involving state
finance, yet the government was keenly interested in its progress
and did all that it could to urge completion. This appears to be
because TAP was seen to be of strategic military significance. It
was a major contribution to self-sufficiency in energy for the USA.

A great project, but . . .

A truly mammoth pipeline project was completed on time, so far as
the engineering, design and construction were concerned, and this
was no mean achievement. Almost all the delays, such as the
requirements of the environmentalists and the restrictive legislation, were due to factors outside the control of the engineers. The
logistic and technical design problems, great though they were,
were overcome within the timetable that had been set. In its
beginnings the project had to ride many storms, and its history was
full of noteworthy events as our historical sketch demonstrates, but
once the project had been authorised by the US Congress in 1973,
there was steady, positive movement towards completion, but at a
price.
    Following the history of the project, we see that in their haste the
construction teams cut corners in relation to the environmental
safeguards, something they had promised they would not do. The
APSC, a consortium of eight oil companies, and the many contractors they employed, frequently violated the State and Federal
environmental rules. There was water pollution owing to improper
sewage treatment and the oil leak detection system may not be
entirely reliable. There was no environmental control whatsoever
built into the TAP system. An internal memo put it rather mildly:
'Greater emphasis must be placed on the environmental work to
bring it into conformance with the stipulations'. It certainly
appears that insufficient emphasis was placed upon these aspects
during construction. Conforming costs time, and time costs
money.
    Let us look at the cost aspect. The various estimates made in the

course of our history have been mentioned, but let us now compare the figures and analyse them. The eightfold cost overrun was almost entirely due to the last start. The cost history is summarised in Figure 11.2. The rise in cost from 1969 to late 1974 was all due to inflation, we are told, so we start at $3.5 billion. The increase of $4.2 billion by mid-1976 was said to be:

| Inflation | $3.1 billion |
| Support systems | $1.1 billion |

The provision of support systems was a late environmental requirement. The original pipeline had been planned to run entirely underground; in the end some 50% was placed above ground, in regions where the oil temperature (100-140°C) might have thawed the permanently frozen ground.

THE ESCALATING COST OF TAP	
Date of estimate	Estimated cost $ billion
1969	0.9
October 1973	3.5*
October 1974	6.0
June 1975	6.4
June 1976	7.7
Final (approx.)	8.0

* This was after the four-year delay due to the environmental controversy.

Figure 11.2 The escalating cost of TAP
This table summarises the escalating cost estimates made for this project over the years.

Now that the pipeline has been built, largely as a result of private initiative, many questions remain. Who will ultimately benefit? What will be the well-head price? Is TAP a commercial success? Some of these questions will get answered in time but it is early days yet.

The private sector's most costly venture

The financial aspects of this project from its inception have been described at length in the technical literature (Ref. 1). Sohio (Standard Oil Company of Ohio), a relatively unknown and minor member in the 'oil company league' had assets of $0.9 billion in 1969, when the project was first conceived. Projections had forecast an oil shortage in the USA by 1975, and a world shortage by 1980, so Sohio made the discovery and production of further reserves their primary corporate objective. When discovered, the Prudhoe Bay oil fields in northern Alaska were estimated to have reserves of some 4.6 billion barrels. More recent estimates put it at 10 billion barrels. This is a sizeable field by any standard and the main problem was to bring this oil to the doorsteps of users in the USA. A Trans-Alaska Pipeline (TAP) was seen as the solution, and Sohio took the initiative, forming a consortium of oil firms to construct such a pipeline. More importantly, they convinced the community as to the merits of the project and this ensured that sufficient capital would be available. Sohio had no clue as to the ultimate cost and one wonders what would have been the reaction if the real cost had been tabled at the beginning. Thanks to the efforts of Sohio, as the estimate grew, so the funds were found.

As a result of this one project Sohio's assets swelled some ten times, from $0.9 billion in 1969, to $8.0 billion in 1977, when TAP went on stream. This phenomenal growth was only possible through the injection of external funds, totalling some $5.0 billion. The initial share of Sohio in TAP, some $0.6 billion, appeared to be within their means, but thanks mainly to the delayed start, this swelled to $2.2 billion. About a dozen oil companies participated in the oilfield exploration and TAP, and the interest of the majors is set out in Figure 11.3. A tentative analysis of the estimated cost of the TAP project is given in Figure 11.4.

The project represents a most significant engineering construction feat. The eight fold increase in cost was not due to any failure in project cost control, or poor estimates as such. Had this occurred, yet another dimension would have been added to what was already a gigantic project. The increase in cost was due to factors outside the control of those engineering the project, such as:

> High rate of inflation;
> High interest rates;
> Environmental issues;
> Government regulations.

Such cost factors are measurable, and no doubt estimators and cost control engineers will take them more into account in the future than they have done in the past. We call that 'backward integra-

ALASKAN DEVELOPMENT – OWNERSHIP		
	Oilfield %	TAP %
Sohio	53	33
Atlantic Richfield	20	21
Exxon	20	20
British Petroleum	–	16
Others	7	10
	100	100

Figure 11.3 Alaskan TAP development – ownership
This table gives the shares of the oil majors in both the Prudhoe Bay oil field
development and the related pipeline across Alaska.

ESTIMATE BREAKDOWN – TAP PROJECT	
	$ – billion
TAP – pipeline	3.1
North slope production	1.8
Reserve tax	0.3
Tankers	0.5
West Coast and mid-continent pipeline	0.5
Working capital (through 1979)	0.1
TOTAL	6.3

Figure 11.4 Estimate breakdown – TAP project
This was the projected capital cost estimate for the TAP system, made some time
prior to completion. Note that the scope of the estimate includes tax and working
capital.

tion'! There certainly seems to be a great deal to be learnt as to the impact on cost of these factors.

Fortunately for the owners a vast increase in the world price of crude oil coincided with the constrution of TAP, helping the profitability enormously, and cancelling out the impact of inflation. Without the 1973 oil crisis TAP would most certainly have been a white elephant. Further, thanks to TAP, Sohio, previously an unknown, has emerged as a major producer of crude oil. This undertaking led to their merger with British Petroleum, to the benefit of both companies. Currently, the profits must be paying off the debts incurred to finance the project, but if Sohio continues to pursue that corporate policy set long ago, in 1969, who knows what project will come. The cycle may well be repeated, since the private sector seems prepared to take on ever bigger challenges. The risk is great, but so are the profits if the risk is well taken, and project managers, estimators and cost engineers can enjoy the excitement!

The design, logistics and construction of TAP

The project was constructed and is run by a consortium. We have named it earlier – code APSC. A host of contractors, more than fifty in all, were employed on the project and the problems of one of them, Fluor, have been described in some detail in a paper in the technical press (Ref. 2). Fluor was awarded its contract in May 1974. It was said to have a value of about $1 billion, and covered:

> A marine terminal at Valdez;
> Eight pumping stations;
> Three mainline refrigeration units;
> Three 'press-through' stations;
> Erection of 62 remote gate valves.

The Valdez terminal is one of the world's largest and includes a master station with radio communication linking all the pumping stations. The infrastructure included a 500 000 barrel oil storage depot, a 37 MW power plant, three loading berths able to accommodate tankers up to 250 000 DWT and a ballast water treatment plant. The installation was designed to handle up to 2 million barrels/day of crude oil. We have already given you an aerial photograph of this installation: see Figure 11.1 on page 173.

The major problems faced by Fluor during the design and construction of their part of the project were those faced by all the contractors. They have all been mentioned previously in this chapter, but to state them once more:

Extremes of temperature, far below zero.
Seismic considerations.
Environmental requirements.
Governmental regulations.

The design was subject to change in order to cater for the latest geotechnical data as it affected the foundations, the treatment of the waste water and protection against external corrosion. An indication as to the degree of government involvement can be had from the fact that Fluor had to prepare and submit over 400 applications to the various governmental agencies: work that required the setting up of a special task force. The worldwide publicity that the project received can hardly be said to have helped. In 1975 alone over 750 requests were received from the mass media around the world, seeking to visit the project site. This in turn led to undue interest and possibly to the intervention by various external groups who sought to 'protect the environment'.

The remoteness of the site and the weather also proved a real challenge. The temperatures at the northernmost sites were as low as −57°C, with a −93°C chill factor in the winter. Precipitation, minimal in the far north, was much heavier below the Yukon river, with an annual rainfall of 70 mm, and 120 mm of snow. In the Fairbanks area temperatures ranged from −51°C to 31°C. During each of the three winters of construction of Valdez there was a snowfall totalling some 900 mm. Most construction equipment cannot be operated below −35°C and synthetic lubricants do not work satisfactorily in arctic conditions. Low temperature service materials had to be developed specially for the TAP project.

Transport was another major problem. The materials of construction were being purchased worldwide and meticulous logistics were required if cost was to be watched and time saved. Steel pipe came from Japan, 48-inch diameter valves from the UK and the mainline pumps from The Netherlands. Most of these materials were routed first to Kenmore, Washington, USA, where a freight staging area was set up. Transport onwards from Kenmore was either by container ship to Anchorage or by barge to Valdez. Until the completion of the permanent bridge over the Yukon river, transport was either by barge, ice-bridge or by hovercraft. During the spring, from early April to late May, no heavy equipment could be transported because the road restrictions limited the maximum weight of trucks to 7 tons, as compared with the norm of 22 tons. A road to the north of the Yukon river had to be specially constructed and until it was completed aircraft (Hercules C-130s) were used, necessitating the building of a 5000-foot landing strip at several northern locations. In order to protect the electronic equipment from the extreme cold, all such equipment was transported in heated vans.

To meet the time targets, construction activity continued even during the peak of winter in 1975-76, when over 8000 people were at work on the project. To carry on through the winter, service facilities, such as the workshops, concrete batch plants and the gravel and sand required, all had to be kept in heated enclosures. When concrete was poured in mid-winter, a heated air-lock building (beluga) was erected over the foundation site where pouring was to take place. The volume of work to be done was in some cases far in excess of the original estimates. For instance, due to inaccuracies in the original soil surveys, the earth and rock excavated was in total nearly *fourteen million* cubic yards, as against an original estimate of eight million. Foundations at the terminal and at some of the pump stations had to be radically revised at a late stage when the original soil surveys proved unreliable.

Having drawn a picture of laying a pipeline in Alaska across the Arctic Circle at sub-zero temperatures we thought a welcome contrast could be to take a quick look at laying a pipeline in the forests of Sri Lanka (formerly Ceylon). We met the story under the headline 'Old way sometimes the only way to get job completed' (Ref. 3). On a pipe-laying project there an elephant was used to lay pipe across an isolated area, where it was impossible to bring in motorised vehicles. Figure 11.5 shows the pipe strung out, ready for welding and later burying, while Figure 11.6 shows the elephant in action. What a contrast with the highly mechanised operation we have just been reviewing. But the contrast demonstrates the adaptability and resource of these major contractors, operating worldwide.

As a closing note, and remembering the debate that took place on the route of the line in Alaska, we recall an advertisement picturing a most attractive girl out in the wilds, and saying 'I can't move mountains, but I can move pipelines!' The point is that she was an anthropologist and environmental specialist working for one of these major contractors (Ref. 4), becoming involved in the project when it was still on the drawing board. To quote her:

> We know building requires change in our environment. But with commitment and proper planning, we can meet the future needs of our society and still respect and preserve the past.

This is true. To win Alaskan oil and get it to the point of use, the

Figure 11.5 Stringing pipe in Sri Lanka
Pipelaying the oldfashioned way, an interesting contrast with the latest methods.
(Photograph by courtesy of Pullmann Kellogg Division of Pullman Incorporated.)

Figure 11.6 Elephant power in Sri Lanka
This, another view of the pipelaying operation illustrated in Figure 10.5, shows the
elephant proceeding to lift a pipe length. (Photograph by courtesy of Pullman
Kellogg Division of Pullman Incoporated.)

environment had to be changed. That was inevitable. Whether the right decisions were taken, involving the least damage, we may never know. But the oil now flows.

What is the moral of the three Ps?

TAP is a multi-billion dollar enterprise, executed across a difficult terrain, under hostile conditions. Thanks to the drive and initiative of private enterprise, it was satisfactorily completed to schedule, once the shackles of 'Politics and People' had been loosened: we dare not say 'taken off', for they never were. The delay and the extra cost, as compared with the initial budget, was almost entirely due to the delays in starting, due to the political restraints, and the extra demands of the environment. Originally conceived in 1969 as the brainchild of a relative minor in the oil league, Sohio, the work could not start until 1973 when the US government, finally appreciating that the project was necessary for survival, put all its weight behind implementation. Perhaps they 'smelled' the oil crisis, which came at the end of that same year. Once given priority from the defence angle, there was no going back.

   Thanks to the ingenuity of the contractors and their design teams, the most difficult and unusual problems were tackled efficiently and on the whole satisfactorily – but at a cost. Was the cost too high? Probably not. The cost would be too high if there were waste and inefficiency, but there was very little of that: people were under too much pressure to waste time. Despite the vast increase in the investment, since much of it was caused by inflation, the project remained profitable, further helped by the substantial increase in crude prices that took place after 1973; and are still taking place. The escalated cost had to be paid because there was a four-year delay in starting, due entirely to people and politics. But these problems are now worldwide, and project management in the coming years will have to learn to take them in their stride. They must look back at projects like TAP and learn the lessons, in order to look forward with clarity of vision. A challenge indeed!

References

1   Phillips, P.D., Groth, J.C. and Richards, R.M., 'Financing the Alaskan project', *Financial Management*, 1979 *8*, Autumn pp. 7–16.
2   Roswell, I. and Stevens, L.G., 'Special considerations in the

design logistics and construction of plants in Alaska', *Process Economics International*, 1979 *1*, Autumn pp. 29–35.

3   'Sri-Lanka – old way sometimes only way to get job completed', *For your information*. Pullman Kellogg, Houston, Texas, USA, 1980, no. 169, April.

4   *Bechtel Brief* – issue of September 1979. A brief review of the environmental problems relating to a coal slurry pipeline route near Zion National Park in Utah, USA. (Bechtel Briefs are published for the employees and friends of the Bechtel Group by the Public Relations Department, Bechtel, PO Box 3965, San Francisco, CA 94119, USA.)

12 The pilot plant *can* be skipped

Now we turn our backs on the USA, the Near and the Far East, the 'overdeveloped' and the 'developing' countries, to look at a certain process plant built in the recent past in Western Europe. This particular plant was very interesting for the project cost control engineer because of a great step that was taken in relation to process design. The usual procedure is for a new process to be first developed in the laboratory. The major chemical and petrochemical manufacturers have research and process development laboratories where new processes are studied on what we might call the 'laboratory bench' scale. Some of the major contractors also have such laboratories, where processes are developed that are then licensed by them to manufacturers. The contractor is looking for the work of detailed design, procurement and construction in plants using his particular process, since that is *his* livelihood. To illustrate what such a 'laboratory bench' installation looks like, a typical laboratory unit is shown in Figure 12.1 We hasten to add, for reasons that shall become apparent a little later, that the equipment illustrated in the photograph is *typical only*; it has no connection whatsoever with the process plant we are going on to study in some detail.

Once the process developed in the laboratory shows promise, it is surveyed in terms of both the technical and economic aspects. This can lead to preliminary market surveys, further laboratory scale experiments and the production of samples of the final product. If this further preliminary work remains promising, the next stage might well be to construct a pilot plant, or some other semi-commercial installation, to provide production experience and the basic data for the development of a full-scale project. All this takes time and the construction of a semi-commercial unit with the benefit of some limited market operation, could well take two to

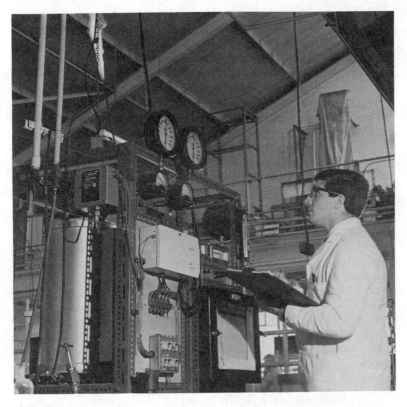

Figure 12.1 Experimental plant
Typical small-scale process unit built for laboratory experiments. (Photograph by
courtsey of Humphreys & Glasgow Limited, London.)

three years at the very least. If, however, you have sufficient experience, sufficient confidence in your process, the knowledge
that the market will readily accept your product, then you might
dare to skip the 'pilot-plant' stage, saving the investment in both
time and money that you would otherwise have to make. The end
result could then well be that you are in the market with full
production at least three years earlier. This bold, brave step was
indeed taken by one company and we would like to show you what
happened and what the consequences were. After hearing the story,
you might feel encouraged to follow in their footsteps, particularly
if you also take the advice proffered in Chapter 15 and 'build
small'. This example is 'big', but it is by no means what some term
a 'jumbo' installation, such as is also discussed in Chapter 16.

Please do not identify us

It is well known that both owner companies and construction contractors are extremely reluctant to publish details of their various
installations and the work that has gone into them, particularly
when they had their problems. This despite the fact that if we all
knew about their problems, and they about ours, we would *all*
stand a better chance of avoiding such problems in the future.
When it comes to success the approach is very different. The Institution of Chemical Engineers, seeking to organise a study of certain
case histories was successful in getting such a seminar off the
ground because they gave it the happy title: 'Successful execution
of overseas projects'. This was in May 1978 and one paper
presented at the conference described the way in which a medium-
sized British chemical engineering company *successfully* bid for
and then managed one of the largest overseas chemical plant
projects ever executed by any UK contractor (Ref. 1). In our view
our story is also a success story, despite the fact that the initial
targets for time and money were overrun.

We did think that cooperation in respect of publicity was
improving in this area. In fact, so *successful* have we been in the
past in securing permission to publish information once held to be
confidential, that this aspect was the subject of comment in a
review of one of our books (Ref. 2). The reviewer on that occasion,
Sir James Taylor, then said of one of us:

> ... gives detailed guidance based on his wide experience in industry
> and as a consultant, and on methods used by companies for whom he
> worked, e.g. Courtaulds Engineering Ltd. This adds to the credibility
> of the procedures described. Moreover, it illustrates an admirable
> trend, namely the growing willingness of large companies to make
> available information which at one time would have been regarded as
> confidential knowledge.

On this occasion we have been less successful. The chairman of one
company whom we approached replied:

> I also think we will be wanting to analyse the lessons to be learned
> within our own management structure before unfolding to a wider
> audience.

We doubt very much whether they ever will 'unfold to a wider
audience'. Their case would have been most instructive, but we
could not get sufficient data to show you the 'whys and
wherefores' of what happened. When it came to the particular case
we are now going to relate, we got on rather better, but we were still

told:

> We would not want _____ to be identifiable and so would not
> wish photographs of our plants to be used in conjunction with the text.
> In addition, I gather that Mr _____ has discussed with you changes
> which would make the text equally unidentifiable.'

We have done our best to comply with these conditions, and trust
that our credibility will not suffer thereby. The plant was indeed
built, in the time stated and with the problems that we describe.

The magnitude of the step taken

Against the background of the laboratory data that had been and
indeed continued to be developed, process design was put in hand
and the approval of the board of directors sought and secured to
design and build the plant that we are going to discuss. Let us call
it, for the want of a better name, Plant X. At that time it was
thought that the plant would be available for commercial production 42 months later. In fact it took another six months longer than
that, a total of 48 months, or four years. The cost? The total investment must not be disclosed, but it can be revealed that the final
cost overrun on the original capital authorisation was approximately 20%. How then can we give you some idea of the magnitude
of the step that was being taken? Figure 12.2 details the basic data
of a plant of the type we are considering. This should give you *some*
idea as to the scale of the project. The plant could be divided up
into a number of process units. For the purposes of illustration, we
take later a total of twelve such separate units, but even that
number is 'designed to deceive'. It was that type of plant, however.
In addition to the process units comprising Plant X, there were also
the various offsite facilities that had to be provided or expanded,
but they are outside the scope of our present study. Perhaps it
should also be mentioned that not all the process units constituting
the plant were the subject of the laboratory experiments that had
proved so encouraging. Many of the units were based, as is usually
the case, on proven and well-established processes, the only
development being that the latest techniques would be incorporated. If the 'new design' section failed, then the whole plant
would be inoperable, so although the process risk was limited to
only a part of the plant, the financial risk was total.

We cannot show you a photograph of the plant, but turn back to
Chapter 6 (A splendid refinery), and the illustration Figure 6.1
shows an overview of the refinery discussed there. The 'volume' of

PROJECT PARAMETERS

Design manhours	1,000,000
Construction manhours	3,400,000
Number of drawings	15,000
Major equipment items	900
Number of piles	4,000
Quantity of concrete, m^3	25,000
Quantity of pipe, metres	200,000
Weight of structural steel, tons	2,500
Length of power cable, km	300
Plant capacity, t/year	500,000
Number of process units	12
Project duration, months	48
Investment, £ million (1980 values)	130

Figure 12.2 Project parameters
The table gives some of the basic physical parameters for Plant X, thus indicating the scale of the project under review.

plant and equipment in Plant X would be similar to that seen in that photograph. For example Figure 12.2 indicates a total of 200 kilometres of pipe; Figure 6.1, although of a completely different installation, nevertheless gives a fair idea of the complexity and size of Plant X in terms of pipework.

Three years later

The project was well into the process design stage when it was approved by the Board of Directors. It had to be, because the estimators needed the plant and equipment sized in order to make their estimate. Total cost was assessed on a statistical basis, using the estimate of plant and equipment made from the details provided by the process engineers. Thereafter, process design continued and detailed engineering design began. The initial estimate of what is sometimes called the 'Home Office' effort, that is, design, engineering and procurement, with related estimating, planning and expediting, was thought to be some 700,000 hours, but as may be seen from Figure 12.2, these turned out to be rather more – we rounded the figure out as an order of magnitude. If you wanted to conjure with the figures that we are slowly bringing before you, you could calculate that while the design effort increased 40%, total cost only increased 20%, and draw a few conclusions from that. These are the sort of relationships that have significance and the way they vary can have real significance. Since these relationships usually hold well together, why in this case did design effort increase so much more than total cost? It would be a fair deduction that a lot of that design effort was concerned with *re-work*, rather than new work, since the relationship between design cost and total cost is usually fairly constant. Now, why was that?

To see the various reasons clearly, we shall look again at the project, two years after construction was first started in the field: about two and a half years from the time that the project first got 'into its stride', following the go-ahead from the Board. The several phases of such a project are illustrated in Figure 12.3 and we should at this point be approaching the end of the 'design, procurement and construction' phase. A large proportion of the pipework has been fabricated and put into place. By this time one unit, a separate entity, is to be started up shortly. It was, in fact, the

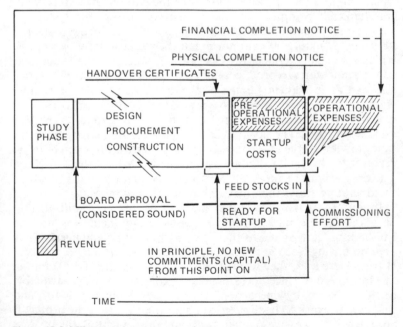

Figure 12.3 Milestones in project development
Here we see the key phases through which a project progresses before the plant is finally 'on stream' and producing the required products.

problems associated with the startup of this first unit that displayed the problems that lay ahead for the units still to be completed. As we have attempted to indicate in Figure 12.3, commissioning a unit or a plant is a gradual process. When a plant is ready for startup, it should be mechanically complete. Mechanical completeness is reached by the contractor(s) finishing their work, a certificate is issued and what is usually called a 'punch list' is drawn up. This is a list of the items of work still to be completed, or regarded as complete but then found to be in error in some way. The certificate is often issued and signed 'subject to completion of punch list items'. It is a fluid situation. At the same time as this is going on, the project manager, dealing with his contractors, has also to look ahead and deal with the commissioning, operating and maintenance staff for the new installation. They will not 'take over' and sign *their* acceptance certificate, until they are satisfied that the plant is safely operable. At this time, then, there exist two parallel streams of effort. The construction team is seeking to complete, and get the plant off their hands, incurring 'start-up costs' in the process. These are the costs incurred in satisfying the requirements of the operating and maintenance staff once the equipment is reportedly 'mechanically complete'. At the same time, the operating staff, as they start to 'handle' various sections, are also incurring costs of a very similar nature. We do not mean their salaries and overheads, which are usually termed 'pre-operational expenses' until such time as the plant starts to produce, but costs arising from the extra staff required as instruments and electrics are set to work. Mechanics stand by to 'trouble shoot'. A great debate can occur as to what extent these particular costs are 'operational' or 'capital' – they are *all* startup costs. The position can be very unsatisfactory from the point of view of the cost control engineer. Here is an 'open door' in relation to the capital budget estimate, which he strives to close. The only way to secure it fast, is to get the plant into the hands of the operating staff; then there is no doubt any more.

In our particular case, this blurred picture was still further obscured by the fact that the process development was not yet finished: at least, that was the view of the process engineers. They kept on having 'second thoughts'. We can enter into their feelings. If truth were told, they were afraid. They were, they felt, standing on shifting sand, since operating plant experience was not available to them. Normally one expects process development to stop and that area of work to be 'frozen' at about the time that the project is authorised. Process *design* will continue, implementing the process and resolving the problems that occur as the detailed design is developed, translating the process design into physical reality. In this case the process itself was still in a state of flux because of the big step that had been taken. The detailed development disclosed problems that would normally have been resolved at the pilot plant stage, but now had to be resolved in relation to the developing design of a major installation. This was the major reason why those 700 000 design hours finally topped a million. Detailed changes are always expensive. Furthermore the later the changes are made, the more expensive they become. We made this point in Chapter 2; look again at Figure 2.2.

What was the result of all this? We shall look at one result immediately: the effect on those start-up costs. Figure 12.4 illustrates the progressive growth of the cost of what are termed 'field changes' over time, as the project approaches completion. The process changes that we have been discussing were to a limited extent made by altering a drawing before the item, or the piece of fabricated pipe (called a 'spool piece' in the field) had been made, but we are more concerned with those changes that had to be made following that stage: in the field, on the site. The cost of the field changes is expressed as a percentage of the total investment. We set what was happening with Plant X against the standard set by the analysis of past projects, the standard of 'experience'. This is what estimators and cost engineers do continuously; it is the basis of all their work. Figure 12.4 illustrates the position 'two years on' from the beginning of construction when it was thought that the plant would be completed and finally handed over some nine months later. Six months later it became very evident that the end-date was not going to be achieved. The changes being made, the afterthoughts – new thoughts, even – were still coming in as fast as ever and new projections had to be made. It now appeared that there were *still* six months to go. The final result is set out, so far as field changes are concerned, in Figure 12.5. Among other things, this experience demonstrates that the S-curve is, even in this context, a most reliable indicator. Going back to Figure 12.4 once again, the forecast assumed that the effort lost would be picked up; the slope of the curve would increase. But it *did not*! The final slope, as seen in Figure 12.5, is the same as that of the 'statistical average'. Once again, the trend is all important. The total of field changes is now a much higher percentage than normal, and the reasons are clear. This is a 'special case' – one result of omitting the pilot plant stage in process development.

Is there surprise at what has happened? There should not be. In the past we ourselves have discussed the problems of cost control in the building of process plants and the risks inherent in changing one's mind while a project is still pliable and capable of change at a

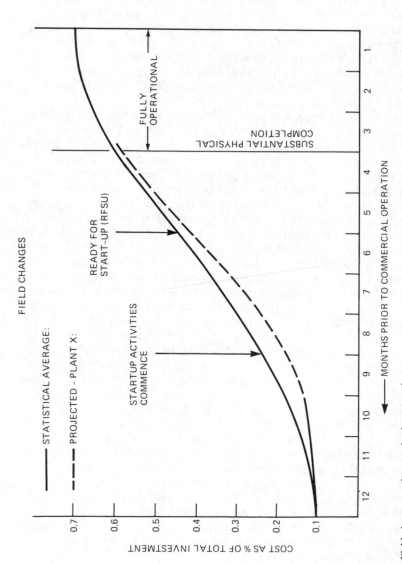

Figure 12.4 Field changes – the standard approach
Here we compare progress on field changes with the statistical average when there are still nine months to go – or so it was thought.

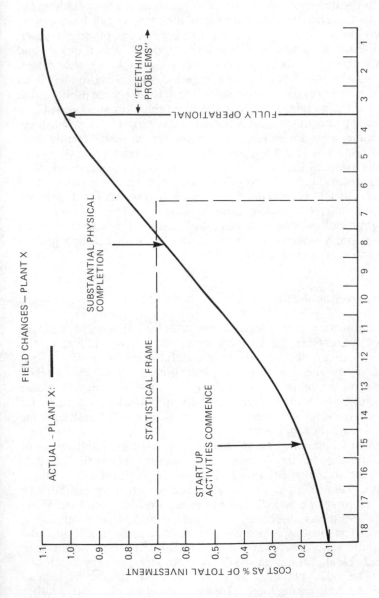

Figure 12.5 Field changes — the actual result
Now the plant is operational and one can see how actuality compares with the statistical average. The slope of the curve is exactly the same.

low cost, while time is still cheap. We warned that changes made late in the day can cost ten times as much as changes made early, that cost overruns, with the related time delay, can have drastic effects on profitability, delaying the break-even point for years. With Plant X, these risks were understood. It was thought, and rightly thought that they were risks that could be well taken. Indeed, when the estimates were prepared, such provision had been made. Some provision was allowed for in the estimate itself, and in addition the margin of error declared on the estimate was wider at Board approval stage than is normally the case. In the event, these provisions were not enough. The estimators at least foresaw what could happen and did happen. But the planners, while they were equally aware of the 'development' nature of the plant, overlooked the time implications entirely. They assumed that the project would progress as all projects do. So we have another lesson. If you are involved in a development project, then remember that there are time implications, as well as cost implications. This comes out even more strongly when we came, as we did in Chapter 5, to a project that was development all the way.

Piping erection the key

To demonstrate more clearly what actually happened during the life of the project, let us look in a little more detail at piping erection, always the key to the successful completion of a petro-chemical or chemical process plant project. We have already referred to the volume and density of the pipework on such plants and with Plant X there were nearly 400 men working on pipework erection at the point of peak effort, out of an overall peak of some 1 500, including supervision.

The initial planning, as we have said, ignored the implications of continuing process development, and was very optimistic. To some extent the argument employed was pyschological: set a target three months ahead of what we really expect, and then we can hope to meet the target we actually have in mind. But that is not our view. We believe that sound, realistic targets should be set at all times; the owner, managing contractor and subcontractor should all know and understand the *realities* of the situation. They all do know in the end. Finally, the facts speak for themselves, as they did in this case. The initial planning for pipework erection is to be seen in Figure 12.6, finishing very happily just before the bad weather would really set in. Compare the forecast with what actually happened. To begin with, piping materials arrived late because

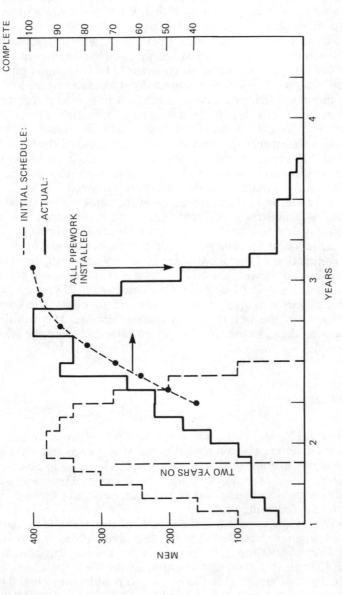

Figure 12.6 Manpower schedule – pipework erection
The many changes resulted in a slow start to material ordering, and pipework erection did not achieve the planned buildup. Then, after rundown, there was protracted re-work.

design was delayed, and design effort in turn had been impeded by change. Fabrication was delayed, since even at that stage the iso-metrics were continually being modified. There never was a project with so many drawing revisions! Figure 12.6 demonstrates that after all the pipework had been installed, it was still some six months before the pipework was finally complete, and even then not to the full satisfaction of all concerned. Not only was piping erection delayed, but it was approaching maximum effort in the winter months, when productivity falls to a low. Everything cost far more than was originally anticipated, although the actual volume and weight of pipework was much the same as had originally been estimated. Then we have what is called the 'knock-on effect'. Because piping erection was delayed, completion of instrumentation and insulation, in particular, were also disrupted and therefore cost much more than was first estimated.

The end result was a transformation of the construction effort in the field, well illustrated in Figure 12.7, where we compare what went on this time in Plant X with what happened on the same site on an earlier occasion. The slow build-up resulting from the delay in the completion of the process design is very apparent, together with the 'hiccup' because the civil works were running down before the mechanical works really got going. Once again, if you see that happening with a project in which you are involved, the curve departing from the normal pattern, then beware. The warning message was there, in the trend, eighteen months before the plant was planned for completion.

The cost

Both figures 12.6 and 12.7 demonstrate that with Plant X we have a significant difference between what actually happened and what we might call the 'average situation'. The graphs show, quite clearly, a 'long tail'. It was the tail that was the surprise. The trend was towards completion by the end of the year, yet it ran on into the spring of the following year.

In terms of the capital investment, it all cost some 20% more than had originally been authorised. On a major project, 20% is a lot of money in absolute terms: perhaps £25 million in this case. We must not forget that the original estimate, the basis for approval, had a margin of error. This fact is all too readily forgotten. The margin of error was originally quoted as –12.5% to +15%. That – 12.5% was a little misleading, since nobody really thought that

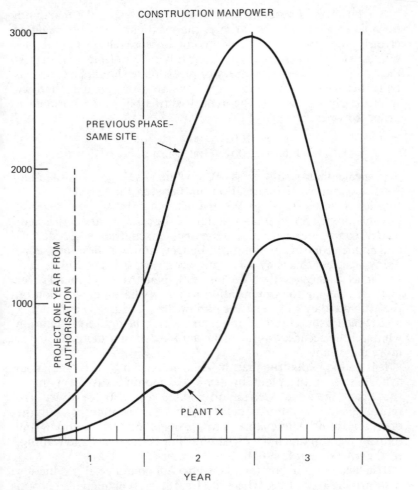

Figure 12.7 Construction manpower
Here we compare the overall manning buildup on Plant X with that achieved on a similar major construction project. Once again, the slow buildup is very apparent.

there was any saving to be made against the estimate, in view of the uncertainties.

When we compare the original estimate with the final result, in the context of uncertainty, we see the problem created by seeking to define with an appearance of preciseness. This matter is discussed in detail in Chapter 14, where we talk about choosing prospects for better business. Theory tells us (Ref. 3) that while the maximum possible positive error is infinity, the maximum possible negative error is only -100%. In practice, commonsense tells us that neither of these statements is true. However, this concept leads to the statement that the range of accuracy of an estimate should be shown as lying between $+x_1\%$ and $-x_2\%$, where x_1 is greater than x_2. Immediately we have a 'theoretical restriction' and a formula is proposed where

$$x_1 = 100x_2/(100 - x_2), \text{ and}$$
$$x_2 = 100x_1/(100 + x_1)$$

This means that $+10\%$ gives -9%, while $+43\%$ gives -30%. Dr. Liddle's scrutiny of the relationship between the 'words' and the 'music' is quite amusing. We have a delightfully wide range of possible names for estimates as far as the 'words' are concerned: tender, conceptual, definitive, semi-detailed, contractor's, order-of-magnitude, control, preliminary, budget, authorisation and scope are typical, but this is by no means a complete list. Dr. Liddle goes so far as to suggest that we just call them A, B, C and D, for instance, leaving the organisation to place what interpretation on the estimate they will, once they know that A is the most accurate, and D the least accurate. Capital cost is not the only consideration whatever the accuracy of the original forecast; time is equally if not more important.

It is undoubtedly true that the delay in reaching the 'commercial availability' of the plant by some six months was much more significant than the overrun on capital cost. Not only was the return on the investment delayed for that six months, but the operating and maintenance staff costs continued without any return. In addition, all the off-site facilities were ready and waiting, further investment failing to bring a return.

The delay in bringing the plant into full commercial production is shown in Figure 12.8, where the final startup planning is set out. While some units were started up more or less on time, in accordance with the original planning, others were long delayed, the final outcome being a delay of some six months in reaching commercial production. Figure 12.8, which was actually version 'E', also demonstrates the complexity of the start-up procedures for a major project incorporating a number of distinct and separate units, twelve in this case. The troubles were by no means over when the plant went into production. Initially, capacity could only be brought up to 60% of design capacity and it soon became apparent that to bring it above 70% could possibly be a major operation. Various operating problems were encountered: not only blocking in

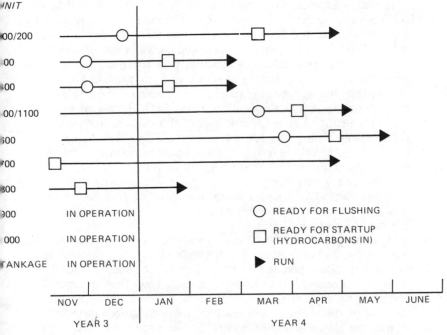

Figure 12.8 Start-up planning
This is the start-up planning, issue E, the last issue. Four earlier plans had to be abandoned. It had been hoped to have all units fully operational six months earlier than was actually achieved.

odd places, but also intensive corrosion in certain areas that was quite unexpected.

The final outcome

Time was overrun; the cost estimate as authorised by the Board of Directors was overrun. But why were those estimates of time and cost made? In the first instance, for project evaluation and in order that an investment decision might be taken. This information was an essential element in the decision-making process – a decision-making process concerned with the generation of wealth. Would the decision have been different had those figures been 20% higher? Almost certainly not. The company was concerned in the *generation of wealth*, and this objective would still have been well in view.

Indeed, we are all concerned with the generation of wealth, and this ought to be the basic objective of the industry we are looking at, as of all industry. Despite the faults so often laid at the door of the oil, chemical and petrochemical industries, some of which we have touched upon earlier, particularly in Chapter 2, there can be little doubt that these industries are, in the main, socially responsible and an integral part of our society. The wealth they create provides the community at large with the social services, while the profits they make are largely ploughed back to maintain their business and the job prospects of their employees. The remainder, when there is any, is distributed as dividend, mainly to employees, insurance companies and pension funds.

In the case we are studying, where the plant had with intent been built in a 'depressed area', a major contribution had already been made in these areas by the time the plant had been built, before it ever went into operation.

When we stand back and look at what now exists, we see that the plant is running (albeit not yet at 100% efficiency); the operating and maintenance people are busy. Indeed they have some challenging problems to face and solve, and keep them happy. The process and materials-of-construction problems are capable of elimination and will be eliminated over some eighteen months: this is well on the way as we write. Consideration of some major problems has to be suspended until items of equipment can be ordered, and then installed at a major shutdown. In another year or so that, too, will be behind them, and the plant will be producing to design capacity and more. In all, perhaps a year has been lost in terms of the original planning for production, but if a pilot-plant stage had been utilised, three years would have been lost, and much money spent. They are in full commercial production with a major installation two years earlier than would have been possible had not these risks been taken. In terms of time it was a risk well taken.

The cost factor? That is more difficult to assess, but we believe that there was most certainly an overall benefit. The plant was built in depressed times, lowering the cost by about 10 or 15%, quite apart from the effect of escalation had it been built later. The increased costs that had to be met owing to all these changes, and the further cost of alterations once the plant was built are certainly far less in total than the cost of the pilot plant that would have eliminated most of them. Once again, the risks were met, contained and overcome. The plant, when complete, was described by those who walked around it as 'impressive'. This must be viewed in the context of an industry well accustomed to large-scale process units.

Was the right decision made? The operational problems are being solved and within two years the plant will, we are sure, be operating to design capacity and beyond. A jump from experiments on the laboratory bench to full-scale commercial production can well be the right decision, provided you have the expertise, particularly as it becomes ever more true that 'time is money'.

References

1   Halford, P., 'The anatomy of a super project', *Process Economics International,* 1978, vol. 1, no. 1, Autumn.

2   Taylor, J., 'The best laid schemes', essay review in *Chemistry and Industry* (UK), November 1973.

3   Liddle, C.J., 'Estimation or procastination?' *Engineering and Process Economics,* Elsevier Publishing, Amsterdam 1978, pp. 165–173.

PART FOUR

THERE ARE LESSONS TO LEARN

13 The cost of indecision

The whole world has heard the saga of the discovery and development of the oil fields in the North Sea, because of their dramatic impact on the economy of the United Kingdom and the very specialised technology and even high drama that has been associated with the recovery of oil and gas under such difficult conditions. The development of the oilfields in the far north, in Alaska, which were examined in some detail in Chapter 11, has also reached the headlines because of the difficulties associated with the transport of the oil across those frozen wastes. But Bombay High – who has heard of that? Yet Bombay High is in fact India's 'North Sea'. It is a gift from God to India, discovered just at the right time. But thanks to Man and his inability in this case to reach quick decisions and to take decisive action, this time in the field of project execution, many of the benefits of the Bombay High field are currently being lost to India. For years gas has been flared away – burnt to no purpose or profit – as it comes to the surface in association with the crude oil that is being recovered and worked. Have you ever seen a gas flare, such as are always associated with oilfields, oil refineries and petrochemical installations? They can be really dramatic when flaring at night. We show you one – a daytime view, and far less dramatic, in Figure 13.1. Of course the objective is to flare, that is, burn the gas as little as possible. At refineries, the flare is really a safety valve, burning the escaping gas when problems arise in operation.

But the gas from Bombay High flares both day and night, although the annual import bill to India for crude oil and petroleum products will exceed Rs. 70 billion, nearly equal to the country's entire import earnings (illustrated in Figure 13.2). That leaves the question: what is left to pay for that country's essential

Figure 13.1 A typical flare stack
This photograph is illustrative only, and shows the tip of a typical flare gas stack, with the gas flaring. (Photograph by courtesy of Escher B.V., of the Hague, The Netherlands, manufacturers of specially designed plant for the oil, chemical, natural gas and process industries.)

imports, such as edible oils, fertilisers, cement, coal, plant and machinery and chemicals? The current foreign exchange reserves of India have been said to be 'considerable', but it would take only the failure of one monsoon or a bout of severe floods, to wipe out that reserve. And then what?

A valuable asset

Fortunately, all the experts for once agree that the best use of the associated gas at Bombay High is as feedstock for the manufacture of nitrogenous fertiliser and petrochemicals. Its use as a fuel gas has a much lower priority, although both contribute to import substitution. The benefit/cost ratio is much higher (nearly five-fold) if the gas is used for the manufacture of chemicals rather than as fuel. India has to import fertiliser, for instance, or the basic petroleum, but the added value of the fertiliser is four or five times

THE MOUNTING OIL IMPORT BILL

Crude Oil	Domestic million tons	Imported million tons	Import Value (a) Rs. billion	Proportion of entire exports As %	Foreign trade deficit Rs. billion
1950	0.3	3.0	0.52	9	0.52
1960–61	0.5	7.9	0.80	12	4.80
1970–71	6.8	12.8	1.40	29	1.00
1975–76	8.4	15.8	12.60	31	12.20
1977–78	10.8	17.7	15.50	29	6.20
1979–80	11.8	21.5	32.70	50	2.70
1980–81	10.9(b)	16.3	52.10	78	26.60
1981–82	16.8(c)	15.4	52.00	70	55.00
1982–83	21.0(c)	14.2	44.00	52	50.00

Notes: (a) Includes petroleum products.
(b) There was a domestic crude loss of 3 million tons due to Assam agitation.
(c) Normalisation in Assam has been assumed.

Figure 13.2 The mounting oil import bill
Here we see how the cost of imported crude oil to India is steadily rising. It is currently some 80% of India's entire export income, and, even on the optimistic forecast we present, could be one and a half times export earnings by 1985.

that of petroleum. It goes without saying that to flare the gas, making no use of it at all, because we are not ready to use it, is just the waste of a most precious asset. Yet this is precisely what India is doing at the moment. As the crude oil is produced at the wells, a certain amount of gas also comes, which must be used then and there – if not, it has to be flared, and is thus wasted. There is no choice! Unlike a natural gas well – and natural gas on its own has indeed been discovered in neighbouring areas – the production of which can be delayed until you are ready, the gas associated with crude oil production has to be dealt with as the crude oil itself is pumped up.

What sort of asset are we in fact talking about? India's current requirement of crude oil is about 30 million tons per year, of which some fourteen million tons per year are produced within the country, the rest imported. Current projections through the eighties indicate that future imports will continue at about this same level, the increased demand owing to growth being met almost entirely by the continuing growth of production from the indigenous sources. Of the present output throughout India of some sixteen million tons per annum, Bombay High contributes around six million tons, this being expected to rise to twelve million tons in 1983, and seventeen million tons by 1984. Associated with this volume of crude oil will be some six million cubic metres of gas per day. This is the asset, and we now want to look at the prospective utilisation of this associated gas. Is it going to be used efficiently?

Production of crude oil from Bombay High has grown quite rapidly. Within three to four years from the time of the discovery of this resource, in 1974, a production rate of 60 000 barrels per day, equivalent to six million tons per year, was being achieved. This came about thanks to the prompt action and forethought of the Oil & Natural Gas Commission (ONGC) who installed a gas trunk pipeline prior to the monsoon of 1978, thus making the gas available to the consumer industries. If this trunk pipeline had been delayed for a year, then the value of the gas that would have had to be flared, and so wasted, would have been simply enormous. Completion of the gas line, and the associated shore terminal on time also meant that costs were being kept within budget. The immediate users of this gas were to be: the Tata Power Company and the Maharashtra State Electricity Board. These were to be temporary outlets, the gas being used as fuel only, to replace coal. The Trombay V Fertiliser Plant was planned to take 1.4 million cubic metres per day at full load; we discussed the history of Trombay in Chapter 8. At that time in the planning stage, the Thal Vaishet Fertiliser Complex project was to take 2.5 million cubic metres per day, at maximum plant capacity.

What has actually happened? The present utilisation is still wholly as fuel, both by the power companies and also at Trombay, which is using the gas as fuel until Trombay V is ready. Since the Thal Vaishet Fertiliser Complex, with two 1350 tons/day ammonia plants, and three 1400 tons/day urea plants, is going to be by far the largest user of this gas, it is interesting to follow the progress of this particular complex. The most convenient approach is to take the events in chronological order, remembering that the 'key date', the date when the gas was not only planned to be but *was* available, was the year 1978, following discovery in 1974.

February 1975   Working Group assigned to recommend opti-
                mum utilisation of the Bombay High associated
                gas. They recommended fractionation, using
                the fractions as follows:
                Methane   –   Fertiliser
                Ethane/propane   –   Petrochemicals
                Propane/butane   –   LPG for domestic use
June 1977   Optimum utilisation plans still under discussion
                by the government.
October 1977   At full production, ten million tons per year of
                crude expected, with 3.1 million cubic metres per
                day of associated gas. ONGC to set up a frac-
                tionating plant at Uran, with production
                expected by May 1979.
November 1977   Submarine and onshore pipeline contract
                awarded to Brown & Root. Work started for
                completion by May 1978, prior to the onset of
                the monsoon. This was 205 kilometres of 30-inch
                and 26-inch pipeline.
April 1978   The associated gas can be used as fuel till the
                pipeline is complete; thereafter, it is available for
                fertiliser manufacture, with any surplus going
                for power production.
                Two working groups are now in action, advising
                the two separate state governments involved,
                Maharashtra and Gujarat, on the best utilisation
                of the offshore gas. Third group is advising on
                the use of the gas for petrochemical production.
May 1978   The total of the gas flared to 15 March 1978 was
                said to be 300 million cubic metres. Its value
                depends on its use, but we are talking of money
                of the order of Rs. 120 million. (This is some
                £7.5 million, or $15 million.)
June 1978   Gas starts flowing from Bombay High (BH field)
                to Uran, followed a few days later by crude oil
                along the other line. These two pipelines were
                commissioned *on time*, prior to the monsoon, as
                per the target programme.

The gas is being produced, but until the Trombay fertiliser plant
can use it as feedstock, it will only be used as fuel both there and at
the thermal power stations. This will save coal, although coal does
not really need saving. It will also reduce pollution in the Trombay
area, notorious because of the high concentration of industrial

plants in the area. Although the pipelines were ready on time, and the gas there, the prime users were not.

Ideally, the gas fractionating plant should have been ready when the gas came ashore, but decision on its location was a long drawn out process, through a plethora of committees and working groups. The unit is now under construction and is expected to be ready by the end of 1982, over four years after the first availability of the associated gas. Meanwhile, there are about three million LPG customers, with a further three million on the waiting list.

Fertiliser plants in prospect

The story may be resumed in mid-1978 because nothing very much has happened in relation to the proposed new fertiliser plants up to then. They are still talking. It is the new fertiliser plants that are going to make the most profitable use of the gas that is now available, some being used as fuel, but largely being flared.

July 1978	The Rewas location for the fertiliser plants is now dropped, because of pollution problems. The Expert Committee expressed a preference for Tarapur, but Thal Vaishet was also acceptable as a second choice.
August 1978	The two working groups that had been appointed to assess the utilisation of the offshore gas, one for Gujarat State, the other for Maharashtra State, made recommendations for a total of four fertiliser plants. Their proposals have been broadly accepted by the Government. The feasibility of petrochemicals production is still being studied by a third group.
November 1978	The task force recommends Tarapur for the proposed fertiliser plants in preference to Mandwa and Thal Vaishet.
August 1979	It is reported that C.F. Braun are 'tipped' for the four ammonia plants at Gujarat: their main competitors, Kellogg, Toya and Humphreys & Glasgow. The World Bank sanctions a $250 million loan in this context.
September 1979	A revised estimate for the Thal Vaishet complex totals Rs. 6080 million, of which half is expected to be funded from abroad. When completed, this complex will represent the world's largest

| | production unit at a single site. A power plant for the complex is included and the infrastructure, which includes a small town, is expected to cost some Rs. 280 million. |
| November 1979 | A high-powered Official Committee proposes a further six plants using offshore gas as a feedstock. These are to be in addition to the four already approved and now said to be in progress. Now we are in a different order of magnitude so far as process plant construction is concerned. Each ammonia plant, of 1350 tonnes/day capacity, needs 1.3 million cubic metres per day of gas. It is expected that a total of 26 million cubic metres per day would be available for these ten plants. This would be 5 million as associated gas from Bombay High and 21 million as free gas from S. Basein. |

To speed up the story:

December 1979	Contract with C.F. Braun is initialled.
February 1980	The issue is reopened by the new Indian government.
August 1980	Amidst reports of 'heavy payoffs' by C.F. Braun, who reportedly had access to all the government files, including the minutes of Cabinet meetings – or so it was leaked to the western press – the Cabinet decided to award the Thal Vaishet plant to Haldor Topsoe and the one at Hazira (Gujarat) to Pullman Kellogg.
December 1980	The World Bank lets the loan agreement lapse. India now gets the 'red tape' treatment instead of the 'red carpet' treatment she normally gets because of her credibility and as the largest single borrower.
January 1981	'Zero date' for the contract. The plants could have been in operation by this date, if ... If ... If!

India already has the capability both to design and engineer ammonia plants up to 900 tonnes/day, and the economy of scale (see Chapter 15) is at best marginal beyond this point for developing countries such as India with weak and costly infrastructure facilities, especially transport. Did the World Bank lobby operating in the various ministries in New Delhi have a hand in this decision?

Would the World Bank loan have been allowed to lapse if the final decision had been in favour of C.F. Braun or another American company? We can only guess. The testimony given before the House of Representatives Committee in the USA put it this way:

> The World Bank ... encourages growth (in the Third World) which increases the demand for US exports, which in turn generates US employment ...

But let us return to our story. The four plants already approved are the two at Thal Vaishet and another two at Hazira, near Surat in Gujarat. This latter installation is to be set up by the Indian Farmers Fertiliser Cooperative (IFFCO), who already own and operate a world-scale ammonia-urea complex at Kandla, Kalol. The IFFCO asked for sanction for Rs. 7000 million, but the Public Investment Board granted only Rs. 6250 million. Why? They only permit three percent for contingency, and allow nothing for escalation. This means that IFFCO will have to approach them again in due course. What a bureaucracy! The World Bank is expected to advance $150 million to cover the foreign exchange requirement.

Since conception of the Thal Vaishet project, there have been perhaps a dozen committees and working groups concerned with location, capacity, the prequalifications of bidders, the preparation of bid invitations, the evaluation of bids – and then re-evaluation *ad infinitum*. The location was changed three times over three years, from Alibag to Tarapur and now Thal Vaishet, thanks mainly to the activities of environmental groups (the Indian 'Ralph Naders' – see Chapter 2). In retrospect the final location is neither better nor worse than the first. But the net result is that construction has started nearly five years late. What could have been the end is now only the beginning. And the final price tag? Perhaps Rs. 12 billion instead of the original Rs. 5.4 billion hopefully estimated. We must say 'hopefully' because we would have had to wait and see how good that estimate was.

What a price to pay for procrastination and indecision! (Ref. 1) All this time the gas has had to be flared away and the shortfall in fertiliser production made up by imports, which use the scarce foreign exchange. Meanwhile, the owners (Rashtriya Chemicals and Fertilisers Limited) are getting on with what can be progressed, so firm dates are given for the completion of the various boiler installations and turbo-generator plants. Work is also under way with warehouses, administrative buildings and the like, although these are also being seriously delayed by a shortage of cement. The investment programme is long drawn out, and assets will lie idle for years. The story remains the same: committees prosper and progress suffers!

Now that the decisions have finally been taken for Thal Vaishet, the picture clears somewhat. Offsites are the owner's responsibility, as we have seen. The foreign consultant, Haldor Topsoe, has responsibility for the ammonia plant within battery limits, but execution responsibility remains with the owner. The detailed engineering work has been entrusted to Fertiliser Planning and Development (India) Limited, and Haldor Topsoe are to ensure transfer of technology in a very real sense. The owners are the erstwhile Trombay Division of the old Fertiliser Corporation of India, but with a difference. They have come a long way from the original Trombay days (we discuss Trombay in Chapter 8). With close co-ordination and a real team spirit between the three parties now involved, there is no reason why the project should not be completed within the target period of 42 months.

The gas still flares

When we looked at the progress made in bringing the gas ashore, we saw that that, at least, was on time. But that was only the beginning. That great day, you remember, was mid-1979. A year later, and where are we? Is the momentum being maintained? The expected availability of associated gas, as of early 1981, is set out in Figure 13.3 A Planning Commission working group has been making studies on the most economic use of the offshore free associated gas, and the optimisation of its utilisation, including a study of the strategy of transportation of the gas. The total estimated recoverable reserves were assessed at some 190 billion cubic metres,

BOMBAY HIGH		
Year	Crude Oil million tons/yr.	Assoc. Gas million cm/day
1978–79	3.3	1.1
1979–80	4.4	1.5
1980–81	5.2	1.8
1981–82	8.4	2.7
1982–83	11.8	4.0

Figure 13.3 Availability of offshore crude oil and gas

of which 30 million were associated with oil, and thus had to be taken as the oil was recovered, and the balance of 160 billion cubic metres was from gas fields. It was said that some 25 million cubic metres a day could be available by 1983. The Group approved the four plants for fertiliser production discussed above, and recommended a further six, all gas based, as we also saw earlier when looking at the fertiliser plant programme. They recommended new plants using gas, rather than the conversion of existing plants, presently running on either naphtha or fuel oil, since production of fertiliser has to be maintained. This programme, do not forget, demands the commissioning of one new plant a year, beginning in about 1986.

The proposed programme of availability in relation to off-shore production is shown in Figure 13.3. This programme is wholly the responsibility of the ONGC. Their 1978 to 1983 draft plan, the sixth, calls for an investment of some Rs. 16 billion, climbing from some Rs. 3.0 billion in 1978–79, to some Rs. 4.0 billion per year at the end of the period planned. The gas separation plant will come on stream, they say, by the end of 1982. Will they do it? Look at the way they performed in relation to their earlier plans. We set out the history in Figure 13.4, from which it can be seen that they have a very creditable record.

Given the will and backed by the appropriate authority, things can be achieved on time, and within the estimates, even in India, with all its problems and imponderables. That 400 km. of pipeline *was* laid on time, and within the estimate of cost. In fact actual cost was below the estimate, this being attributed to a glut of pipe worldwide, enabling purchase by the ONGC below their estimate. This project must rank as an outstanding achievement by the ONGC, although we most not forget the efforts of the main contractor, Brown & Root. But without the owner's full support and active backing, a contractor is helpless to prevent a project going 'sour'. The importance of the work of the ONGC and their role in the economy can be gauged from the fact that since 1972, the demand for crude oil has risen from 23 million tons to 30 million tons per year in India. Of this, local production accounts for nearly half, having risen over the same period from seven million tons per year to about fifteen million tons per year. The result has been to hold imports down. The import of crude oil and petroleum products is costing India nearly Rs. 70 billion a year in foreign exchange – and this is still growing as the price rises. Even this bill is only half what it would have been, if India's own production had not doubled during those same seven years.

There are two major oil fields and a major gas field to be

	ONGC – INDIA EXPLORATION AND PRODUCTION PROGRAMME OFFSHORE ONLY				
	Investment Rs. million	Crude oil tons/yr. million	Gas cm/day million	Execution	Completion date
Phase I	2000	2.0	–	6/75-5/76	9/1976
Phase II				11/76-12/77	1/1978
Phase IIIA	5540	4.0	–	6/77-6/78	6/1978
Phase IIIB		7.0	2.10	1978-79	5/1979
Phase IV	4860	12.0	4.00	6/78-5/80	3/1982
Phase V	3330				

Figure 13.4 Exploration and production programme – ONGC, India
Work has gone forward in a series of planned phases. Phase VI, now under planning, is discussed in the text.

exploited. Thanks to the urgent sense of purpose, and the strong support received from the central government in New Delhi with respect to funds and the chosen policies, ONGC have done a really creditable job, meeting practically all their targets. But to what purpose if the consumers are not ready to take up the resource as it becomes available? This is not the first time that this has happened. ONGC had to hold back production in Assam because neither the crude oil pipelines nor the associated refinery at Bongaigon were ready on time. Much greater harm is done when there is gas associated with the crude oil, as we have at Bombay High, for the gas that cannot be used has to be flared away and is lost for ever. Crude oil is different, since it can be seen as a 'bank', which is not drawn upon until it can be used, so there is no actual loss, only the ever increasing cost of imports. The Bombay High field was discovered in 1974, and its full potential was known as early as 1976, yet there is still no single agency charged with ensuring the timely use of the associated gas coming from this field. It is available, it is being flared. Look again at that flarestack in Figure 13.1 and think of it lighting the sky, day after day and night after night, month after month – and year after year, it would seem!

A plethora of committees

Will it ever come to an end? There has been a plethora of committees and working groups looking at the issue of utilising the gas that comes free from time to time, but unfortunately an 'ad-hoc' approach has been adopted. A group is called together to consider one specific aspect, or perhaps a few aspects, of the central issue. But the maximum potential of this valuable resource is far too precious to be treated in such a haphazard manner. In our view it is *essential* that one single agency be charged with the vital task of defining the priorities clearly, making proposals which amount to a master plan and then having the authority to see those proposals through. We have considered at length earlier the vital role that the project manager plays in any project and its successful completion, and we have seen full well the disaster that results if he is not given the appropriate authority. Indeed, the projects that we have been looking at in India, in particular, suffer much from that very fact; action is hamstrung by the rule of committees and government departments. What we now have before us is, in relation to gas utilisation in India, a project on the grand scale and it should be treated as such. Having once decided to set up a committee, or working group, the least one should do is to see that their recommendations are implemented. Never mind that their decisions are not necessarily the best, never mind that they have to cut across a wide range of conflicting interests. The last thing that should be done, just because their advice is disputed in certain quarters is to set up yet another group, to rework the problem yet again. That is like having a new project manager on a project every three months or so; we know how disastrous that would be in terms of cost and time. Most contracts with managing contractors have clauses to ensure continuity with staff engaged on the project: certainly not the opposite.

What is our view? One single organisation, say the Bombay High Authority, should be charged with the task that we have just described. A successful operation could easily add some Rs. 10 billion yearly to India's gross national product (GNP). In other words, there should be a unified approach instead of a specialised committee for each function. To quote from an article in the *Times of India* (Ref. 2):

> *Issue of gas landfall for panel*
> A committee of experts is to be appointed by the Government of India to examine the economic and technical feasibility of locating the land-fall point of the Bombay High gas pipeline. An early report is expected. An earlier committee (Satish Chadran) suggested utilisation pattern of Bombay High gas but did not go into the question of the landfall point.

Some can see the implications. The *Economic Times* (of India) wrote early in 1980 (Ref. 3):

Priority decision on conflicting claims vital
One of the first tasks of the Petroleum Ministry in the new government is to sort matters out relating to the colossal output of natural gas and associated gas from Bombay High, otherwise most of the gas will have to be flared for the next three to five years. It is Hobson's choice: either to allow the gas to be used now for the vital power generation or to reserve it for the distant future and 'better use' for fertilisers and chemicals. It is unfortunate that the government should have fought shy of striking a happy mean between these two conflicting interests – urgent 'low level' use for power or the not so urgent 'high level' use for fertilisers and petrochemicals.

Need we say more? This is in fact a worldwide problem, now that oil is becoming far too costly to be used as a mere fuel. Use of the gas for petrochemicals – where, when and how – is at the centre of current debate both in Maharashtra and Gujarat States. It is agreed – or is it? – that two world-scale petrochemical plants should be set up to exploit to the fullest extent the Bombay High and Basein resources. But firm decisions and final clearance are still awaited. Will the previous history in respect of fertiliser plants now be repeated for petrochemicals? We feel that it is unfortunate that India has opted for world-scale ethylene plants just when the developed world is beginning to doubt the wisdom of these. There is much to be said, particularly in a developing country such as India, for 'small is beautiful' – an aspect we discuss later, in Chapter 15. These days the variable cost, which is mainly raw materials, has become the predominant cost, and economy of scale in that context may be a mere mirage.

The final decisions and then the construction of these proposed petrochemical plants may well take a decade. Industry has meanwhile suggested an interim plant (MEDC 1980) whereby the ethane and propane fractions in the associated gas are used in existing petrochemical plants now run by National Organic Chemicals of India, Union Carbide, Polyolefins and Polychem, requiring but nominal investment for conversion facilities. This appears to be a sensible and pragmatic approach and it could add perhaps Rs. 5 million to India's GNP in return for a nominal investment (Ref. 4). It also ensures optimum utilisation of this valuable resource. Such a decision and its implementation would have to be on a 'crash' basis, since the ethane and propane fractions will become available by the end of 1982.

Time is money

We do not think that we can find a stronger lesson than this to demonstrate the money value of time. It is a powerful lesson because it is so clear and so vivid – you can *see* the money being *burnt* as time passes!

To sum up, there exists an extremely valuable resource, first discovered in 1974, whose full potential was known within the next couple of years. Yet this resource, it seems, may very easily be 'frittered away', especially the associated gas, the gas that *has* to come as the crude oil is recovered – and all because of lack of decision. Those in authority have taken so long trying to decide what is the best course for the utilisation of this associated gas. Why? Primarily because there is no single authority charged with the task. We can see quite clearly that this lies at the root of the problem, because where we do have a single authority, as in the case of the recovery of the crude oil and the gas, the ONGC, positive and purposeful action *has* been taken. Divided responsibility has brought lack of decision, and the gas has been flaring for years. The gas not flared is more likely to be used as fuel than for the manufacture of fertiliser or petrochemicals, although this is most certainly not the best use for this precious resource. The gas-based fertiliser plants first mooted in 1976 are only now taking shape and the decision on the fractionating plant has been still further delayed (Ref. 5).

Meanwhile, 'as Nero fiddles, Rome burns'. India will continue to import fertiliser, currently costing the country many billions of rupees per year, continue to import excessive quantities of crude oil and petroleum products – items that are already a very heavy drain on the meagre foreign exchange resources of that country. Disaster has been averted by further major discoveries of petroleum, particularly offshore, and the pricing of local crude oil at more realistic levels, approaching current international prices. This has made coal as fuel even more attractive, stopping the switchover from coal to oil, and encouraging the conservation of oil.

There is one silver lining. We have seen that *even in India* (an Indian wrote those words!) – even in India projects *can* be completed on time. We can see what is necessary: the appropriate power and authority to get on with the job. ONGC have shown us this very clearly. Who is going to listen now? There is still time. Who is going to listen to their past failures, or the failures of others and so turn failure into success?

References

1   *Chemical Weekly* (India), 'Delay in know-how, consultancy selection – Thal fertiliser project suffers', 4 March 1980. Also other articles in issues up to April 1981.
2   *Times of India*, 'Issue of gas landfall point for panel', 5 April 1980.
3   *Economic Times* (India). 'Priority decision on conflicting claims vital', 11 January 1980.
4   C.P. Bhambi, *World Bank of India*. Vikas, 1980. 137 pp.
5   Maharashtra Economic Development Corporation. *Petrochemicals from Bombay High – Industrial Opportunities and Challenges*, Bombay, India, December 1980, 142 pp.

14 Picking prospects for better business

In a fiercely competitive and highly technological area such as the process industries one of the main preoccupations of senior management is that of deciding which products and product areas are likely to be profitable and, alternatively, which products should be phased out. The rate of return on capital investment is the traditional manner in which the viability of new ventures is assessed. The methods whereby this has been done have been highly developed and have become ever more sophisticated over the years. Many books have been written on the subject, to guide accountants and others who undertake the intricate calculations that are required.

The recommended approach is extremely complicated and becomes almost unintelligible to those who have not got a degree or more in mathematics or accountancy, or both. We learn from one recent book on the subject (Ref. 1) that we are concerned, as we read it, with the economic analysis and selection of industrial projects. We are also told that the level of presentation in the book is such that readers are presumed to have a working knowledge of differential calculus, linear programming and statistical theory through regression analysis. It would also be helpful, we are told, if we had a background in economics, or had taken a course in intermediate microeconomics. That, apparently, is where one *begins*. You need all that just to get started!

The blunt truth

The book mentioned above has a section on 'Single, risky projects' and that is what it is all about. That is the type of project we have frequently been discussing – single, risky – occasionally *very* risky –

projects. The important thing in any project is to get your money back and then make a profit. To do that there has to be a 'cash flow', so Bussey's book discusses cash flow at some length.

The discussion introduces a variety of complex tables, diagrams and charts, supported by a series of extensive mathematical equations which have to be solved before there is enought information for a decision to be reached. What is the background to this highly sophisticated mathematical approach? Let us consider the chemical and petrochemical industries for a moment, whose management are continually faced with the need to make decisions about what, when and where to build. These complicated mathematics are designed to guide such decisions, remove the 'risk', and make the decisions much more informed.

Earlier, in Chapter 12, we discussed the profound step that was taken by one company in this business, in jumping from laboratory bench data to commercial production on a very large scale. The basic area of doubt, and hence the greatest area of risk, was the process, in that particular case. But that area of uncertainty was only one of many. When it comes to profitability calculations, certain areas, such as those of sales volume and price, are not only uncertain; they are uncontrollable, qualitative and often highly subjective. On the other hand, the ability to achieve a definite output on the basis of a particular process and engineering design is fairly certain. With well-known processes it is more than that; it is precisely controllable. There is no trouble at all in predicting the capacity in such cases within $\pm 20\%$. In the case mentioned just now, more than 60% of the design output was achieved at startup, and not too much money would have to be spent to bring the plant up to design capacity. Basic plant sizing was sound. This is almost invariably the case. But what of all the other, equally important factors involved in an investment decision, which form the basis for the detailed mathematical calculations leading to an assessment as to feasibility and desirability? Their reliability is far less than that.

Look at the following table, which has been abstracted from a book by Professor L.M. Rose (Ref. 2):

	Margin of error %	
Capital cost estimate	−10	+ 25
Sales volume	−50	+ 150
Sales price	−50	+ 20
Raw material prices	−25	+ 50
Inflation rate	−10	+ 100
Interest rate	−5	+ 50
Scrap value	−100	+ 10

With such a background, how dare we call an evaluation made with such data a *quantitative* evaluation? The most detailed calculations give the answers an air of authenticity, but that is only while their background is forgotten. Further, as already stated, the production capacity of a plant can be predicted with reasonable certainty: that plant has to operate at least 70% of its rated capacity if it is going to break even on costs. With a large plant, if that plant turns out to have been oversized by some 30% because of false predictions in other areas, then the profit margin has disappeared – just like that. This type of risk merely grows and becomes steadily more disastrous the larger the plant, and is a fundamental reason for turning to smaller plants – a subject discussed in some detail in the next chapter.

However, what happens in practice? Using data such as we have just described, supported by the mathematical wizardry that gives it authenticity, detailed reports are made to the boards of companies, full of firm numbers. It is against this background that the vital decisions are then made. As we have seen, such reports can well be, and it is notorious that they are, extremely unreliable and much subject to the bias of those who prepared them. This is one reason that more and more independent consultants are being used at this stage. This approach at least eliminates the in-built bias of the servants of the company. There is no doubt at all, as the use of independent consultants confirms, that the uncertain value of the data they have before them *is* appreciated in many cases by the Boards of Directors who have to act. To take but one instance, Union Carbide no longer look for a fixed number for ROI (Return on Investment) when evaluating their new projects, having found that almost all the proposals meet (or are forced to meet) their minimum. Let us now look at another approach.

The directional policy matrix

The two key questions to be considered when investment in a new project is under review are: what will it cost? Will it show a profit?

As can be seen from the table above, there is not too much difficulty in answering the first question with a degree of certainty (−10 to +25%), but what of the second? In our view, and not only in our view, as shall be explained, the answer to the second question in the present economic climate is no longer a matter of calculation, if it ever was. It is, without doubt, a matter of entrepreneurial judgement. As we have already indicated, the traditional approach to answering the second question has been to 'calculate' the rate of return on the capital being invested. In the present world situation such calculations can no longer be relied upon, even in the most basic of industries. Markets for instance can and have collapsed dramatically, almost overnight. Worldwide inflation, too, has severely weakened the validity and hence the credibility of financial forecasts, particularly for businesses that are affected to any material degree by oil prices. In addition, such calculations do not really provide any insight into the underlying dynamics and balance of a company's individual business sectors, or the balance between them. Let us not forget that the desire to spread risk has resulted in more and more companies diversifying their interests, so that this question of 'balance' within a company becomes ever more important. Single product companies are rare these days, on any scale.

Corporate managements who recognise these shortcomings bring a variety of other qualitative and quantitative considerations into the equation, to guide their decision-making processes, other than the financial yardsticks that can be 'calculated'. This 'entrepreneurial approach' is growing in use and is now attracting the attention of the major multi-nationals (Ref. 3). The technique proposed, called the Directional Policy Matrix (DPM) owes some of its features to various practitioners and members in this particular field of management science, such as the Boston Consulting Group (USA) and the PIMS programme of the Strategic Planning Institute. But computer programs and differential calculus are *out*!

The technique being proposed, DPM, allows the systematic analysis of some of the qualitative considerations we have been discussing, and which are so important – more important than any of the financial answers on offer. Comparison becomes possible between business sectors and company positions in a way that is largely independent of financial forecasts.

What is the procedure?

There are two key factors in any decision to proceed with a particular investment, especially in the process industries. They are:

> Which area of activity of the several I can choose will be the most profitable?
> In the preferred area, how does my product compare with that of its competitors?

Let us deal, first of all, with the selection of an area of activity: a 'business sector'.

In building up a corporate plan a company will normally have available a number of plans and investment proposals for individual business sectors. These will include historical data on the company's past performance in that sector and financial projections embodying the future investment plans. Such projections will reflect the expectations of those responsible for the company's business in that particular sector in relation to:

market growth
industry supply/demand balance
prices and costs
the company's future market share
manufacturing competitiveness
research and development strength
the activities of competitors
the future business environmment

These are all things that can be 'weighed and measured' to some extent, but how can their respective values and influence be compared?

The basic technique of the DPM is to identify the main criteria by which the prospects for a business sector may be judged to be favourable or unfavourable, and then those by which the company's position in that sector might be assessed to be strong or weak. One first evaluates the business sector, then the prospective position of the company in it: first the 'sector prospects' are rated, then the 'company capability'. What we are looking for all the time is high profit and sound growth potential; that is the 'favourable' aspect of a business sector. To sort these things out, a matrix is drawn, in three columns and three rows, as shown in Figure 14.1, and the ratings as assessed are plotted on this matrix. There are various ways in which this matrix can be used, but in the example set out on the matrix the positions of a number of different business sectors in a company's portfolio are displayed. Examples of applications of this technique would be a chemical company having a range of products to offer, each product being a 'business sector'; with a shipping company it would be the different types of cargo; with an engineering company its range of products and services. The best sectors for the company are those in the bottom right hand corner, while the worst are at the top left hand corner. Our example is not doing too badly – his sectors are generally well towards the bottom right hand corner – but you can see how quickly, vividly and clearly an impression of the business can be gained.

When it comes to product assessment, the same approach can be

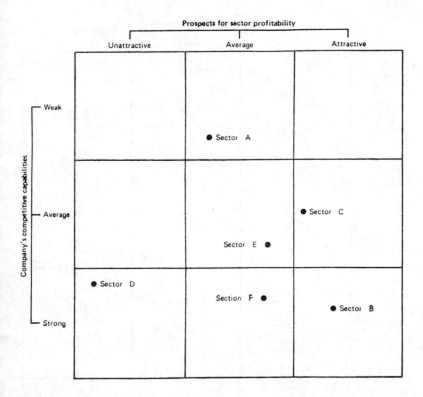

Figure 14.1 The directional policy matrix
This matrix is concerned with the selection of a business sector, as discussed in the
text. (With acknowledgements to the Shell International Chemical Company
Limited, London.)

adopted, and this is illustrated in Figure 14.2. Here the situation is
studied with respect to Product X in a particular business sector.
There are three major competitors in the sector, the firms A, B and
C. Each firm has been assessed, and it is very apparent that firm A
has the advantage. Firm A, therefore, should go ahead and build.
But how do we establish these various dots on the matrix?

Evaluation of product 'X'

The first thing that has to be done is to formalise the method of
assessment of the product. This is done under three headings:

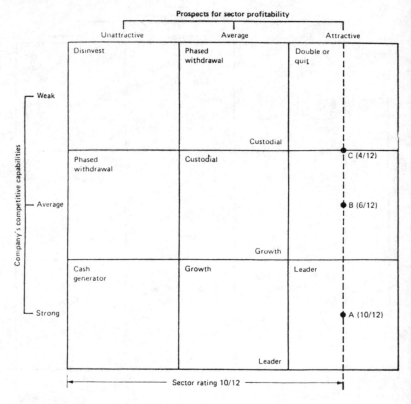

Figure 14.2 An assessment of Product X
The directional policy matrix as developed for product X, which is comparable to that of Competitor A. (With acknowledgement to the Shell International Chemical Company Limited, London.)

Market position
Production capability
Product research & development

Under each head a total of five points (or stars) can be awarded. To take the assessment of the market position as an example, the five levels could be:

*****   *Leader.* This would be a company which, from the mere fact of its pre-eminent market position is likely to be followed by others in pricing;

****   *Major producer.* The position where, as in many businesses, no one company is a leader, but two to four competitors may be so placed;

*** A company with a strong viable stake in the market but below the top league;

** Minor market share. Less than adequate to support R&D and other services in the long term;

* Current market position negligible.

A total of four marks is awarded, a 5-star counting as four marks, while our one-star gets nothing. A similar approach is adopted to the other two aspects we mentioned above, so that a total of twelve marks becomes available. You will see from Figure 14.2 that our three companies, A, B and C, received 10, 6 and 4 marks respectively. They all had the same sector rating, from Figure 14.1, that is they were 'strong' companies, so that the sector was 'attractive'. So, once again, it is the company in the bottom right hand corner who should go ahead with confidence. The further you are away from that right hand bottom corner, the more difficult life is going to be.

How do we arrive at those points? Quite a detailed description of this method of project assessment has already been published (Ref. 4), but this last practical aspect is not mentioned. They say:

It has to be recognised of course that the zones covered by the various policy key words are not precisely defined by the rectangular subdivision arbitrarily adopted for the matrix. Experience suggests that (i) zones are of irregular shape (ii) they do not have hard and fast boundaries but shade into one another (iii) in some cases the zones are overlapping.

The problem of fixing the dot in an area becomes that much more difficult. The practical way to deal with the problem is to distribute matrix forms to all those who are likely to have a sensible opinion on the matter within the company: the economists, marketing, research and manufacturing personnel. Put all the opinions on to one form, and then see where the 'centre of gravity' is. That is the point we are looking for. This *works* – even though it sounds rather like picking a race winner from a list with a pin. This approach is being both used and recommended. (See Ref. 4 again.) How different this is to the 'mathematical' analysis referred to earlier. The beauty of the matrix is that it gives, even to the uninitiated, a 'feel' for the situation and the philosophy is: if it looks good – bottom right hand corner – get on with it fast! Remember, however, that we are discussing a technique designed to facilitate choice. When the tool has been used to assist that choice, management still has to use its own 'entrepreneurial judgement' in making up its mind whether to proceed or not.

Theory and practice

We have just looked at a case where theory would take you along one route, but practice along another and much simpler path. This is project selection. How do theory and practice compare when we come to *build* a project? That is indeed the theme of this book. The theory was set out in those original estimates of time and money, in the end – in practice – so sadly overrun. There are a multitude of books dealing with the theory. The British Broadcasting Corporation in the UK have a weekly radio programme called 'Analysis', sent out at a peak listening time (Ref. 5). One theme dealt with was the matter of cost and time overrun on major projects. Their interest was limited to plants being built in the UK, and the special problems of the UK in this context were naturally highlighted, but it was made clear that while many major projects did indeed overrun in both time and cost, there *were* other major projects that were built within their budgets. Seemingly if such a theme was chosen for broadcasting at a peak time it was considered to have considerable popular appeal. It certainly appealed to us!

Many of the comments made by those interviewed, all experienced project managers, were down to earth and practical. A key point was that it was vital to keep down the number of people on a construction project *and* to keep them busy. This avoided inefficiency and helped to minimise industrial relations (IR) problems. When one of us entered the industry 'IR' was never heard of; now we have a standard term that everyone in the industry recognises immediately. One speaker said: 'I would rather run a man "light" than a man "heavy" any day'. Another piece of worldly wisdom was to tell the truth about the probable length of time that a project would take. The only problem there, it appeared, was that 'management', and particularly the 'accountants' did not like such truths, and would not listen. They had to hear it in the end; eventually it happens.

We were very impressed once with a booklet produced by the Central Electricity Generating Board (CEGB) in the UK. Its subject was project cost control. It was published a while ago, around 1960. It was a most impressive booklet full of coloured diagrams. They described the way the Board *rigidly controlled* cost, for the benefit of others. They used a computer program called SNAP, as we remember it, and the booklet that was published was called 'Measuring the spend rate'. The background to the booklet was a National Working Party, set up in 1958 by the CEGB, charged with the responsibility of developing a budgetary control procedure for power station construction. 'Within twelve months the completed procedure was commended for implementation'. Let us quote what they had to say about it.

> The central feature was that all future capital payments should be made only on the basis of achievement against programme. This meant a re-negotiation of payment conditions with the major trade associations in the heavy engineering industry. In parallel with these developments, computer programs were developed to assist in the monitoring and control of physical and financial programmes, initially in respect of bar charts and more recently with networks, i.e. the CEGB development of the SNAP program.
>
> An important feature of the computer budgetary control is that no separate financial reporting is required since the financial expenditure is related directly to the physical programme. Progress information for up-dating the physical programme and its interrelated financial programme is collected via a questionnaire sent monthly to each contractor. Actual achievements or anticipated movements of events or activities on the network are recorded. This input data is fed to the computer and the output provided not only a report on the physical progress of the contract but also, when allied to budgetary control, its financial state.
>
> The principles of project control already described make it clear that each main plant contract is planned, monitored and controlled at the detailed level as a separate programme in either bar chart or network form. In the programme planning stage attention should be given to the structure of the programme to ensure that it is adequate to provide financial control avoiding both generalisation and excessive detail. The budgetary control procedure has so far only been applied to the principal contract areas but its range of application is being extended.

It sounds wonderful, doesn't it? Give them time to settle the details, of course. In 1960 it was a new toy and they had to learn how to operate the program and teach their suppliers and contractors how to cooperate. Is ten years enough? It ought to be. Ten years later the CEGB started to build a power station, using oil as feedstock, called INCE B, on Merseyside in the UK. A straight forward station, estimated to cost some £110 million. What is the position now, with many years' experience of SNAP? Completion is now expected in 1982 and the cost will be at least twice that original budget cost. In those ten years the cost of oil has risen so much that word has gone round that they couldn't care whether the 'thing' was ever completed because it will cost so much to operate. What happened to that basic statement: 'all future capital payments should be made *only* on the basis of achievement against programme'? We are not surprised and we hope that *you* are not surprised either, by now. This history demonstrates yet once again that wide gulf between theory and practice. Theory looks beautiful on paper, but practice is with *people*. To succeed, to learn from your mistakes, or those of others, this wide gulf must be seen, recognised and its significance fully appreciated. As we showed you in Chapter 7, in particular, human relations are far more important than systems and computer programs, although these latter have their place. But put them in their *proper* place!

Predicting the future

Now where is all this taking us, and taking the cost engineer in particular? The world is now going through an era of unprecendented change and uncertainty. Technological changes, political and economic problems proliferate and the prospect of holocaust cannot be completely discounted. Though many people attempt to predict the future, cost engineers among them – that is part of their job – it should be recognised that this is absolutely impossible to do with any certainty. It is, indeed, highly dangerous to believe that you *can* predict the future. Dear cost engineer, dear planner: every S-curve should be drawn somewhat 'tongue in cheek'. S-curves indicate the potential trend. Let us paraphrase a well-known saying in this area:

> 'A trend is a trend. The problem is – when will it bend? Will it go higher and higher, or just expire?'

That is indeed the question. A naive but very common mistake in predicting the future in relation to economic development is to assume that past growth will continue unabated. This was the assumption of the fifties and the sixties, but it all collapsed in the seventies. What will the eighties bring? No one knows. Never forget that growth is an S-curve and that there is a limit to growth. When we build a plant, the project comes to an end and the S-curve flattens out; so it seems do many other things in the economic sphere. The problem for the cost engineer, and it appears also for the economist, is to determine when that S-curve is going to flatten out and how long that 'tail' is. The cost engineer has this problem with all projects. It is not new to him. Now the economist finds himself with a similar problem. So far as the cost engineer is concerned, and indeed all those involved in the design and construction of new manufacturing facilities, their immediate task is to recognise that current trends are going to affect the nature of their work. The very plants they are building are changing quite rapidly. Energy conservation, increased automation, the computer and micro-processor revolution – all these will play their part. The impact of some of these things is so fundamental that it is difficult – nay, impossible – to conceive how and to what extent they will eventually affect the plants we build, the way we build them and the techniques to be used for project cost control. But revolutionise them they most certainly will.

References

1   Bussey, Lynn E., *The Economic Analysis of Industrial Projects*. A book from the Prentice-Hall International Series on industrial and systems engineering. Prentice-Hall Inc., USA 1978.

2   Rose, L.M., *Engineering Investment Decisions*, Elsevier, Amsterdam, 1976.

3   Thomson W.C., 'A rational approach to corporate strategy in the chemical industry'. An address to a Group of the Verband der Chemischen Industrie in Rotterdam, 19 November 1975. (Reprint available from the Shell International Chemical Company, London.) Mr Thomson was at that time a Director of Shell International Chemical Company and Chairman, Shell Chemicals U.K. Limited.

4   'The directional policy matrix – a new aid to corporate planning'. A booklet published by the Shell International Chemical Company Limited, London, November 1975.

5   British Broadcasting Corporation. Programme 'Analysis', on BBC4, 8.45 to 9.30 p.m., 25 June 1980.

15 Small is beautiful

It was in 1973 that Dr. Schumacher first published his book *Small is Beautiful*. Since then it has appeared as a paperback; evidently this is a subject that has broad appeal and the book has certainly been very widely read (Ref. 1). It was a study of economics as if *people* really mattered, and was most timely. The author sounded a warning: to build *bigger* is not necessarily to build either cheaper or better. The publication of the book has over the years led to some serious rethinking on the subject of the size of plants (Ref. 2) and there is no doubt that management in the process industries in particular should question their policies in this area. The approach till now has always been to build plants as large as current technology would permit or the total market demands. The result of the pursuit of this policy over the past 40 years is illustrated in Figure 15.1 (Ref. 3). The point has to be appreciated that there are both qualitative and quantitative aspects to the assessment of the economic viability of process units. In the previous chapter, we saw how suspect even the qualitative aspects could be: so much so that they were being replaced by 'subjective' and 'entrepreneurial' feelings when decisions have to be made. We have also seen that even the most careful calculations still come adrift in terms of both cost and time much more often than would at first be expected. Where, then, do 'qualitative' evaluations get us? Not very far, it seems. Then there are still a number of qualitative factors which seem never to be taken into account. It can be far better to build two plants to meet a market than one big one, for quite a wide range of reasons that cannot be given values – yet they exist. In the light of the many problems we have discussed as we examined our several case studies, it can even be that to build two instead of one will be cheaper in terms of the actual capital investment. Let us see the way it works.

TREND IN PLANT SIZE **(AVERAGE – AMMONIA & ETHYLENE)**					
	1940s	50s	60s	70s	80s
Ammonia, Tons/day	150	300	600	1700	2500?
Ethylene, Tons/day	–	150	500	1950	2500?

TECHNICAL LIMIT (TURBO MACHINERY) TO CAPACITY

Plant	Maximum capacity (Tons/day)
Ammonia	2500–3000 compressor
	2000 steam turbine
Ethylene*	3000
Methanol	2500

* 3 × 2300 plants under construction

Figure 15.1 Bigger and bigger
These two tables show first the trend in maximum plant size over the years, and then the limits to size currently imposed by technology.

The cost/capacity relationship

Why did anyone ever say that bigger plants were more economic than smaller plants? It all begins with the capital investment. The capital cost of a process plant is seen to vary in relation to capacity in accordance with a well-known formula:

$$\text{Cost } \alpha \text{ (Capacity)}^n$$

Although this formula has been extremely helpful to process designers, cost engineers and the like, it has also been badly misunderstood and widely misused. It is very common for that exponent 'n' to be taken as '0.6', and as a constant. That is where talk of the 'six-tenths rule' comes from. But in fact this is *not* a 'six-tenths rule'. That value 'n' varies with capacity and its value for any particular type of plant or process ranges all the way, quite possibly, from 0.4 to 1.0, and even over 1.0 in some cases. Once the value of 'n' is 1.0 or more, of course there is no longer any economy of scale at all.

If the value of 'n' is taken as 0.6, then doubling the capacity of a plant results in an increase in capital cost of only 50%, instead of 100%. That is where this 'economy of scale' comes in. Unfortunately, things are not really as simple as that, and the manner is which 'n' varies with capacity is not really known. Its intrinsic value will also depend quite significantly on the type of plant with which we are dealing. A typical variation of 'n' with size is given in Figure 15.2 (see Ref. 3). Note that 'n' starts at 0.4 rather than at 0.6, and moves through the value of 0.6 to 1.0. It does indeed so happen that for the normal capacity range of many plants the value of 'n' is very nearly always 0.6. This finding led to the general belief that an empirical law had been discovered and that 'n' would be, or should be 0.6 in all cases, at all capacities. So the paper on the 'six-tenths' rule was published, all of thirty years ago

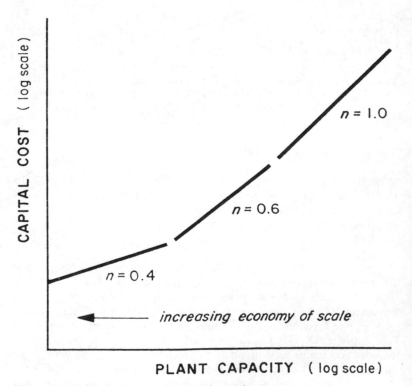

Figure 15.2 Relationship between cost and capacity
Ths graph illustrates the way in which the exponent 'n', discussed in the text, varies with capacity.

now. More recently, however, it has been shown that this is most certainly *not* a universal law. If the value of 'n' increases with capacity as has now been shown, then the economy of scale begins to disappear as one builds larger and larger plants. A study has been made of this in relation to ethylene plants, and the result of this work is presented in Figure 15.3. For each specific case there is then an optimum size of plant, and we find that the capital cost of that plant, in terms of cost per ton of product, plays a far less significant role that we are at first led to expect. Account must be taken not only of the economy of scale, which is where the capital cost of the plant comes in, but also of a number of other factors, such as the cost of transport, the effect of the infrastructure and so on. All these are factors which seem in general to work in the opposite direction. So we have various 'opposing forces' as it were, which lead to an optimum size of plant in any particular location. This effect has been thoroughly analysed (Ref. 4).

VARIATION OF 'N' WITH CAPACITY – ETHYLENE	
Tons/day	Cost-capacity exponent 'n'
400	0.5
600	0.7
1200*	1.0
2000	1.1

* At this capacity heat exchangers have to be in multiple units and large towers must be field welded.

Figure 15.3 Variation of exponent with capacity – ethylene
This table demonstrates that for plants producing ethylene, at least, there is no further economy of scale above a capacity of 1200 tons per day.

Capacity versus production cost

The point has just been made that the capital cost of the proposed plant is only a part of the story. Let us then look at a few other aspects that contribute to the final cost of the product we are going to make. These days very significant factors indeed are the cost of raw materials, and the cost of operation. We find that the relative magnitude of these elements of cost vary quite considerably in their influence on product cost, not only from plant to plant, but also over time. However, let us consider a case where we have a weighting of 75:15:10 for those three elements: raw materials, depreciation (the effect of capital cost) and operating costs. That is quite normal, and the average overall exponent related to size then becomes 0.11, because the cost of our raw materials changes so little with volume. Then with that exponent, we increase a plant tenfold in size and what do we find:

$$(10)^{0.11} = 1.30$$

In other words, despite this vast increase in size, tenfold, our production cost is only 1/1.30, or some 75% of what it is before. And we still have not considered the effect of freight, for instance. Well, others have done some sums (Ref. 5) and we find, as we show in Figure 15.4, that a tenfold increase in capacity of a manufacturing plant brings no saving at all in the price of the end product to the user. In fact, in the case set out in Figure 15.4, the exponent of size, in terms of product cost at the factory gate, is not even the 1.30 that we calculated above, but 1.18. How do we get that? That is the ratio of production costs − 150.2/127.1. When we look at the situation in a developing country, we find that in terms of the final cost to the farmer the smaller plant built near the point of product use provides him with fertiliser some ten per cent cheaper than would be the case with the large plant.

All this is very relevant to the problems we have discussed at length in earlier chapters. You will remember the gas from Bombay High, flared and lost for years on end, because decisions could not be made. Here is one aspect leading to indecision. We read an article (Ref. 6) questioning the location of the Thal fertiliser plant. It was to be located at Thal, we are told, because of its proximity to the gas terminal at Uran. But the product volume is far greater than the input volume of raw material, so such plants should be located near the market, not near the source of raw material. So, they say, the implementation of the Thal project would put a heavy burden on the already overstrained railway system, which would have to move many thousands of tons of fertiliser from the west coast of India, where the gas is available, to the northern states, where the fertiliser is actually needed. They think it a rather expensive way of generating traffic for the Konkan railway!

The physical limitations

So far we have been looking at the end result and its effect on cost,

PRODUCTION AND DELIVERED COST (ECN)
(Urea – $/T)

	Industrialised country		Developing country	
	1,500 T/day	150 T/day	1,500 T/day	150 T/day
Fixed costs				
Fixed Inv. Fin. Charges — Depreciation	29.6	41.6	44.4	49.9
	2.1	–	3.6	–
Interests on loans on w. capital	7.5	11.5	13.5	13.8
	2.0	2.4	2.3	2.9
Labour	16.2	23.9	8.4	12.8
Maintenance	7.1	10.0	9.7	14.0
Overheads and Ins.	4.2	2.4	3.4	2.4
(A) Total fixed costs	68.7	91.8	85.3	95.8
variable costs				
Natural costs	51.4	51.4	17.2	17.2
Chemicals	1.0	1.0	1.0	1.0
Bags	6.0	6.0	6.0	6.0
(B) Total variable costs	58.4	58.4	24.2	24.2
Production costs (A) + (B)	127.1	150.2	109.5	120.0
(C) Distribution cost	30.0	8.0	40.0	15.0
Total cost at farmers site (A) + (B) + (C)	157.1	158.2	149.5	135.0

Figure 15.4 The relationship between plant size and product cost
This set of figures clearly demonstrates that, particularly in a developing country, increase in size of plant, even ten times, brings no cost benefit to the ultimate user. (Acknowledgements to ECN – Ref. 5.)

when comparing large and small plants. There are also many problems on the way when building large plants. We have seen the end-result of these problems: overruns in time and cost. Our case studies have shown us this quite clearly. The bigger the plant, the more men are needed at site; a process that finally becomes self-defeating. We find we have ever more men, but ever less work. The end result is that the plant *never* gets finished – and this has actually happened (Ref. 7). This is yet another reason why economy of scale is so quickly lost. Among the other risks that have to be taken are those in relation to the reliability of key items of equipment, such as compressors or other very large rotating machinery. Such equipment is always crucial to the continuing operation of the plant, yet it is usually considered far too expensive to duplicate. A failure results in total shutdown; a bad failure can shut a plant down for a year, waiting for replacement parts.

Another aspect is the uncertainty that exists in scaling. We could quote many examples from our experience, but perhaps one simple one will suffice to illustrate this point. Those great circular concrete cooling towers are a familiar sight at a power station. In Chapter 9 Figure 9.2 shows two of them: one built, the other just begun. Figure 9.5 shows another two behind one another, standing out boldly against the skyline, in the background. In the late fifties the Central Electricity Generating Board (CEGB) in the United Kingdom built a power station at Ferrybridge in Yorkshire. This had eight cooling towers of this type, the first to be built of their size – 375 feet high and 300 feet in diameter (some 110 metres by 90 metres). In 1965 three of the eight collapsed! So there is always the element of surprise and the experts in the field are far from immune to expensive mistakes. Thus the apparent initial economy of scale can be more than offset by the many additional problems that sheer size brings with it. Let us list a few:

> organisational complexity;
> suspect reliability – failures are expensive;
> increased threat to the environment;
> startup is most complex;
> difficulties in maintaining steady operating conditions;
> excessive off-grade material can be made;
> disruption in supplies to or from the plant, is most expensive;
> better quality operators and maintenance are required;
> longer construction period;
> more damage in the event of fire or explosion.

It is quite a list, is it not? The problem of 'tuning in' the plant and maintaining steady operating conditions is interesting because that aspect gets no publicity. Large plants now have process computers to 'control' operation – a substantial extra cost that large plants can 'afford', but life seems no easier for the operating staff. Highly specialised personnel, knowledgeable in computer techniques, have to be on hand, so the difficulties in recruiting the appropriate staff only grow.

So that is where the money goes

Because of the inherent risks, which can but grow with size, there is strong temptation for process design engineers in particular to 'play safe'. They are building bigger, so they have no finite design and operating experience over a period of years: no history to study and learn from. They have to extrapolate. The basic justification for the increase in size is, as we have shown earlier, the reduced capitalisation per installed ton of capacity. Such an approach ignores the realities of the market place by assuming that the plant, when built, operates continuously at flowsheet capacity. The basic falsity of this assumption these days has become all too apparent. In Figure 15.5 the effect of running below flowsheet capacity is shown (Ref. 7). Here two plants are compared, one with a flow-sheet capacity of 20 000 tons per year, the other half that size, 10 000 tons per year. We see from the graph that if the larger plant, double the size, operates at but 80% of its design (flowsheet) capacity, then the capital cost per annual ton is the same as for the plant half its size. That is all it takes to wipe out the economy of scale. On the other hand, we have only to get an increase of some 12.5% in capacity on the half-size plant, to have the capital cost per annual ton of capacity the same as if we had built a plant double the size. This exposes the fallacy very clearly. Of course, with the smaller plant – with any plant – there is a very good chance of getting that increase in capacity at marginal cost, perhaps even at no cost at all. With the smaller plant there is also the likelihood of needing the extra capacity, and so running the plant very eco-nomically. Mr Arnold, who wrote the article that caught our eye, had a rather different objective in view. He was actually criticising process plant designers, whose conservative attitudes to design can put up costs so much. Because of their conservative, play it safe approach there is rarely any difficulty at all in increasing capacity in a plant, once built, by some 15%, by what is called 'de-bottlenecking' – removing one or two minor constraints on operation at marginal cost. Our major point is made yet again: small IS beautiful.

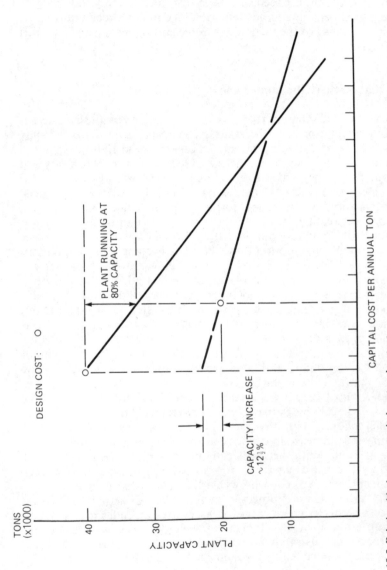

Figure 15.5 Relationship between capital cost and output

This graph shows the effect of lowered production on the capital cost in relation to production. It assumes an exponent 'n' of 0.5 (see Figure 15.2). With acknowledgements and thanks to Mr. M.H.M. Arnold, of Arnold Services, Warrington, UK.

Some typical examples

Reference has already been made to *Chemical Insight*, a specialised news sheet published by Mike Hyde from London (Ref. 2). In his issue 189 of early January 1980 it was pointed out that since he had extolled the virtues of smaller plants in issue 187 there had been feedback from a number of readers. One producer pointed out that the cost penalty involved in running a plant at less than optimum capacity put their sales staff under tremendous pressure. Costs could only be reduced by increasing the volume of sales. Such pressure could be tolerated when markets were growing, but could be disastrous in times of slump. It just led to a lowering of prices –a vicious circle. The Managing Director of Shell Chemicals U.K. Limited, Mr. K.H. Walley, was quoted as saying that when he praised the virtues of smaller plants in the field of ethylene manufacture, one of our examples in Figure 15.1, as long ago as 1972, no one listened to him. Although what he had to say then is even more relevant today, still no one seemed to want to listen. Indeed, as he wrote Shell were just starting up the world's largest single-train ethylene plant at their petrochemical complex in Texas, USA. It was the last of a series of four large-scale ethylene plants to be built for Shell by Pullman Kellogg, and is described as a 'billion-pound-a-year' plant by them. That puts it in the 1500 tons/day bracket, looking at our Figure 15.3. But notice those words 'single-train'. That is done to give the maximum possible economy of scale, but it increases the difficulty and risk of maintaining production very considerably.

A recent study of the scale of production of ammonia, a basic material for chemicals and fertilisers, disclosed that small units could be economical in several countries including Brazil, India, New Zealand and Zambia. We managed to find out a little more about that Indian installation, designed to produce some 90 000 tons per year of liquid ammonia, mainly for the manufacture of nitric acid and other chemicals. The cost was estimated at $51 million and the project is expected to save India some $25 million every year in foreign exchange. The unit will use Bombay High gas – the flared gas we discussed and deplored in Chapter 13. Production is confidently expected within two years of approval, thanks to the enterprise of departments in the public sector. What a difference this makes when compared with the progress being made on the major large public sector fertiliser plants being built in India discussed in Chapter 3. Compare this story – two years only – with the periods given in Figure 3.2. There is no doubt at all that the biggest research and development (R&D) challenge facing the traditional producers of chemicals over the next few years is to discover and devise ways of manufacturing commodity chemicals and plastics cheaply and efficiently in small plants. The task is not difficult, but whether it will be undertaken is another matter.

Some companies have already seen the light and are moving in this direction. There is a brochure (Ref. 8) with the title 'Sugar and the chemical industry'. This illustrates the way in which ethanol, a base product for many chemicals and plastics, can be produced by the fermentation of sugar extracted from vegetation. Ethanol can be used as a 'building block', synthesised to produce liquid fuels, solvents, plastics, rubber, foodstuffs and textiles. India pioneered in this and lately Brazil has taken it up seriously. The plants are very small in relation to the current scale on which ethylene plants are being built worldwide, producing only some 50000 tons per year of ethanol, but they are economically sound. Such a plant would use some 5000 tons per day of sugar over a period of some 180 days. The cane is processed to sugar juice, which is stored and further processed over the year (360-day operation) by fermentation and distillation to produce the ethanol. The plant has of necessity to be located close to the growing source, since this time the products are smaller in volume than the raw material, so there is the possibility of wide-scale small industrial units. Several small plants, built in sucession, allow experience on the earlier plants to be transferred along the line and built into the later plants. There is a high degree of flexibility and there is no need to worry about market capacity and optimum size. The optimum is chosen in relation to local conditions.

Of course there are snags. There always are. One came to us via a newspaper headline 'Alcohol from crops may hit food prices'. The reporter had studied a paper entitled 'Food as fuel: new competition for the world's cropland', which said:

> if cropland is shifted to the production of fuel for automobiles, it will come at the expense of grain for export (in the USA).

Here an entirely different objective is being pursued. Ethanol is seen, not as a base product for a range of chemicals, not as a means of spreading chemical production over a wide area in developing countries, but as an 'oil saver'. So comes the danger of a choice – food for cars or food for people.

Jumbo projects

A chapter on 'small is beautiful' can hardly be complete without some reference to what are called 'jumbo projects'. They are being built – but why? The term 'jumbo' is descriptive and speaks for itself. There are a number of jumbo projects scattered around the world; we referred to the Saudi-Arabian 'dream' in Chapter 10. Outstanding in this field and thus a good example, and a most practical illustration because they are being built, not merely dreamed about, are the Sasol Two and Sasol Three projects in South Africa. These are plants to produce oil from coal. Earlier jumbo projects, such as the North Sea (UK) oil projects and the trans-Alaskan pipeline have been cited in earlier chapters and you will remember that they have had a most unsatisfactory history, so far as completion on time, or within budget are concerned. We have sought to draw the lessons for you. But it does not have to be like that. The major problem with such big undertakings is logistics, and the logistics problems have been met and overcome with the Sasol Two project. It was indeed a jumbo project, costing Rands 2458 million (say $3 billion). Our authority for the success of the project, despite its jumbo size, is the client himself, in a paper 'A client's view on project planning and cost control as applied to jumbo petrochemical projects'. (Ref. 9) He is fully confident that this project will be completed within the budget and within the allotted time.

The Sasol Two project is being immediately followed by the Sasol Three project. The Minister for Economic Affairs for the Republic of South Africa announced on 22 February 1979 that the production capacity of Sasol Two was to be doubled by the construction of Sasol Three adjacent to Sasol Two at Secunda, near Johannesburg in South Africa. The estimated final cost, including provision for escalation, was said to be Rands 3276 million. This figure, as with the estimated figure for Sasol Two, excludes interest, working capital and the cost of housing. They say they are going to use the existing designs and also the existing temporary construction facilities established for Sasol Two. So now we have a project (Two plus Three) effectively handled as one, and totalling in all some Rands 5800 million or more (at 1980 prices). This is roughly equivalent to some $7 billion – truly a multi-*billion* dollar project which, on completion, will use some 70 million tons of coal per year!

Some of the conclusions that have been drawn from the handling of such jumbo projects are:

> The only corporate techniques that are appropriate to project management on this scale are 'management by exception' and 'management by objectives'.

Cost increases on jumbo projects are almost invariably related to schedule slippage, so strict design change control procedures are vital. The elements of such projects are so closely related that if any one of them fails to achieve the scheduled objective, then probably the entire project is in jeopardy;

The key to effective project management on this scale lies in *leader-ship*, together with the innovative skill and dedication of all the people involved;

Successful completion of a jumbo project within the allocated time and budget is possible, but a comprehensive team effort is required for this. A weak link brings failure every time.

Why do we mention jumbo projects at all? There does still remain the situation where small is not *really* beautiful. In the case we are just considering, the only way for South Africa to achieve independence in relation to fuel supplies is by an effort of the scale and magnitude that is now being made there. Sasol Two was already the world's largst 'oil from coal' installation, and it is now being more than doubled. It will have a peak construction workforce of some 20 000 and all is expected to be ready by 1982. The economics of the conversion process are a closely guarded secret. When Sasol Two was started there were hints that it was only marginally profitable, but since then oil has risen still further in price and is still rising faster in cost than the average rate of inflation. The firm Sasol itself insists that its new plants will be comercially viable, but while that may well become true it is not really the point. The plants have a strategic importance to South Africa that overrides every other consideration. The real proof of viability will come if the process is adopted elsewhere in the world for the large-scale production of oil from coal. While South Africa has embarked on a most ambitious time-targeted programme, it is so ambitious that at the end of the day the availability of both men and materials may well become basic constraints.

Conclusion

Although bigger can be cheaper, in terms of the initial capital investment, we have seen that there are today a growing number of factors which place very definite limitations on bigness, if the operating plant is to be an economic success. Beyond a certain size the economy of scale, of which so much has been made over the years, becomes but nominal and other costs can completely offset the initial saving in capital investment. Unfortunately, not all these 'on-costs' are necessarily borne by the manufacturer himself, so that it is possible for him to be making a profit while the end user receives no benefits. There is no doubt at all, therefore, that a comprehensive – and we really mean *comprehensive* – assessment of *all* the relevant factors will show that, for each project, for each location, there is an optimum size which can be well below the maximum size technically possible. Unfortunately in the economic studies which are made when an investment is being proposed, this aspect is not even mentioned, let alone studied in depth. The location of the optimum point may well be difficult to determine, but some indicative figures have already been suggested for certain processes. For developing countries as has already been clearly indicated in Figure 15.4, it is perhaps but a half, or even a quarter, of that which is to be found for the same process in a developed country. This arises because there are a number of factors other than the capital investment itself which play an increasingly significant role. Typical of these are the costs of transport – perhaps even a complete inability to transport large volume – the costs of distribution and other similar infrastructure costs. Our exhortation, then, is to management: ensure that these aspects are considered and weighed in the balance; you may then make more profit in the long run.

References

1   Schumacher, E.F., *Small is Beautiful,* Blond & Briggs Limited, London 1973.
2   *Chemical Insight,* No. 187, December 1979. (Published by Mike Hyde at 6 West Grove, Greenwich, London, SE10 8QT.)
3   Ball, D.F., and Pearson, A.W., 'The future size of process plants', *Long Term Planning,* vol. 9, August 1976, pp. 18–28.
4   Rose, L.W., *Commercial Investment Decisions,* Elsevier Publishing, Amsterdam 1976.
5   *European Chemical News,* 'Small urea plants economic', 20 October 1978, p. 23.
6   *Chemical Weekly* (India) 'Thal fertiliser plant – is West Coast suited?' 10 June 1980, p. 69.
7   Arnold, M.H.M., 'So that's where all the money is going', *Process Engineering,* 10 February 1971. M.H.M. Arnold is a Consultant and Principal of Arnold Services, of Warrington, Lancs., UK.
8   'Sugar and the chemical industry'. Informative brochure

published by Humphreys & Glasgow Limited, London, international contractors and consultants to the chemical, petrochemical oil, gas, mineral, metal and food industries.

9   Mostert, D.F., 'A client's view on project planning and cost control as applied to jumbo petrochemical projects'. An address presented by Dr. Mostert, of Sasol Limited, at a symposium on project planning and cost control, organised by the South African Institute of Building, September 1979.

16 Let's listen now – or we shall never learn!

We began by pointing out that many projects that overrun in either cost or time, or both, are in effect 'development projects'. We asserted that in all probability the final cost was much closer to the 'proper cost' than the first, unrealistic estimates, so grossly overrun. Much may be due to the motivation of those who prepare those first estimates. Most of the estimates are made by the very people who want to undertake the project. When we say this, no one can prove us wrong, so we are in the position of the statistician who asked: 'What is it you want me to prove?' Indeed, it was a famous physicist, Einstein, who once said: 'Cost is supposed to be based on facts, but – the facts are wrong!' The only 'fact' that is ever established is the final cost of the project. Whether or not it should have cost that sum of money depends on the efficiency with which the project was carried out.

Take the time

Without being able to prove anything, we remain of the opinion that those early cost and time estimates are often suspect and so we put forward a few basic rules for an approach to a new project:

1 Take the time to make a sound assessment of project cost and duration *before* you start;
2 Always ask yourself to what extent this project is a 'development' project, and if it is of that nature allow for it in terms of both cost and time.

This approach requires project definition, and by this we mean not only the process route, the plant output, the actual site, the product quality, but also some meaningful engineering development and design on that basis. Experience shows that some three to five percent of total project cost needs to be expended in order to establish a realistic estimate of cost and time, which in turn will establish its viability. Unfortunately, such expenditure can well prove abortive if the decision finally taken is not to proceed. Nevertheless, the work should be done, and some of the major companies do approach projects in this way. It is by no means unusual for a Board to release sufficient funds for the design of a major project to proceed to a point where everything is defined and the estimates firm, before the total project is authorised for detailed engineering and construction. Sometimes, long delivery items are authorised for purchase, pending final definition, while the total project is still not approved and could even be aborted. This obviously involves a degree of financial risk, but it is a risk well worth taking, for from them on you *do* know where you are going.

The first lesson we learn is that there will be fewer overruns in cost and time if the estimates are better in the first place. It is not always the fault of the site construction people, who come last and have to 'pick up the pieces'. Get the estimates right in the first place; take the time to get them right.

Change costs dear

Another theme with which we started and which has kept coming to the fore in the case studies that we took as our examples, is that change is always expensive. The later change occurs, the more expensive it becomes. Going back to Chapter 2, and Figure 2.1, you will remember that in that diagrammatic flow of events on a project, we called scope changes 'that lump of lead in the middle'. Change is terrible, however it is caused. We inhibit change by making up our minds before we start and resolving that we shall not make changes once we have started. In spite of a firm resolve to make no changes, changes can still come for a variety of reasons. Mistakes in detailed design can have devastating results, giving rise to as many changes and delays as poor definition of the project in the first place. Indeed, we know of one project that was cancelled following discovery of a design fault. That was an undersized compressor and the corrected design would have cost so much that the project would no longer have been economic.

Change can be drastically reduced if a step-by-step approach is adopted, although mistakes can never be entirely eliminated. For instance:

1 Complete the basic project definition;
2 Do not proceed with detailed engineering and procurement until the process flowsheets and line diagrams have all been finalised;
3 Delay start on site until detailed design and procurement for the whole project is within six to nine months of completion.

If this procedure is followed, change will be minimal and the targets for cost and time will almost certainly be met. Unfortunately this approach prolongs the design and construction period very considerably, and that can cost money. If a capital venture is to be successful, the project must be completed in time to meet the market. Telescoping a project, once defined, into as short a period as possible by having a sensible overlap between the various phases set out above may well be essential if the whole process from project inception to project completion is not to become so long as to make the investment totally uncompetitive. So we sit on the horns of a dilemma.

Are they learning?

As we bring this book to a conclusion, we continue to watch the technical journals, to see what is happening to the projects we have reviewed for you, so that we all may learn. We looked, you may remember, amongst others at the fertiliser plants being built in India. The Haldia Fertiliser Plant was on our list – refer to Figures 3.2 and 3.4, in Chapter 3. The plant was completed, but now what do we have? We are told (Ref. 1) that a power shortage has almost paralysed the Haldia Fertiliser Plant, though the plant was ready for commissioning from 1 January 1980. The West Bengal State Electricity Board, with a contractual obligation to provide for the plant, has now told the plant management that full power will not be available until early 1982. The Haldia plant took more than five years to complete, it was one year behind schedule, yet when it is ready to come on stream there is no power. The delay in construction pushed the cost of the plant up from Rs. 2280 million to Rs. 2600 million. The 1978 flood and the lack of experience of local (that is, Indian) equipment suppliers were said to be the two main reasons for delay in completion of the plant itself but now, with power problems, the plant is likely to take at least one more year to get into full production. Full production means 165 000 tons of urea and 500 000 tons of NPK fertiliser in a year, together with the methanol and soda ash that come as by-products.

In the same week (Ref. 2) we find another headline, relating to the flared gas from Bombay High. We made this a subject for study earlier, in Chapter 13. This report has as its headline: 'States vie for Bombay High gas – controversy continues'. The article below the headline tells us that they are still 'grappling with the issue'. It was pointed out that as crude oil production increases, more and more of the 'associated gas' becomes available. Meanwhile, the debate goes on and the concluding sentence in that article was:

> Mr. S.N. Desai, president of Ratnagivi District Industries and Economic Development Council, said that only economic yardsticks, shorn of political overtones, should govern the equitable distribution of Bombay High gas for industrial use.

Maybe, but did not George Bernard Shaw once say:

> If all economists were laid end to end, they would not reach a conclusion.

So what hope has Mr. Desai? Even the 'political overtones' might serve him better. What *we* should like to emphasise is that a bad decision is almost invariably better than no decision at all. If you make up your mind and act, you may well make mistakes, but at least you are on the move. Indecision is always terribly expensive.

Development projects galore

Almost all the cases that we have studied have been development projects in some way or another. If we had proven technology, as for instance with our fertiliser plants, then it was being applied in an unproven area, a developing country. If new technology, then it was being developed to meet the needs of climate or process. It looks, however, as though development projects are going to increase still further in frequency as the current energy problem grows. The energy problem is crystallised in the statement that current oil consumption per head was some 64 bbl. per year in the US, 32 bbl. per year in Europe, 4 bbl. per year in producer countries and only 2 bbl. per year in developing countries. The demand for energy is bound to increase in the developing countries – that will bring a steady flow of development projects. On the other hand, in the US and Europe every effort will be made to diminish the use of energy, and that will bring another flow of development projects, of a different type.

   Already the technical press is starting to talk about the 'refinery of the future'. A basic requirement is the development of processes for the conversion of the heavier fuel oil materials to the light, more valuable fuels and base products. This trend is already appearing in Europe. We know, for instance, of one refinery that two years ago had no prospect of expansion. Now, all of a sudden, it becomes economic to install a cracker and related process units designed to turn heavy oil products into lighter ones – the products valuable as base materials for a wide range of chemical products, rather than for use as fuel. There will soon be no by-products with less value than the crude that comes into the refinery. Even the low-value tars will be upgraded.

At the same time, every effort is being made to reduce energy requirements and to satisfy these without using the crude oil charged into the plant. This may be a formidable task, but it will mean a steady inflow of new technology and the problems will remain for the cost control engineer. As we have seen, when it comes to producing a reliable estimate of time and cost, the aspects always requiring clarification and clear definition are:

> project scope;
> materials of construction;
> environmental regulations;
> process optimisation;
> process de-rating (that is, assessing the loss of capacity through the use of pollution control systems).

These problems remain with us and to the extent that they are not resolved when we start our detailed design, they give our project a development character, with all that implies in terms of extra cost. Change will come, and costs – extra costs – will result as inevitably as night follows day. So there is no justification for optimism. In fact, if the past holds any lesson, it is: 'Expect the worst, even if you dare to hope for the best'.

Hubble, bubble, much less trouble

This was the headline above an article on the latest moves in pollution control in the USA (Ref. 3). We said, when we looked at what was going on in that over-developed country, in Chapter 2, that something would have to happen if they were not to be 'killed by kindness'. Now we have a 'straw in the wind'. We dwelt at length on the ever-increasing cost of complying with the environmental regulations. These costs are an ever-increasing and ever more significant factor in both the initial capital cost of the plant and also its running costs. Since the regulations are constantly changing, and become ever more costly to comply with, they were a significant factor in overexpenditure. We warned that 'something ought to be done'. Here, at last, is evidence that something is being done.

The headline quoted above was inspired by the fact that the US Environmental Protection Agency has now put into action a policy – a new policy – for controlling industrial pollution that allows individual companies a degree of flexibility, while still requiring them to meet the statutory requirements. The policy, known as the 'bubble concept' (hence the headline) differs from previous EPA requirements in the regulation of the sources of emission of polluting products. The previous approach regulated each individual source of emission from a plant. Now according to the bubble concept, an individual company can treat each plant that it owns, or even several plants together, as a single source of pollution. Instead of regulating the specific sources, such as the emission from each smokestack or drain and ensuring that that is within the regulatory limits, the bubble approach merely requires that the *total emission* from the plant, or group of plants, shall not exceed the overall limit set by the EPA. This allows the company to deal with the problems in the most economical way, by tackling the sources of emission which are the cheapest to clean. 'We want the skill and creativity of business's engineers turned to the environment's business', said a spokesman for the EPA, 'and that's exactly what this policy will do.' It was said that DuPont, the chemicals giant in the USA, could through this concept reduce the cost of complying with anti-pollution standards from $136 million per annum, to $55 million.

Of course, some environmentalists are unhappy. They suspect that it will further complicate the already baffling task of checking that emissions are within the legal limits. So the 'war' goes on. There is no doubt that the man-in-the-street has no conception at all of the contribution that the chemicals industry makes to his daily well-being. The media tend to focus on the bad news. This means that the coverage that the industry receives in the media is broadly negative and it is this fact that induces over-reaction first by the public, and then by the governmental regulating bodies, who are very sensitive to public opinion. This is a worldwide phenomenon, in no way restricted to the United States. Chemicals producers should realise that they have no need to apologise for what they make and the way they make it, even though it is the profit motive that is their prime incentive. Rather they have much reason to be proud of what they do, and some of the multi-nationals have indeed now adopted this attitude to the public in their advertising. 'See what we are doing for Britain' is, for instance, the theme of a series of full-page advertisements in the daily newspapers in the United Kingdom. It seems that public relations in the widest sense should be one of the main responsibilities of the senior executives in all such companies. There should be an on-going dialogue with the public both in good times and in bad. Management has a role to play in society, as management, just as have their many critics.

It would seem from what we have learnt that the major environmental challenge to the chemical industry in particular in the eighties is to avoid excessive regulatory costs, seeing that these are inhibiting growth, reducing productivity, restraining innovation and inflating costs. Probably the best way of securing reasonableness in this sphere is to seek any and every opportunity to co-operate with the appropriate governmental bodies, so as to ensure that the legislation that results is both sensible and reasonable.

Conclusion

We have attempted, in this concluding chapter, to highlight a few aspects of the many we have seen playing a role in cost and time overruns in the course of the design and construction of new manufacturing facilities, but we still feel that the best lesson lies in the case studies themselves. If you find a 'case' that parallels your own situation to some degree, then the dangers you may have to face become apparent. That is why we have sought out such a wide range of very different illustrations. We ourselves have had a lifetime of experience and yet we never dare to think that there will come a time when we can say invariably: 'I have seen this situation before'. But the more you can say that, the happier you can be. Experience is undoubtedly the key to success. Having seen it before, you know how to handle the situation, what to expect and, one hopes, how to avoid the pitfalls you met last time. Our objective has been to broaden *your* experience by laying hold of the experiences of others, reluctant though they were to discuss them at times, and so learn with them the lessons that they had to learn 'the hard way'.

The most important point of all, we believe, is a realisation of the profound significance of those first, early estimates of time and cost, especially when they are used for the authorisation of funds. Those who authorise the money, whether it be a Board of Directors or a government department, inevitably look to and take those first figures as their standard of reference in all subsequent discussion. It is of no use saying later that 'it was only an estimate', that not enough time had been spent on development, that the scope had been changed. You know all these excuses; they are made all the time. The one thing that is never said, though so often true, is: 'We underestimated because we wanted to do the job'. So then, management must ensure by whatever means open to it that those early estimates are *sound*. From then on, make sure that *every change* in scope is identified, recognised and authorised – and publicised right to the top! Then, and only then, do you, and your management with you, begin to know where you are going. The end result will then be a plant, operating to the satisfaction of its owners and perhaps, sooner or later, making a profit.

References

1   *Chemical Weekly* (India), 'Deadline for panel on gas-based fertilisers', 3 June 1980, p. 66.
2   'States vie for Bombay High gas – controversy continues', *Chemical Weekly* (India), 3 June 1980, p. 66.
3   *New Scientist* (UK) 'Hubble, bubble, much less trouble', 10 January 1980.

Annotated bibliography

A number of references to books, technical papers and both the technical and popular press have been given throughout this book, at the end of each chapter. These have been cited largely to demonstrate the authority of the text and the case studies but they can always be looked up and studied by those interested in a particular aspect of a particular case.

In addition, below is a list of journals and books for general reference on the various aspects of project management that we have highlighted in the course of our survey. This list is not intended to be complete, nor to present what might be the best book on any particular subject. We have inevitably had to be highly selective and we are also limited by our own reading. Fully detailed and much more comprehensive listings are prepared on an ongoing basis by the professional bodies involved in the various aspects of project management. But for those interested, a 'browse' through books such as we have listed could be very instructive.

Aczel, J. and Morris, G. (1978), 'Future trends in world trade (a review of the Lima target).' *Long Range Planning, 11*, pp. 19–24, April, 1978. Discusses ways of speeding up the industrialisation of the developing countries. The target formulated, if achieved, could have far-reaching implications for the entire world.

Altman, E.I. (1971). *Corporate bankruptcy in America*. Heath Lexington Books. A classic and the first serious work on this subject in the USA. Uses modern techniques, such as multivariable statistical analysis, for linkage between failure and economic trends. The aim is to predict failure.

American Association of Cost Engineers. *Cost Engineering*, their bi-monthly journal. *Transactions*, an annual publication containing the papers presented at the annual meetings of the Association. Both these publications contain informative articles on all aspects of cost engineering, including estimating and cost control. The AACE's prime objective: the application of scientific principles to the problems of cost estimation, cost control and profitability.

Argenti, J. (1976). *Corporate collapse*. McGraw-Hill. 193 pp. The first serious work on this subject in the UK. Collapse never appears suddenly though it always seems as though it does. Clear signposts leading to collapse go unnoticed. An analytical and constructive book to help rescue ailing companies. The Rolls-Royce collapse is analysed.

Association of Cost Engineers (UK). *The Cost Engineer*. The journal of the Association, which has similar objectives to those of the American Association of Cost Engineers, already outlined above. *'Fundamentals of cost control'*. A booklet giving a brief outline of the basic tools for project cost control and cost reporting. One of a number published by the Association.

Ball, D.F. and Pearson, A.W. (1976), 'The future size of process plants'. *Long Range Planning*, *9*, pp 18–28 (August 1976). Large plants pose problems for contractors. They are few in number but have high values. A framework for a reasonably accurate assessment is discussed.

Beaven, P.R., Green, G.J.L. & Russell, J.G. (1979). 'Developing a strategy for an industrial training Board – a participative approach'. *Long Range Planning*, *12*, pp. 41–55. (February, 1979). Particular reference is made to the UK chemical and allied products industry.

Bentley, T.J. (1976). *Information, Communications and the Paperwork Explosion*. 183 pp. McGraw-Hill. This book gives a systematic analysis of paperwork needs and methods for developing the most appropriate and efficient system for dealing with those needs, based on common sense. The aim: reduced clerical cost and increased effectiveness. Really enjoyable reading.

Bentley, T.J. (1978). *Making Cost Control Work*. 152 pp. Macmillan. A delightful little book and extremely well written. Presents a commonsense approach to accounting and cost control problems. Informative and enjoyable. The author, an accountant, feels that accountants can hardly control costs.

Bussey, L.E. (1978). *The Economic Analysis of Industrial Projects*. 491 pp. Prentice-Hall. A sound theoretical basis for the economic analysis and selection of industrial projects. Gives worked out examples and has an extensive bibliography. Covers the interface between engineering and economics.

Caudle, P. (1977). 'UK Chemicals – Strategic Planning or Industrial Strategy'. *Long Range Planning, 10*, pp. 31–39. (December 1977). Close collaboration is required of the industry with the government and the unions. Joint planning process formalised through planning agreements and an industrial strategy. There is identification of some major strategic issues.

Central Office of Information, London. (1979). *Concorde*. Publication SN 6032, revised April 1979, 4 pp. Historical development, technical characteristics, production and sales, operations and future developments.

Clark, W.C. (1978). 'Concept to completion'. *Hydrocarbon Processing, 57*, pp. 87–89. (March, 1978). Have money available to meet actual invoices and no more. This can mean millions of dollars gained or lost when the annual capital expenditure is of the order of $500 million. (Dow Chemicals background.)

Coussement, A.M. (1978). 'Investment & financing in a new era'. *Long Range Planning, 11*, pp. 2–10. (October 1978). Thanks to politics, currencies no longer obey economic laws. The world of finance is becoming ever more international. How to cope with the financial needs of the future.

Dean, H.W. (1978). 'The process plant contractor's view'. *Chem. & Ind.*, pp. 249–253. (April 15, 1978). One of the major problems of process plant contractors is the cyclical nature of their industry. It is a service industry and labour intensive. Specific details are given in regard to a London-based American company.

Finch, W.C. and Postula, F.D. (1979). 'Benefits of probabilistic cost estimating for nuclear power plants'. *Transactions American Association of Cost Engineers*, July 1979. PCE does not predict future cost outcomes but provides management with the information necessary to control uncertainties in cost, scheduling and performance.

Finch, W.C., Postula F.D & Perry, L.W. (1978). 'Probabilistic cost estimating of nuclear power plant construction projects'. *Transactions American Association of Cost Engineers*, July 1978. PCE as applied to nuclear power plants. Provides an insight into areas of greatest cost uncertainty and a knowledge of the factors which can cause costs to vary.

Fiske, H.W.M. (1977). 'Cost controlling a North Sea oil field development project'. *Cost Engineer, 16*, pp. 1–5 (March 1977). Describes the setting up and administration of cost control procedures. The role of accounting is detailed, and a code of accounts given. The types of reports and their circulation are also discussed.

Goldhabe, G.M., Dennis, H.S., Richetto, G.M. and Wiio, O.A. (1979). *Information Strategies – New Pathways and Corporate Power*. 323 pp. Prentice Hall. Communications are assumed to be 100% efficient. The actual optimistic efficiency is 25 to 50%, but mostly it is a mere 1 to 5%. Not much more than random! This book explores the fallacies that cause complacency and the eventual communication breakdown.

Guthrie, K.M. (1977). *Managing Capital Expenditures for Construction Projects*. 624 pp. Craftsman Book Company, USA. Has five sections: cost estimating and financial planning, project planning and control, management and supervisory functions, and total system integration. An Appendix of 150 pages presents typical project organisations, project execution functions, project personnel requirements, project control systems, typical cost account codes and the report of a 'round table' discussion on project control. Gives valuable detailed guidance. Should be used as a work of reference.

Hackney, J.W. (1977). *Control and Management of Capital Projects*. 300 pp. McGraw-Hill. The standard work in this field for over a decade. A very useful work of reference. Has been republished in 1977.

Hall, W.K. (1979). 'Changing perspectives on the capital investment process'. *Long Range Planning, 12*, pp. 37–40 (February 1979). Changes in corporate practice are slow and evolutionary, responding to trends such as increased regulations, increased worldwide competition, slow erratic growth in consumer markets and the limited availability of capital, raw materials, new technology and management resources.

Harrold, K.G. and Nicol, S.I.R. (1979). 'The prediction of design and development costs of civil airplanes'. *Cost Engineer 18(2)*, pp. 6–18. For research and development projects the experimental method of summating assessments of the smallest task elements is most likely to give acceptable accuracy. Unfortunately, too little information is available on past projects to allow estimators to develop methods which would yield acceptable accuracy. (UK background.)

Hodgson, M. (1978). Chairman ICI Limited. Talk given to the American Chamber of Commerce, London on 14 November 1978. They have an olefin project in the USA three months ahead of schedule and likely to be completed within budget. A very similar project in the UK is two years behind schedule, with substantial cost overrun.

Howenstein, E.J. (1972). 'Productivity trends in the Construction Industry – a comparative international view'. Paper presented at the Conference on measuring productivity in the construction industry, Washington DC, USA, 14 September 1972. During the postwar period at least seven countries (Austria, France, Netherlands, Hungary, Poland, USSR and Portugal) showed for substantial periods of time higher rates of productivity growth than the economy as a whole. In the majority of countries, including the USA, the reverse has been true.

Hydrocarbon Processing. A monthly magazine which carries interesting articles from time to time on project management and control. Publishes the worldwide HPI Construction Boxscore in October of each year, giving details of plant construction in the process industries worldwide.

Institution of Chemical Engineers. (1977). *A New Guide to Estimating.* One of a series of booklets published by the Institution. Designed primarily for the student or the young practising chemical engineer. Can give a real 'feel' for the cost relationships within the estimate if studied carefully.

International Cost Engineering Congress (1980). *Transactions.* Various national cost associations are members of the ICEC. The International Congress is held every alternate year at various places around the world. The latest was in Mexico in 1980. It is a useful forum at which to learn of the progress being made in cost management, via its *Transactions.*

Kerzner, H. (1979). *Project Management – a Systems Approach to Planning, Scheduling and Controlling.* 487 pp. Van Nostrand.

Kharbanda, O.P., Stallworthy, E.A. and Williams, L.F. *Project Cost Control in Action.* 272 pp. Gower Publishing 1980, and Prentice-Hall (USA) 1981. International reviews have described this book as authoritative, a rare book, down-to-earth, practical, refreshing and simple. It deals with cost control in relation to the process industries.

King, R.A. (1977). 'How to achieve effective project control'. *Chem. Eng.* pp. 117–121 (July, 1977). This article presents a typical project schedule and the points at which major changes may be made are indicated. Carefully drawn guidelines can protect a construction project from cost overruns, delays and poor workmanship.

Likierman, J.A. (1977) 'Analysing project escalation – the case study of North Sea Oil'. *Accounting and Business Research, 8,* pp. 51–57 (Winter, 1977). The methodology of the study group of which the author was a member is presented. Typical calculations with the causes of escalation; main causes are identified as being low productivity and an unexpected increase in quantities due to the project being the first of its kind. While out of the common run, the lessons are there for those building a 'first-off' plant.

Merrell, V.D. (1979). *Huddling – the Informal Way to Management Success.* 208 pp. American Management Association. This book demonstrates that results are not produced by organisations but by people, by a special kind of people – the 'huddlers', who are able to work intimately and informally in small groups.

Molleson, A.V. (1979). 'Investment control'. *Chem. Eng.* no. 340, pp. 47–50 (January 1979). Competent project management can result in investment savings of up to 10%, or a shorter schedule, or both. Opportunities for saving money in the field are more difficult to find, but the dangers of losing money there are immense. This article is typical of those that appear in this American journal from time to time on project management.

National Economic Development Office (NEDO) (1976). *Engineering construction performance.* This is the report of a Comparative Construction Performance Working Party. The report demonstrates that so far as the UK is concerned there is very considerable scope for change and improvement in site working in particular. Although now several years old, it is still worth reading so that its lessons may be learnt.

Oliver, E.D. and Moll, A.J. (1977). *Preliminary Feasibility Studies in times of rapid cost escalation.* The cost of development processes may be affected by factors other than escalation such as project scope and auxiliaries, materials of construction, yield, process variables. Environmental considerations and energy shortage are more recent additional major factors.

Patrascu, A. (1978). *Construction Cost Engineering*. 302 pp. Craftsman Book Co., USA. A very practical guide on all aspects of cost engineering. There are two chapters (154 pages) on cost control as such.

Phillips, P.D., Groth, J.C. and Richards, R.M. (1979). 'Financing the Alaskan project'. *Financial Management, 8,* pp. 7–16 (Autumn, 1979). Growth of Sohio with assets of $0.8 billion in 1969 to $8.0 billion in 1977 through judicious financial planning of the Trans-Alaskan Pipeline System. Sohio has emerged as a major producer of crude oil.

Process Economics International. A journal for the international interchange and dissemination of ideas and information on process economics.

Rose, L.M. (1976). *Engineering Investment Decisions*. 477 pp. Elsevier, Amsterdam. A sound theoretical background with extremely useful practical applications. In the closing chapter the author notes: 'the professional boundaries are largely artificial . . . has this book been about chemical engineering or production engineering or operations research or econometrics or economics?'

Snowdon, M. (1977). *Management of engineering projects*. 134 pp. Newnes Butterworth. A sensible little book. The author is a civil engineer but seems to have had exposure to process plant projects. The management and engineering aspects of maximising the value of the capital investment are given.

Spellman, K. (1978). 'Predicting the failure of a construction company'. *Accountancy, 89,* pp. 54–56 (August 1978). Attempts to evolve mechanical, quantitative techniques to substitute for qualitative and intuitive type of analysis, in order to predict failure.

Starr, M.K. (1978). *Operations management*. 618 pp. Prentice-Hall, USA. Presents production/operations management techniques in a simple and very readable style, without much complex mathematics. The main theme: how to choose and use the best possible production configuration.

Taylor, W.J. and Watling, T.F. (1979). *Successful Project Management*. 269 pp. Business Books. 2nd Edition. A practical down-to-earth guide to the subject. Demonstrates an outstanding grasp of financial and strategic considerations. A new chapter has been provided in the second edition on the golden rules for project management. There is an extended bibliography.

Trimble, E.G. (1978). 'Project cost control case studies'. The

Project Manager (Internet UK), *1*, pp. 5–8 (January, 1978). Five case studies based on the author's experience, intended to demonstrate the breadth of the subject and the very different approach necessary in each case. Concorde, which we discuss, is used as an illustration of a high technology project.

Turner, L. and Bedore, J.M. (1979). *'Middle East Industrialisation'*. 220 pp. Royal Institute of International Affairs. These economists bring a refreshing objectivity to their subject along with a sympathetic understanding of the aspirations of the oil producers. Their overall conclusion is pessimistic, particularly in view of the expectation of slower growth in major markets.

Willis, W.F. (1979). 'TVA's first ten years of nuclear plant design and construction experience.' *Cost Engineering, 21*, pp. 5–13. (Jan/Feb. 1979). The assumption that building a nuclear facility is like building a conventional plant proved to be wrong. Additional problems were largely due to regulations and environmental considerations. Nevertheless, the TVA's decision to have a major stake in nuclear power has proved a wise one.

Index